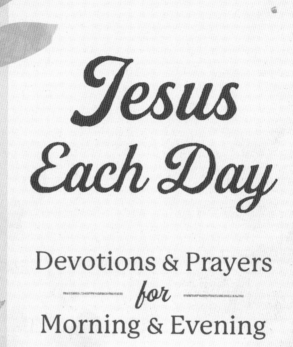

Jesus
Each Day

Devotions & Prayers
for
Morning & Evening

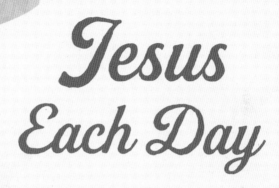

Jesus Each Day

Devotions & Prayers *for*
Morning & Evening

BARBOUR
PUBLISHING

Published by Barbour Publishing, Inc., 1810 Barbour Drive, Uhrichsville, Ohio 44683, www.barbourbooks.com

Our mission is to inspire the world with the life-changing message of the Bible.

 Member of the
Evangelical Christian
Publishers Association

Printed in China.

Introduction

**There's no greater personality than Jesus—
so why not make time each day
to know Him better?**

This 365-day devotional highlights many aspects of Jesus' life and work, touching on His teaching and example and ongoing impact on our lives. You'll find powerful insights for every day of the year.

The brief readings are not heavily theological, but inspirational pieces that provide food for thought each morning—and each is accompanied by an inspiring prayer for bedtime.

Monthly themes tie the daily messages into the annual calendar:

- JANUARY: Beginnings
- FEBRUARY: Love
- MARCH: Rebirth
- APRIL: Blessings
- MAY: Growth
- JUNE: Joy
- JULY: Freedom
- AUGUST: Perseverance
- SEPTEMBER: Guidance
- OCTOBER: Change
- NOVEMBER: Gratitude
- DECEMBER: Nearness

The Creator, Sustainer, Lover, and Redeemer of humanity is worthy of every moment you devote to Him. . *Jesus Each Day Devotions & Prayers for Morning & Evening* will help you do just that.

January 1

If anyone is in Christ, the new creation has
come: The old has gone, the new is here!
2 CORINTHIANS 5:17 NIV

How appropriate that New Year's Day arrives just a week after Christmas! January 1 is traditionally a time for new beginnings, though our resolutions to lose weight or go back to school or find a better job pale in comparison to the life change Jesus offers.

Christmas celebrates the Incarnation—that point in history when God became man, when Jesus "became flesh and made his dwelling among us." And because of this "one and only Son, who came from the Father, full of grace and truth" (John 1:14), we enjoy the unparalleled opportunity to be made new—no matter what traumas, mistakes, failures, or personal bad behaviors darken our memories.

Christmas means Jesus and Jesus means new beginnings. Let's spend some time this year, just a few minutes each day, pursuing the One who always pursues us. You'll soon find that Christmas is much bigger than December 25—it's a reality we live out all year.

EVENING

Jesus, I know that any resolutions I could make to
improve my life pale in comparison to the newness you
offer through Your forgiveness. Show me how to turn
away from old habits, sin, and disappointments and
look fully toward Your grace and healing in this new
year. Please give me a renewed heart and mind as I walk
in Your forgiveness and mercy. I want to end each day
knowing that I have fully honored You. But even when I
fail, remind me that Your mercies are new each morning.

January 2

> The Word (Christ) was in the beginning. The Word was with
> God. The Word was God. He was with God in the beginning. He
> made all things. Nothing was made without Him making it.
>
> JOHN 1:1–3 NLV

In order to have a new beginning, there must be an "old beginning."
You can read all about that in the Bible's first book, Genesis.

This remarkable universe, filled with untold galaxies and planets
and stars, sprang from the even more remarkable mind of God. This
incredible earth, teeming with life from amoebas to human beings,
reflects the even more incredible life of its Creator. And that Creator is Jesus.

The sweet little baby of Bethlehem, the helpless infant wrapped
in cloths, and lying in a manger, was actually the immense power
behind everything we see, hear, feel, taste, and are. He can offer us
new beginnings because He is the almighty God who commanded
the old beginning.

Nothing exists beyond Jesus' creative decree. Nothing lies beyond
Jesus' re-creative capability.

EVENING

> Lord, I am so thankful that You're willing to re-create
> me and allow me to become the person You meant for
> me to be all along. Only You know what is truly best for
> me. You know the end from the beginning, and I trust
> that what You see in me and what You have planned for
> my life is for my good and Your glory. I pray that my life
> honors You as You mold and make me new day by day.

MORNING

The LORD God said to the serpent... "I will put enmity between you and the woman, and between your offspring and hers; he will crush your head, and you will strike his heel."

GENESIS 3:14–15 NIV

In a perfect world, we wouldn't need new beginnings. But we don't live in a perfect world.

Blame Adam and Eve if you must, though we've all played a role in the conflicts, failures, and disappointments of this life. The psalm writer David could hardly have been clearer when he proclaimed, "there is no one who does good, not even one." As if to emphasize the point, David recorded those words twice (Psalm 14:3; 53:3).

Like Adam and Eve, we all make foolish, selfish choices. We all fail. We all need help. And that's why Jesus came to earth—not to make it perfect (not yet at least), but to set us on the path of perfection. When we hear Jesus' voice and accept His invitation, we can stop listening to Satan's words and doing his bidding.

Listen carefully.

EVENING

Thank You, Jesus, that You did not leave me in my failure, but You died for all my sins, to forgive my sin and give me access to Your perfection. Help me to listen to Your voice and walk in Your ways. As I reflect on my actions and thoughts of today, I ask You to show me the areas in which I didn't heed Your voice. Teach me to hear You above all the distractions of the enemy, and to follow what You lead me to do.

January 4

"For God so loved the world, that he gave his only begotten Son, that whosoever believeth in him should not perish, but have everlasting life."

JOHN 3:16 KJV

Only God knows the true number of souls on earth. But current scientific estimates place the world population between seven and eight billion. Around the globe, people's styles, beliefs, and experiences vary widely—but all human beings share the commonality of birth. And we all share a need for rebirth.

That was Jesus' message to a man named Nicodemus: "ye must be born again" (John 3:7). This conversation between the Lord and a highly placed Jewish religious leader was recorded and passed down through history as "John, chapter 3." It provides us with perhaps the best-known and most quoted of all scriptures, and for good reason. Verse 16 is a sublime summary of God's love, of Jesus' work, and of our opportunity for the ultimate new beginning.

How important we must be to God!

Jesus, sometimes I find myself as confused as Nicodemus. I think I know the truths of Your Word, then realize I'm stumbling on some of the most basic concepts of the faith. Please give me a rebirth into Your grace and forgiveness every single day. As I wrap up this day, I turn my failures and disappointments over to You, looking forward to tomorrow's sunrise with Your fresh mercies.

MORNING

*For [God] has rescued us from the dominion of darkness
and brought us into the kingdom of the Son he loves.*

Colossians 1:13 niv

Knowing Jesus changes everything. As we've already seen, anyone who is "in Christ" is a "new creation" (2 Corinthians 5:17). Sure, we still live in a broken world in aging (actually dying) bodies. But salvation through Jesus means this life—so often hard and disappointing—is only the beginning of a perfect life that will never end, a life without "death or mourning or crying or pain" (Revelation 21:4).

Jesus is the doorway to that life. Every one of us is welcome to enter real life through Him. Every one of us can enjoy the new beginning that He purchased for us by His death on the cross for sin. Every one of us faces a question: *Have I accepted that gift—will I?*

Knowing Jesus changes everything. Forever.

EVENING

*God of Righteousness, You have rescued me from
darkness and brought me into Your marvelous
light. I no longer despair about this life, or the life to
come, since I know that You hold me in Your hands.
You have made me new so that I can live a life that
honors You. May I never turn back to the things
of my past. May I always honor Your sacrifice and
give You the glory that You are due. I look forward
to the promise of eternal life in Your presence.*

January 6

And he is the head of the body, the church: who is the beginning, the firstborn from the dead; that in all things he might have the preeminence.

COLOSSIANS 1:18 KJV

Today's verse calls Jesus "the beginning." The beginning of what? The next few words provide the answer. As "the firstborn from the dead," He is the beginning of new life.

Jesus wasn't the first person to be raised from the dead. You can find Old Testament examples of resurrection in 1 Kings 17:17–24; 2 Kings 4:32–37; and 2 Kings 13:20–21. And before Jesus' own resurrection, He had brought back from the dead His friend Lazarus (John 11:39–44), Jairus's daughter (Mark 5:35–43), and the widow of Nain's son (Luke 7:11–17).

But Jesus is the "firstborn" from the dead in the sense of the permanence of His resurrection. Unlike these other Bible figures, He didn't come back to life only to die again. Jesus lives forever—and because of that, so will all of us who accept His gift of life!

EVENING

Jesus, may I use this evening time to reflect on Your goodness and the way You went before me. Thank You for loving Your children enough to endure death on the cross, taking our deserved punishment and instead offering us eternal life. Because You rose again and live forever, I will too! Remind me of Your wonderful hope, even in death. Prepare me for the beautiful forever I'll enjoy in Your presence.

MORNING

*For since the beginning of the world men have not heard, nor
perceived by the ear, neither hath the eye seen, O God, beside
thee, what he hath prepared for him that waiteth for him.*

ISAIAH 64:4 KJV

Jesus' name doesn't appear in the Old Testament. But He's certainly all through it.

In fact, many called the book of Isaiah "the fifth Gospel" because Jesus is so prominent throughout. It was Isaiah who prophesied of Jesus as "Immanuel" (or "God with us," 7:14) and as the Suffering Servant of chapter 53, who would be rejected and beaten, bearing the sins of many for their salvation.

Isaiah 64, specifically a message to the sinful Israelites, includes a promise that the apostle Paul later applied to all sinful people whom Jesus forgives: "As it is written, Eye hath not seen, nor ear heard, neither have entered into the heart of man, the things which God hath prepared for them that love him" (1 Corinthians 2:9).

All those incredible, yet-to-be-seen things are yours through Jesus.

EVENING

*God, I thank You for the things that You prepared
for me even before the world was created. You
planned for things that I cannot even imagine for
myself, yet You offer them to me as I live to honor
You. May I never fall into the trap of thinking
that the good in my life comes from anything I do.
Remind me, Lord, that You prepared good things
for me because of Your mercy, grace, and love.*

January 8

MORNING

From the rising of the sun unto the going down of the same the Lord's name is to be praised.

PSALM 113:3 KJV

Do you begin your day with a workout to get your blood moving? Maybe you need a ridiculously large cup of coffee to open your eyes. Whatever your morning routine looks like, scheduling time for prayer and praise will improve your whole day.

King David, the writer of many psalms, began his day in prayer. Psalm 5:3 says, "My voice shalt thou hear in the morning, O Lord; in the morning will I direct my prayer unto thee, and will look up."

Even Jesus started His day in prayer. "And in the morning, rising up a great while before day, he went out, and departed into a solitary place, and there prayed" (Mark 1:35).

Prayer is more than asking God for help—it's recognizing who is in charge. Praising God shifts your focus from your troubles to God's goodness. Be like Jesus—begin your day in God's presence. Then watch Him make something good of the rest of your day!

EVENING

Lord, teach me to dedicate the first moments of my day to You. I know that whatever may come I can take in stride because of the time I've already spent in Your presence. May nothing be sweeter to me than time spent praising and thanking You. I want to consciously acknowledge how good You have been to me, Lord. Help me to make the most of my days by praying and praising without ceasing, from the rising of the sun to the going down of the same.

MORNING

For no one can lay any foundation other than the
one already laid, which is Jesus Christ.
1 CORINTHIANS 3:11 NIV

Buildings are constructed in a certain order. The roof goes on after the walls. Insulation happens before drywall. Plumbing must be in place before the sink is installed. But everything begins with a strong foundation.

Christianity is built on the foundation of Jesus Christ. As His disciples, we build on that foundation by practicing what we read in scripture and hear from faithful teachers. Jesus said, "Everyone who comes to me and hears my words and puts them into practice, I will show you what they are like. They are like a man building a house, who dug down deep and laid the foundation on rock. When a flood came, the torrent struck that house but could not shake it, because it was well built" (Luke 6:47–48).

Are you building your life on Jesus' foundation? If so, your "house" will protect you from the storms of life—and help to shelter those you love.

EVENING

Jesus, show me whatever parts of my life that I've
built on sand rather than Your sure and immovable
foundation. I don't want to rely on the things of this
world, the things that crumble and sink and leave me
in danger. Teach me to stand fully on You as my strong
foundation. Reveal Your truth in my moments of doubt.

January 10

After his baptism, as Jesus came up out of the water, the heavens were opened and he saw the Spirit of God descending like a dove and settling on him. And a voice from heaven said, "This is my dearly loved Son, who brings me great joy."
MATTHEW 3:16–17 NLT

Jesus began His earthly ministry with a heavenly encounter. Although He had no sins to repent of, He initiated His mission by partaking of John's baptism. This foreshadowed His death and resurrection, His payment for and victory over sin.

When you began your new life in Christ, the heavens probably didn't open. But the Holy Spirit showed up. And because of His presence, you can have strength in weakness (Romans 8:26), peace in troubled times (Romans 15:13), and the freedom to see God (2 Corinthians 3:17).

The Holy Spirit is the seal of our salvation (2 Corinthians 1:22), so we can have a hope and joy this world can't understand. What Jesus began at His baptism led to a new beginning for us. Praise God!

Lord I thank You for sending Your Holy Spirit to fill me with hope and joy. No matter what tomorrow brings, I know that I have every opportunity to experience Your presence. When troubles come, as I know they will, please provide the strength and peace I need. Help me to know You even more tomorrow than I did today.

MORNING

Then Jesus was led by the Spirit into the
wilderness to be tempted by the devil.
MATTHEW 4:1 NIV

Trouble began for Jesus as soon as His baptism was over. Following His heavenly encounter, now empowered by the Holy Spirit, Jesus was immediately faced with Satan's temptation. Can you relate?

Temptations often feel strongest the moment we repent of sin and accept the Lord's forgiveness. Can't we have just a few minutes of peace? Well, yes, if we do what Jesus did. When tempted by the devil, Jesus answered, "It is written: 'Man shall not live on bread alone, but on every word that comes from the mouth of God'" (Matthew 4:4).

When we respond to temptation with God's truth, we prove that the devil has no power over us. He is no longer lord and master of our lives. *Jesus* is. He knows what temptation feels like, and He has proved that He is stronger than anything we might face.

What scripture will you quote the next time you face temptation?

EVENING

Lord Jesus, as I strive to live a life set apart and pleasing
to You, I know that the devil is working against me.
He wants to see me fall into old patterns of sin that
dishonor You and keep us apart. But You set the example
of fighting temptation with scripture. Help me to respond
to each of Satan's attacks with Your powerful Word.

January 12

Jesus was walking by the Sea of Galilee. He saw Simon and his brother Andrew putting a net into the sea. They were fishermen. Jesus said to them, "Follow Me. I will make you fish for men!"

MARK 1:16–17 NLV

In New Testament times, fishermen had a hard—and often unrewarding—job. They stood on the shore or went out in boats and threw nets into the sea. Then they would haul the nets up, see if they'd caught anything, and toss the nets again. It was monotonous and physically demanding. . .and there were no guarantees of success.

No matter what work we do, we've all experienced difficult and unrewarding times.

But when Jesus called Simon, Andrew, James, and John to abandon their fishing career to become His disciples, this new beginning was no herald of an easier life. Jesus walked among sick, selfish, sometimes violent people—and was eventually murdered.

After He rose again, Jesus told His disciples to keep fishing. . .for men. The work could be monotonous and physically demanding, and there were no guarantees of success.

Fortunately, it is God's responsibility to provide the catch. Ours is simply to continue fishing.

Lord, You have called me out of my same old routine and into a new life of making disciples! Like the men You called two thousand years ago, I have no guarantee that I will see fruit from the seeds I plant. But I know that You have called me to be a "fisher of men." You will give me the tools I need to reach others for Your kingdom and glory!

MORNING

As he walked along, he saw Levi son of Alphaeus sitting at the tax collector's booth. "Follow me," Jesus told him, and Levi got up and followed him.

MARK 2:14 NIV

The Jewish tax collectors of New Testament times were considered traitors. They collected money for the Roman government, and many used their position for extortion, threatening Roman retribution if the Jewish people didn't pay. Many of them were educated men, and they knew how to get what they wanted.

It must have come as a shock to everyone when Jesus called Levi the tax collector to become His disciple. But Levi got up and followed the Lord. Then he used his training and skills to write the first Gospel. He communicated convincingly to his fellow Jews that Jesus was the Messiah.

Jesus offers us a similar new beginning, redeeming our skills for His service. What did you do before your life in Christ that can now be used for His glory?

EVENING

Though my skills may seem small, Lord, help me to use each one for Your glory. Turn everything I do well into something I can do for You. I don't want to be successful or famous in my field if it means that I am not serving for Your glory. Teach me how to honor You in all that I do.

January 14

Looking at his disciples, he said: "Blessed are you
who are poor, for yours is the kingdom of God."
LUKE 6:20 NIV

Jesus' teachings are often counterintuitive. Luke's account of the Beatitudes—or "blessings"—lists groups of people who don't sound very blessed at all. Blessed are those who are poor, hungry, crying, and insulted? It's a strange way to begin a sermon. Then Luke includes a list of woes. Woe to those who are rich, well-fed, laughing, and spoken well of. Did Jesus get it wrong?

It may feel that way. . .until you realize that Jesus' vision is bigger than this world can hold. His perspective is eternal. Being poor may not feel like a blessing, but when we willingly depend on God for our care, we show Him (and the world around us) what it means to belong to the heavenly kingdom. Alternatively, if we are rich on earth, we may learn nothing about our true position before God. . .and have no part in the eternal blessings that come with dependence. The question isn't one of blessing, but of perspective.

EVENING

Jesus, I thank You for showing me that I must have
a heavenly perspective rather than an earthly one.
I know that You use all things—wealth or poverty,
health or sickness—to teach me more about Yourself
and how to live faithfully. I trust You with all my life.
As I prepare for tomorrow, remind me to thank You for
not only the blessings but the hardships of life too.

MORNING

> *"Come and see a man who told me everything I
> ever did! Could he possibly be the Messiah?"*
>
> JOHN 4:29 NLT

An exit strategy is a way out of a troubled situation, a way to survive to fight another day. Exit strategies are a common feature in spy novels and action films, but they aren't reserved for life-or-death situations. Exit strategies are also on the minds of people who are caught up in sin.

That describes the Samaritan woman at the well (see John 4:1–42). Her exit strategy involved avoiding people by getting her needed water while the town's well wasn't busy. But she couldn't avoid Jesus.

Jesus offered the woman a new exit strategy. Instead of trying to hide her sin, she accepted forgiveness and brought others to Christ. She stepped out of the darkness of sin and let the light of the world expose and heal her.

Do you need an exit strategy from sinful choices? Just turn to Jesus, accept forgiveness, and enjoy a new beginning.

EVENING

> *Lord Jesus, I accept Your mercy and forgiveness—
> and thank You for it. Even on my best days, I know
> I could still fall into temptation and need Your exit
> strategy to save me from wrong choices. Please grant
> me forgiveness for this day's sins and empower
> me to walk in Your mercy and grace tomorrow.*

January 16

He came to His own town and taught them in
their places of worship. They were surprised and
wondered, saying, "Where did this Man get this
wisdom? How can He do these powerful works?"
MATTHEW 13:54 NLV

People who have visited their hometown after some time away have often felt that little is as they remembered it. And sometimes the people in the town feel the same way about their old neighbor.

Jesus' old neighbors thought they knew Him, so when He tried to show them who He really was, they couldn't believe it. *Isn't this only Jesus, the carpenter's son?* they thought. Their preconceptions prevented them from experiencing Him as God's Son. Jesus knew that would happen, but He tried to reach them all the same.

When you experience a new beginning in your life, people from your old life may not recognize you—or they may not trust the new person you've become. Still, it's worth reaching out, as Jesus did, to help them see God's truth. Maybe in small ways at least, if not in large ones.

EVENING

Lord, I pray that You will give me grace to deal with
those who knew me before I knew You. Show me
how to love others and point them to You. Give
me Your heart for the lost and struggling. May
many in my circles come to the saving knowledge
of You and enjoy the blessings of eternal life.

MORNING

As Jesus was walking along, he saw a man who had been blind from birth. "Rabbi," his disciples asked him, "why was this man born blind? Was it because of his own sins or his parents' sins?"

JOHN 9:1–2 NLT

Some beginnings are harder than others. Is God unfair? Are our disadvantages related to sin?

The Bible makes clear that everyone is born equally sinful before a holy God (see Romans 3:23; 1 John 1:8; and Psalm 51:5). So one person's earthly advantages over another's disadvantages cannot be because the first person is holier than the second.

"It was not because of his sins or his parents' sins," Jesus said of a man's lifelong blindness. "This happened so the power of God could be seen in him" (John 9:3).

We don't know why God allows some people to face more challenges. We do know, however, that He provides His strength in our weakness, and that He calls us to trust Him at all times. Hard beginnings are not a reason to doubt but an opportunity to trust.

EVENING

Lord Jesus, may I never criticize anyone's disadvantages, but instead see Your hand in all situations. I know it's not because of my own holiness or simple luck that I've been given advantages—it's because You have specific purposes for each one of us. Allow me to learn from those who've had different experiences, that I may grow in understanding, patience, and mercy.

January 18

*As he neared Damascus on his journey, suddenly a light from
heaven flashed around him. He fell to the ground and heard
a voice say to him, "Saul, Saul, why do you persecute me?"*

ACTS 9:3–4 NIV

Saul of Tarsus—later known as Paul the apostle, author of most of the
New Testament—didn't begin his religious career as a Christian. Far
from it! Saul was a zealous defender of the Jewish faith, who was out
to kill off Christianity by any means necessary. . .until he met Jesus.

Encounters with Christ will fundamentally change the direction
of a person's life. Saul went from "breathing out murderous threats
against the Lord's disciples" (Acts 9:1) to saying that "to live is Christ,
and to die is gain" (Philippians 1:21).

At one time, Paul was zealous about keeping the Jewish faith
pure. Then the Lord repurposed Paul's passion to bring Gentiles
and Israelites alike to Himself. What were you passionate about
before you encountered Jesus? How have you seen Him repurpose
your passions?

*Lord Jesus, You have given me passions that I need
to use to honor You. Show me how I can best use
my talents to advance Your kingdom. I don't want
to use my gifts in self-serving ways. May I employ
every advantage You've given me to honor You, to
help others, and to promote the gospel message.*

MORNING

But the Comforter, which is the Holy Ghost, whom the Father will send in my name, he shall teach you all things, and bring all things to your remembrance, whatsoever I have said unto you.

JOHN 14:26 KJV

God has set a pretty high standard for Christians: "As obedient children, not fashioning yourselves according to the former lusts in your ignorance: but as he which hath called you is holy, so be ye holy in all manner of conversation; because it is written, Be ye holy; for I am holy" (1 Peter 1:14–16).

Fortunately, we have help. Our holiness is not dependent on our own efforts but on Jesus' actions. Our decisions and thoughts are not only guided by our whims, but by the Holy Spirit Jesus sends to live within us.

In John 14:26, Jesus offered comfort to His disciples by assuring them that even after His ascension, they wouldn't be on their own. God sent the Holy Spirit to help them, comfort them, advocate for them, and live inside them. He's done the same for you.

EVENING

Thank You, Jesus, for Your ever-present guidance, comfort, and conviction through the Holy Spirit. Help me to listen for Your voice through scripture and Your Spirit's gentle promptings. Thank You for redirecting me when I stray from Your truth. Please guide and comfort me every day.

January 20

> *The father instantly cried out, "I do believe,*
> *but help me overcome my unbelief!"*
>
> MARK 9:24 NLT

Remember when the heavens opened at Jesus' baptism and God affirmed Him as His Son? The incident was repeated at Jesus' transfiguration on the mount. Mark 9:7 says, "Then a cloud overshadowed them, and a voice from the cloud said, 'This is my dearly loved Son. Listen to him.' "

You would think this affirmation of Jesus' identity could make anyone a believer, but not everyone was there to hear it. After He came down from the mountain, Jesus encountered the desperate father of a demon-possessed boy at the center of an argument between the scribes and Jesus' disciples.

This father believed that God could help his son, but when the disciples proved unable to cast out the demon, the man appealed to Jesus. He healed the boy and the father's belief grew.

Whether you're beginning your faith journey with a mountaintop experience or you're desperate for help, faith in God's goodness will always result in growth.

EVENING

> *Lord, I do believe in Your goodness, but there*
> *are moments when I still doubt. Difficult times*
> *should push me even closer to Your side, so I*
> *pray that You will remind me of Your love and*
> *power. May my times of doubt become fewer and*
> *more fleeting, my trust in You ever stronger.*

January 21

The fear of the Lord is the beginning of wisdom.
To learn about the Holy One is understanding.

PROVERBS 9:10 NLV

Wisdom is the combination of knowledge, intuition, and resolve to achieve a specific goal. It is active, always striving toward something better. But where does it begin?

According to today's verse, wisdom begins with "the fear of the Lord." Properly understanding our relationship with God should do more than inspire us toward awe; it should frighten us to see the contrast between His perfection and our imperfection. And yet Jesus has made us holy by His perfect sacrifice, so we need not live in fear. Now we can simply ask God for the wisdom we lack (James 1:5).

When we ask, here's what we receive: "the wisdom that comes from heaven is first of all pure. Then it gives peace. It is gentle and willing to obey. It is full of loving-kindness and of doing good. It has no doubts and does not pretend to be something it is not" (James 3:17).

The wisdom of God is necessary for us to live well and bring others to Jesus. It begins with fear, but it leads to peace.

Jesus, because I know You as my Savior, I do not need to fear judgment. Thank You for sharing Your wonderful goodness with me when I accepted You. Your peace passes all understanding, and it belongs to me when I seek Your wisdom. Please help me to be exactly who You have called me to be, and never pretend to be anything else.

January 22

*And he said unto them, When ye pray, say, Our Father
which art in heaven, Hallowed be thy name. Thy kingdom
come. Thy will be done, as in heaven, so in earth.*

LUKE 11:2 KJV

Prayers from the Old Testament were usually addressed to God by His personal name, YHWH, rendered as Jehovah or LORD in our Bibles. Addressing God this way honored His holy nature since God's personal name was considered too holy even to write down.

When Jesus taught His disciples to pray, He addressed God differently: "Our Father." This was no less respectful of an address, and God's name is still regarded as holy—"Hallowed be thy name"—but it was much more personal than the name Moses or the prophets typically used.

Jesus came to reunite God and man by giving His holiness to us, by making our adoption into God's family permanently possible. As such, God is still holy. . .but we are able to connect to Him personally as our Father. So when you begin prayers with "Our Father," thank Jesus for making it possible.

EVENING

*Jesus, thank You for Your sacrifice which makes
it possible for me to address a holy God with such
familiarity. To be seen as a daughter of the awesome
God of the universe is a gift and a treasure. And
if I'm God's child, Jesus, I'm also Your sister!*

January 23

MORNING

Let us think of ways to motivate one another to acts of love and good works. And let us not neglect our meeting together, as some people do, but encourage one another, especially now that the day of his return is drawing near.

HEBREWS 10:24–25 NLT

Church attendance has been declining for decades. People busy with work, family, and life started taking time for themselves where they could. And while attending church *is* important, it isn't because God cares whether you are warming a pew.

Attending church, especially when it requires sacrifice, puts you in closer touch with Jesus—and in touch with people who need your encouragement. It allows you to stop focusing on your own concerns and gives others an opportunity to show their concern for you.

Being a follower of Jesus means attending family gatherings, not because God *needs* us in church, but because He *wants* His children to be better family members. If it's been a while since you've been in church, it's time to head back. Begin your week with the family, motivating one another to acts of love and good works!

EVENING

Lord Jesus, I'm grateful that my new life with You is much bigger than just us. I thank You for the community You've provided for me through the local church. Guide me into the best place and style of service in Your family as we worship You together!

January 24

Your Word have I hid in my heart, that I may not sin against You.
PSALM 119:11 NLV

Beginning any new practice takes intention and commitment. Well, beginning any *good* new practice takes those things. Left to our own devices, anyone can begin bad habits without intending to (which will then take commitment to undo).

Here's something worth pursuing intentionally: memorizing Bible verses. Knowing God's Word helps us keep His truth at the front of our minds, so we can live it out intentionally—the way Jesus did every day of His life here on earth. Making time to commit scripture to memory protects us from using that time selfishly. . .and when we come against specific temptations, we'll be equipped to fight them.

Take a few moments to look up 2 Timothy 3:16–17; Hebrews 4:12; Psalm 119:105; Mark 13:31; and Romans 15:4 for biblical reasons to memorize scripture. Then look for some verses to "hide in your heart." You might even start by memorizing the powerful verses about Jesus found in this devotional!

EVENING

*Jesus, I know it's important to hide Your Word
in my heart. That doesn't mean I'm keeping Your
Word from others, just that it's safe and secure
inside me, a part of my very being. I don't want to
sin against You, Lord. As I fall off to sleep tonight,
please bring Your Word to my mind—and make
it my first waking thought in the morning.*

MORNING

Your heart should be holy and set apart for the Lord God.
Always be ready to tell everyone who asks you why you
believe as you do. Be gentle as you speak and show respect.

1 PETER 3:15 NLV

Beginning new practices like regular church attendance or memorizing scripture can be intimidating. But few things feel as monumentally nerve-racking as sharing your faith. Why is that?

Perhaps because we've been told from our earliest days not to talk to strangers. Or maybe we're afraid we won't be able to answer a person's questions perfectly and we may do more harm than good. And what if we offend others by suggesting their current belief system is wrong?

If sharing the gospel of Jesus Christ makes you uncomfortable, remember how uncomfortable it was for Jesus to provide it for you. If you have been set apart for God, you must be ready to do what He asks. If you speak with gentleness and respect, most people will appreciate the fact that you care enough to share your life with them.

EVENING

Jesus, it's a great honor to share the gospel with others—
lead me to people who need to know You and empower
me to speak Your truth. You have changed my life, so
use me to encourage others to consider You too. May
many in my circle experience Your peace and power.

January 26

Jesus said, "How can I describe the Kingdom of God? What
story should I use to illustrate it? It is like a mustard seed
planted in the ground. It is the smallest of all seeds, but
it becomes the largest of all garden plants; it grows long
branches, and birds can make nests in its shade."

MARK 4:30–32 NLT

Mustard seeds are tiny, but they can grow into plants up to ten feet tall. Mustard plants were considered weeds in Israel because they could quickly overtake a garden. Farmers would have worked hard to keep them out!

When Jesus compared God's Kingdom to a weed, He meant it wasn't going to grow in orderly, controllable ways. Its hidden beginnings in a small Judean town were going to change the world.

When life isn't as orderly or controllable as you'd like, remember the mustard seed. God is still in control, and He may not want your garden to be orderly. He may be looking for ways to grow your faith from a tiny seed to an overtaking force of nature.

EVENING

Lord Jesus, I trust You to make even the disorderly
seasons of my life a testimony of Your goodness.
Use me, like a tiny mustard seed, to grow in
faith and spread Your gospel. Show me the
people I need to reach for Your name's sake.

MORNING

> *The crowds that went ahead of him and those that followed shouted, "Hosanna to the Son of David!" "Blessed is he who comes in the name of the Lord!" "Hosanna in the highest heaven!"*
>
> MATTHEW 21:9 NIV

The beginning of a week can look very different from its end. Crowds welcomed Jesus on Palm Sunday with shouts of "Blessed is he who comes in the name of the Lord!" Crowds called for His crucifixion days later (Matthew 27:22).

Though the whims of a crowd can change dramatically, God never changes. His plans cannot be thwarted. It is only our perspective that needs to change for us to recognize God's perfect plan acting in our lives. After all, our redemption couldn't have happened without Jesus' crucifixion.

When it seems as if things are heading downhill, look up! You'll see that God's love is constant in all circumstances.

EVENING

> *Jesus, I thank You for the new beginning You offered by Your free gift of salvation. You changed the course of my life in a moment, and You continue to change me day by day. You understand my trials because You've gone through unimaginably difficult things, and You promise always to be by my side. Whatever tomorrow may bring, You can redeem it for Your own glory.*

January 28

*"Suppose one of you wants to build a tower. Won't
you first sit down and estimate the cost to see if
you have enough money to complete it?"*
LUKE 14:28 NIV

The first step of any project? Figure out what you're getting yourself
into. Action without forethought invariably leads to regret. Whether
you're building a tower as in today's scripture, or remodeling a bath-
room, or even thinking of fast-food at the drive-thru, it is wise to
count the cost first.

But Jesus wasn't offering pocketbook advice. The context of this
scripture is found in verse 26: "If anyone comes to me and does not
hate father and mother, wife and children, brothers and sisters—yes,
even their own life—such a person cannot be my disciple."

Following Jesus isn't just expensive, it is exclusive. To be a Christian means laying down everything—money, relationships, pride,
goals—at the foot of the cross, knowing that what we get in return
is worth incomparably more.

*Lord, when I first came to You, I didn't recognize the full
cost of faith. But I know the value of it, because nothing
in this world compares to Your love. May I be like the
woman in Bethany who poured out her expensive jar
of perfumed oil on Your feet, Jesus. You were blessed
by her sacrifice, and You blessed her in return. Help
me to freely lay down everything I have for You.*

MORNING

> *"Don't misunderstand why I have come. I did not come to abolish the law of Moses or the writings of the prophets. No, I came to accomplish their purpose."*
>
> MATTHEW 5:17 NLT

When did Christianity begin? The early movement can be traced historically and archeologically to within a few years of Jesus' death and resurrection, but it didn't begin then. Not really.

Although the Lord's incarnation forever changed the way people interact with God, to say Christianity started with Jesus would disagree with what He said in today's scripture. Jesus wasn't looking to start a new religion, but to finish what had been promised in the garden of Eden.

Christ's role in God's rescue plan is recorded in the serpent's curse: "And I will cause hostility between you and the woman, and between your offspring and her offspring. He will strike your head, and you will strike his heel" (Genesis 3:15).

When the devil whispers half-truths to entice you to sin, remember that Jesus came to set you free—and He has already accomplished His purpose.

EVENING

> *Lord, I know that You came to redeem me, to cause me to pursue righteousness and follow those things You want me to do. You didn't abolish the law, You fulfilled it—and You'll help me to live up to it. I thank You that Your guidelines protect me from harm.*

January 30

Be very careful, then, how you live—not as unwise but as wise,
making the most of every opportunity, because the days are evil.

EPHESIANS 5:15–16 NIV

In 1923, a bank in Coshocton, Ohio, published an advertisement that said, "Half the game of getting ahead is getting started." Not only is that sound financial advice—the Bible echoes the statement in Proverbs 13:11—it applies to anything you may be putting off. Even sharing the gospel of Jesus Christ.

It's time to begin. Investing in others now will yield heavenly rewards later, which are infinitely more valuable than money (Matthew 6:19–21). Plus, opportunities to bring others to Jesus are swiftly passing by—and no one knows when they will end completely.

How can you get started? By living wisely: confess your sins (1 John 1:9), take care of widows and orphans (James 1:27), love God and your neighbor (Matthew 22:37–39), and think about godly things (Philippians 4:8).

You're halfway to success!

EVENING

Lord Jesus, I want to walk in Your wisdom and
live out Your Word at every opportunity. Keep
my mind and heart on the things You have for
me. May I reflect Your light in this dark world,
and point many people to the life You offer.

MORNING

Better is the end of a thing than the beginning thereof.
ECCLESIASTES 7:8 KJV

Beginnings are essential, and new beginnings are wonderful. But neither comprises the full story.

As we close out the first month of this new year, consider the words of the Preacher of Ecclesiastes: a successful conclusion excels the beginning of any endeavor.

Believers know that God the Father will finish what He started in their lives. As the apostle Paul wrote, "he which hath begun a good work in you will perform it until the day of Jesus Christ" (Philippians 1:6). And Jesus Himself guarantees our safety and security to the very end: "My sheep hear my voice, and I know them, and they follow me: and I give unto them eternal life; and they shall never perish, neither shall any man pluck them out of my hand" (John 10:27–28).

When you begin with Jesus, you are assured of a very good end—a perfect one, actually.

EVENING

Lord, I trust that my new beginning in You will have a glorious ending—eternity in Your presence. Endings on this earth are often painful or bittersweet, but I know that You are always working all things for my good as I love and follow You faithfully.

February 1

> *"There is no greater love than to lay down one's life for one's friends."*
> JOHN 15:13 NLT

Love takes center stage in February, with Valentine's Day at the midpoint of the month. The holiday is named for a third-century Roman Christian martyr. Though, like Christmas, Valentine's Day has become secular and commercialized, it can prompt us to ask good questions—like, "What *is* love?"

Of course, there are plenty of lighter, less-serious aspects to love: we "love" pizza, puppies, and parades. We experience junior high crushes and think we'll die if our "love" doesn't reciprocate. If we eventually marry and have children, we begin to plumb the deeper wells of love, drawing slowly closer to the dictionary definition of Jesus' type: "unselfish loyal and benevolent concern for the good of another."

What else can you call Jesus' choice to leave the glory of heaven, to live as a man on this sin-cursed earth, to face the opposition of far lesser men, and ultimately to die on a cross as payment for human sin? Just *love*.

EVENING

In You, Jesus, I see the perfect outpouring of love. May I follow wherever You lead because I know that all the plans You have for me come from a place of deep and sacrificial love. The way You love me is the model for how I should love others. . .and most importantly You!

MORNING

Dear friends, let us continue to love one another, for love comes from God. Anyone who loves is a child of God and knows God. But anyone who does not love does not know God, for God is love.

1 JOHN 4:7–8 NLT

Humans need love. Babies who don't receive loving touches have higher mortality rates. Adults are constantly searching for love, sometimes in unhealthy ways. Why is love so integral to the human experience?

Consider what today's verse means in light of Genesis 1:27: "So God created human beings in his own image. In the image of God he created them; male and female he created them."

We were made in the image of God, and God is love. We were created by, for, and to resemble love itself! When sin broke the world, we humans tried filling our love needs by ourselves, but we were made to love and be loved by God. Nothing else can satisfy our innate desire for love. Praise Jesus for making it possible for God's love to live in us!

EVENING

Lord Jesus, only You can satisfy my need and desire for love. Your love is a treasure that fills my heart and overflows into the lives of others. May I honor You, Your Father, and Your Holy Spirit by accepting and sharing the love You are.

February 3

We love him, because he first loved us.
1 JOHN 4:19 KJV

Jesus' love takes initiative. It doesn't wait for someone else to take the first step. It doesn't sit near the phone, waiting for the ring. Jesus' love reaches out first.

Jesus' love is bold. It isn't nervous about rejection, although rejection is a possibility. And only because we are able to reject Him does it mean anything when we choose to love Him in return. We may deny His love, but there's no denying that Jesus reached out first.

When we accept His love, we are filled to overflowing, boldly initiating relationships with others. Jesus' love inspires action first. It opens us to the possibility of rejection but also to the possibility of true connection.

When we love as Jesus loves, we forgive before the apology. We choose kindness while facing hostility. We turn the other cheek, give more than is requested, and go the extra mile. We realize that our love for others may not change them. . .but we do it because Jesus' love has changed *us*.

EVENING

*Lord Jesus, I ask for strength to grow in love. I want
to be known for demonstrating Your love even in the
most difficult situations. Forgive me for those moments
today when I didn't show Your kind of love. I thank
You for the new mercies You'll give me tomorrow.*

February 4

*Therefore, as God's chosen people, holy and dearly loved,
clothe yourselves with compassion, kindness, humility,
gentleness and patience. Bear with each other and forgive
one another if any of you has a grievance against someone.
Forgive as the Lord forgave you. And over all these virtues
put on love, which binds them all together in perfect unity.*
COLOSSIANS 3:12–14 NIV

What's the important step that comes after getting cleaned up for the day but before going out in public? Getting dressed! We don't live in a pre-sin Eden anymore. Decent society expects us to be clothed.

In the same way, now that we've been made clean in Jesus, we need to get spiritually dressed before we interact with the world. But we're not talking socks and pants. Christians are called to put on kindness, humility, gentleness, patience, and forgiveness. And on top of everything, we put on love. Love completes the holy ensemble.

When we're dressed for success, we'll be ready to focus on others more than ourselves, and in doing so, we'll resemble Jesus Himself.

EVENING

*I want to be clothed in the things that represent You,
Jesus. May my life look like the life You lived on this
earth. Clothe me in Your compassion, kindness,
forgiveness, patience, and most importantly, Your love.*

February 5

> *There is no fear in love. Perfect love puts fear out of our hearts. People have fear when they are afraid of being punished. The man who is afraid does not have perfect love.*
>
> 1 JOHN 4:18 NLV

Obedience happens for different reasons. We might follow rules for logical reasons—for the love of the person who gives the rules or to avoid the punishment that results from breaking said rules. If the rules are being obeyed, does it matter why?

On one hand, it does, because our motivations matter to God. On the other hand, we were born into disobedience, so we already deserve punishment. Romans 3:23 (KJV) says, "For all have sinned, and come short of the glory of God."

But thanks to Jesus, who has taken our punishment, we have been declared holy before a perfect God. We obey Jesus' commandments, not for fear of punishment or even because they make sense—they won't always—but because we love Him. And we know our obedience pleases Him.

EVENING

> *Lord, obedience doesn't come naturally, but I know I need to do Your will. Help me to walk on Your path because the rules You've given are for my good and the advancement of the gospel. You always know what's best for me. When I obey You, even when the rules don't make sense, I know that I'm honoring You with my life.*

MORNING

But God showed his great love for us by sending
Christ to die for us while we were still sinners.

ROMANS 5:8 NLT

Think of a sacrifice you've made for love. Maybe you went to a restaurant you don't like because your significant other wanted to eat there. Maybe you scrimped and saved to afford a really nice gift for someone. Maybe you did a household chore you hate because you know your loved one hates it even more. It's easy to make these kinds of sacrifices for someone you love who loves you in return.

Now imagine making the ultimate sacrifice for someone who doesn't even know you, maybe even for someone who hates you. That's the sacrifice Jesus made for us. While we were still His enemies, He laid down His life to make us right with God. That's the love we are called to show others.

If you ever find yourself with someone you don't like, pray for Jesus' love to fill your heart. Then make a sacrifice that reflects the "great love" of God.

EVENING

Lord, it's hard to imagine Your love. Thank You for
seeing beyond my sin to the salvation You would offer.
May I view others with the same love with which You
see them, with the same love with which You saw
me. Your kindness draws people to repentance. May
my kindness and love draw others to know You.

February 7

> *Most important of all, continue to show deep love for each other, for love covers a multitude of sins.*
>
> 1 PETER 4:8 NLT

It's good that Jesus doesn't hold grudges. We sin constantly. We make mistakes and promise never to be trapped by sin again only to find ourselves sinning almost immediately. Jesus could be skeptical when we repent—He knows every sin we have committed and will commit in the future—but He isn't.

Being forgiven is wonderful, but if it doesn't result in forgiving others, then we haven't truly understood Jesus' love. Jesus said, "If you forgive those who sin against you, your heavenly Father will forgive you. But if you refuse to forgive others, your Father will not forgive your sins" (Matthew 6:14–15).

When you truly experience Jesus' love, grudges melt away and forgiveness comes easily, covering "a multitude of sins" done against you. Ephesians 4:32 says it like this: "Be kind to each other, tenderhearted, forgiving one another, just as God through Christ has forgiven you."

EVENING

> *Lord Jesus, I don't want to hold grudges. Remind me that I have sinned much, but You didn't hold that against me. Let me be a gracious forgiver like You, leaving the sins of the past—other's and my own—far behind.*

February 8

MORNING

Husbands, love your wives. You must love them as
Christ loved the church. He gave His life for it.

EPHESIANS 5:25 NLV

Marriage is a relationship that reflects the union of Christ with His church. Today's verse may be addressed to husbands, but the call to love self-sacrificially is applicable to every Christian, whether you're married or not.

The purpose of marriage is given in Ephesians 5:26–27: "Christ did this so He could set the church apart for Himself. He made it clean by the washing of water with the Word. Christ did this so the church might stand before Him in shining-greatness. There is to be no sin of any kind in it. It is to be holy and without blame."

Marriage exists to make people holy, not happy. This call to holiness applies to every believer and is achieved in part by our relationships with others. They often reveal the sin present in our own lives! As we allow Jesus to make us holy, we are increasingly able to put the interests of others ahead of our own. We can be more like our Lord, who gave Himself for us.

EVENING

Jesus, You make me holy before Your Father, but I
still have a responsibility to obey Your commands.
As part of Your bride, the church, I want to be pure
and true and honoring to You in every way. May You
empower my efforts and be pleased by the results.

February 9

If ye love me, keep my commandments.
JOHN 14:15 KJV

God's laws were given to the nation of Israel as proof that they were His chosen people (Deuteronomy 7:9). When Israel obeyed these laws and loved God properly, they prospered. When they defied God, they suffered.

By the time of Jesus' arrival, Jewish leaders took God's laws very seriously—to the point of adding their own rules into the mix to make them appear to be the holiest men around. But these new laws made life unnecessarily difficult for people.

In Matthew 11:29, Jesus had a better idea: "Take my yoke upon you, and learn of me; for I am meek and lowly in heart: and ye shall find rest unto your souls."

Jesus doesn't want to make our lives harder. He's all about making peace between us and God, offering rest for our souls. The commandments He mentioned in John 14:15 are quite simple: love God above all else, and love your neighbor as yourself (Matthew 22:37–39).

EVENING

You've made it so simple, Jesus. When I love You I find peace. I don't need to strive, because You have done the work I never could have. Now it is my privilege to love You and others. Please keep my motives pure and shed Your love abroad through my words and actions.

MORNING

*If I could speak all the languages of earth and of angels,
but didn't love others, I would only be a noisy gong or
a clanging cymbal. If I had the gift of prophecy, and if I
understood all of God's secret plans and possessed all
knowledge, and if I had such faith that I could move
mountains, but didn't love others, I would be nothing.*

1 CORINTHIANS 13:1–2 NLT

First Corinthians 13 is sometimes called the "love chapter" of the Bible. While the theme for this month of February is love, we're going to look specifically at this passage from today until Valentine's Day.

To put 1 Corinthians 13 in context, understand that chapter 12 describes how people in the church—Jesus' beautiful bride—have different gifts (for example, prophecy, hospitality, and wisdom), and all of them are needed for the church to be complete. Today's passage refers to the fact that gifts alone are useless if not carried out in love.

When our personal gifts are empowered by Jesus' love, the world will be drawn to Christ. They will see His love exuding from our words and actions, and others will want to know Him too.

EVENING

*Jesus, may all that I do be done in love. I want to honor
You and draw people to Your name by showing others
how much You love. May I put off every self-interest,
and be motivated purely by love—Your pure love.*

February 11

Love is patient, love is kind. It does not envy, it does not boast, it is not proud. It does not dishonor others, it is not self-seeking, it is not easily angered, it keeps no record of wrongs. Love does not delight in evil but rejoices with the truth.

1 CORINTHIANS 13:4–6 NIV

You've probably heard today's scripture quoted in marriage ceremonies. But how do we apply it to our everyday lives?

Read through these verses again and consider the focus of each of love's attributes. For love to be patient and kind, it must look beyond itself. For it not to be envious, boastful, or proud, it must look beyond itself. Love is not concerned with self; it is set on the good of others.

To this end, Jesus was the ultimate example of love. He humbled Himself for our sakes (2 Corinthians 8:9), forgave others freely (Luke 5:20), and is the embodiment of truth and grace (John 1:14). To apply today's passage to your life, look to Jesus. . .then attend to the needs of those around you.

EVENING

Lord Jesus, help me to look beyond myself and focus on You instead. May I follow Your example and try to fulfill the deepest needs of others. Teach me to champion others, never seeking to put them down to lift myself up. I ask for Your perfect love and pray to be like You as I share that love with others.

February 12

Love never gives up, never loses faith, is always hopeful, and endures through every circumstance.

1 CORINTHIANS 13:7 NLT

True love cannot be shaken. It doesn't matter if circumstances change, if tragedy strikes, or if loving someone is no longer convenient. Love doesn't give up when the loving gets tough.

The love of Jesus is again the best example. For love, Jesus left the perfection of God's presence to come to our broken world (John 1:14). For love, He wandered from town to town without a place to rest His head (Matthew 8:20). For love, Jesus reached out to those society rejected (Luke 15:2). And for love, Jesus went to the cross to pay for our sins (John 3:16).

To love as Jesus does, we must be intentional. Let's lay aside our comforts, accept those whom others reject, and keep loving even when it costs us everything. Real love isn't easy. It requires endurance. But when we endure, we prove that Jesus' love dwells within us.

You never give up or lose faith, Jesus. I want to be like You. Give me endurance to stay hopeful not only in the easy times but in the times of deepest sorrow and pain. I know that You will never give up on me or love me any less—Your sacrifice on the cross proves that. Thank You for such love.

February 13

Love never fails. But where there are prophecies, they will cease; where there are tongues, they will be stilled; where there is knowledge, it will pass away.

1 CORINTHIANS 13:8 NIV

We live in a world of natural entropy and planned obsolescence. Cell phones are designed to fail in time, so you need to buy another. Cars can be meticulously maintained, but their parts eventually wear down. Ultimately, everything breaks down. Well, everything except love.

The love of Jesus is as timeless as God Himself. Hebrews 1:3 says, "The Son is the radiance of God's glory and the exact representation of his being, sustaining all things by his powerful word. After he had provided purification for sins, he sat down at the right hand of the Majesty in heaven."

Jesus is waiting for the Father's "go" to bring us as His followers to our ultimate rest. . .and He never stops loving us. As this broken world continues to crumble, His love is as pure and whole as He is Himself. Jesus, and His love, will never fail.

EVENING

Lord, I'm so grateful for Your unfailing love. Even when I fail, time and time again, Your love does not grow weary. It is the same today as it was the day I came to the saving knowledge of You. Show me how to love like You do, with constant faithfulness and joy.

February 14

*And now we have these three: faith and hope
and love, but the greatest of these is love.*

1 CORINTHIANS 13:13 NLV

Faith, hope, and love are all pretty great. The apostle Paul explained how they overlap in the Christian's life. First Thessalonians 1:3 says, "While praying to God our Father, we always remember your work of *faith* and your acts of *love* and your *hope* that never gives up in our Lord Jesus Christ" (emphasis added).

But it is only in today's scripture that Paul recognizes love as the greatest of the three. Why is love the greatest? Because if Jesus didn't love us through His obedient sacrifice, we would have no reason for faith. If His love had stayed in the tomb, we would have no reason for hope. But because Jesus' love took Him both to the cross and out of the grave, we have faith, hope, and love altogether.

On this Valentine's Day, don't forget the One who made *love* the greatest thing of all: Jesus!

EVENING

*Lord, I thank You for Your sacrifice on the cross—
I can enjoy faith, hope, and love because of Your
selfless work. Since You loved me first, what can I
do besides love You in return? Take my life—body,
mind, and spirit—and make it Yours, I pray.*

February 15

> *See what great love the Father has lavished on us, that we should be called children of God! And that is what we are! The reason the world does not know us is that it did not know him.*
>
> 1 JOHN 3:1 NIV

Adoption goes back to ancient times. In the Roman world of Jesus' day, it was fairly common, with both family adoptions (in which one family would legally become part of another) and individual adoptions (which is more commonly seen today). In either case, adoptees were legally considered part of the adoptive family, subject to the authority of the family head, and able to inherit that family's estate. In all cases, adopted persons ceased to belong in any way to their original family.

Because of Jesus' love and sacrifice, we have become children of God (John 1:12–13). We no longer belong to the family of this world. Our love, then, shouldn't be for the world, but for our Father in heaven, our Lord Jesus, and our new family in Him.

EVENING

> *Jesus, I want people to know that I belong to Your family. May I never live as if I'm still part of this world. Forgive me this evening for the times I've loved this world today. I pray that tomorrow I will be fully committed to Your beautiful family.*

MORNING

"Love your enemies! Do good to them. Lend to them without expecting to be repaid. Then your reward from heaven will be very great, and you will truly be acting as children of the Most High, for he is kind to those who are unthankful and wicked."

LUKE 6:35 NLT

Loving your enemies is hard. They're your enemies! They are the last people on earth you would naturally feel like loving.

Ah, you may think, *what if by loving them, I can change them and make them more lovable?* Unfortunately, that misses the point in two ways. First, *your* love cannot change anyone; only Jesus' love can. Second, loving your enemies isn't supposed to change *them*; it is supposed to change *you*.

When Jesus came to save the lost, He sought out tax collectors, prostitutes, and people considered to be enemies of society. He reached out with a pure love, and they were changed because of Him. We can only love our enemies when we stop thinking of them as enemies and love them with Jesus' love. . .just as He has loved us.

EVENING

Lord, You know how difficult it is for me to love my enemies. Teach me to see even those who've hurt me through Your eyes of love. Empower me to pray for my enemies and believe that You can and will transform them into loving, faithful believers, my own sisters and brothers in Christ.

February 17

> *Love each other as Christian brothers.*
> *Show respect for each other.*
> ROMANS 12:10 NLV

It's easy to slip from brotherly love into sibling rivalry. Just ask Cain and Abel. But it doesn't have to be that way. As followers of Christ, we are united by family bonds that are stronger than the blood in our veins. They are as strong as the blood of Jesus.

So what do we do when rivalries form between brothers and sisters in Christ? We don't ignore them; we must surrender them to God. When we find jealousy or anger within, the Bible tells us to go to God in prayer. If God won't honor our request, it may be because our desires were selfishly motivated. Only by giving up our selfish desires and respecting our siblings in Christ will we show the world that the family of God means something special (James 4:1–3).

Jesus made us children of God so we could love each other well, not engage in rivalries.

EVENING

> *Lord Jesus, I have brothers and sisters around the world through faith in You. You prayed that all Your people would be unified as You are with Your Father and the Holy Spirit. Please give me patience and understanding for my fellow believers, so we can present a beautiful image of Your family to the world.*

MORNING

No, in all these things we are more than conquerors through him who loved us. For I am convinced that neither death nor life, neither angels nor demons, neither the present nor the future, nor any powers, neither height nor depth, nor anything else in all creation, will be able to separate us from the love of God that is in Christ Jesus our Lord.

ROMANS 8:37–39 NIV

Jesus doesn't write break-up letters. He's in it for the long haul. Nothing can separate us from the love of Christ. Not your worries. Not your doubts. Not your fears. Not your finances or the lack thereof. Not your mistakes. Not your sins. Not the size of your social media following. Not "trouble or hardship or persecution or famine or nakedness or danger or sword" (Romans 8:35). Not bears with chainsaws for arms or sharks with laser eyes or a zombie apocalypse.

When Jesus says He loves you, He means He loves you *forever*. When you are "in Christ," you are in His love. . .no ifs, ands, or buts. Rest easy in such love!

EVENING

Jesus, as this day ends, I thank You for the reminder that nothing can separate me from Your love. You knew and loved me before I was even born, and You will love me for all eternity to come. This truth gives me comfort, peace, and rest, and I praise You for it.

February 19

> *But the Holy Spirit produces this kind of fruit in our lives:*
> *love, joy, peace, patience, kindness, goodness, faithfulness,*
> *gentleness, and self-control. There is no law against these things!*
>
> GALATIANS 5:22–23 NLT

Fruit is the naturally occurring, self-replicating, delicious evidence of God's love and provision for humanity. Yes, there are things that fruit farmers must do to cultivate and protect their crops, but farmers don't create fruit. God does.

And just as physical fruit is a naturally occurring phenomenon, the fruit of the Spirit happens naturally when we allow Jesus to work in our lives. In John 15:5, He said, "Yes, I am the vine; you are the branches. Those who remain in me, and I in them, will produce much fruit. For apart from me you can do nothing."

In today's scripture, love is listed as the primary evidence of the Spirit's work. It is a naturally occurring, self-replicating, delicious way that we show others what Jesus has done for us.

EVENING

> *Lord Jesus, I thank You for the Spirit You've sent into*
> *my life. May my heart be a fertile garden that produces*
> *much fruit and brings honor and glory to You. Help me to*
> *remain in You at all times so I can be healthy and strong*
> *myself and provide blessing and nourishment to others.*

MORNING

But because of his great love for us, God, who is rich in
mercy, made us alive with Christ even when we were dead
in transgressions—it is by grace you have been saved.

EPHESIANS 2:4–5 NIV

If you've ever taken a trip through a hard place—whether a minor detour of life or the valley of the shadow of death—you know it's life-giving when a traveling companion comes along and shows you love. Perhaps someone offered a note of encouragement, a hug, or fulfilled an unexpressed need. No matter the act, the love behind it breathes new life into us when we feel almost dead.

When Jesus came to earth, it wasn't simply to give hugs or words of encouragement. He came to give *life* to those who were truly dead in their sins. Our new life in Christ may still include paths through the valley (we still live in a broken world), but we can always trust that the path will ultimately lead where He wants us to go. And we can be certain that He walks beside us every step of the way.

EVENING

Lord Jesus, where would I be now, apart from Your
love? You have given life to my days and filled my empty
spirit. Even in hard times, I know that I'm never alone.
You are my ever-present companion, and I trust that
You will lead me exactly where You want me to go.

February 21

> *Dear children, let's not merely say that we love each other; let us show the truth by our actions.*
>
> 1 John 3:18 nlt

An elderly couple was having dinner with some newlyweds when the young husband turned to his bride and said, "I love you." The elderly wife looked at her husband and said, "Why don't you tell me you love me like that?" The elderly husband responded, "I told you I love you years ago. I'll let you know if anything changes."

Saying "I love you" *is* important. It's good to be reassured, even if nothing has changed in the years since you heard it last. But words alone are not enough. Jesus could have pronounced His love over humanity until He was blue in the face, but if He hadn't followed through with the crucifixion, His words would have been simply that—words.

Thanks to Jesus' fully enacted love though, the love shown by both His words and His actions, we know without doubt where we stand with God. And now we have the ability to love others in word and in truth, following His example.

EVENING

> *Jesus, I am so grateful that You didn't just say You loved us, but that You sacrificed Yourself and truly proved Your love to all humanity. I need never doubt Your love or worry about it changing because You proved on the cross that it's real and lasting. I praise You for loving me so fully!*

MORNING

Then Christ will make his home in your hearts as you trust in him. Your roots will grow down into God's love and keep you strong. And may you have the power to understand, as all God's people should, how wide, how long, how high, and how deep his love is. May you experience the love of Christ, though it is too great to understand fully. Then you will be made complete with all the fullness of life and power that comes from God.

EPHESIANS 3:17–19 NLT

Try explaining double-digit multiplication to an average preschooler and you'll end up frustrated. The child doesn't have a basic understanding of math, so she can't grasp the higher concepts. But start with simple addition, and you can build up to more complex functions in time.

When Jesus came into your life, you began a different kind of education. As you trust Him and live in His love, your understanding of God's nature and power will grow deeper and more complex. You'll begin to realize "how wide, how long, how high, and how deep his love is."

Of course, you'll never fully understand Jesus' love for you. But you were made to experience it all the same!

EVENING

As I rest this evening, Lord, please remind me of the extent of Your love. I can never fully understand it, but I want to learn more about You each day. You know everything about me, Jesus—help me to know You better with every passing moment.

February 23

> *Live with love as Christ loved you. He gave Himself for us,*
> *a gift on the altar to God which was as a sweet smell to God.*
>
> EPHESIANS 5:2 NLV

Baked apple pie, fresh-cut grass, peppermint, pine. Agitated skunk, an outhouse on a hot summer day, rotten eggs. The nose knows what it likes and what it doesn't. When you smell something good, you take a deep breath and smile. When you smell something bad, you grimace, hoping the odor dissipates soon.

According to today's scripture, loving others with the unconditional love of Jesus is "a sweet smell to God." Imagine Him breathing deeply and smiling as He watches you treat others with kindness, forgive their offenses, and sacrifice your preferences so they will feel loved. It's a much better image than that of God seeing you and holding His nose.

How can you improve the "scent" of your life? By living out the love of Jesus. He produces within your heart and life the sweet-smelling, fragrant fruit that brings Him pleasure.

> *Lord, I want my life to be a pleasing aroma to You.*
> *May the fruit that You produce in me by Your Spirit*
> *bring joy to You and to those around me. I want to*
> *honor You with everything that I say and do and am.*

MORNING

"I have loved you just as My Father has loved Me. Stay in My love."
JOHN 15:9 NLV

You are the house that God built. First Corinthians 6:19–20 says, "Do you not know that your body is a house of God where the Holy Spirit lives? God gave you His Holy Spirit. Now you belong to God. You do not belong to yourselves. God bought you with a great price. So honor God with your body. You belong to Him."

When you invited Jesus into your house, He didn't show up as a cleaning service. He came to set your affairs in order. He became a permanent roommate. He's even laid out some helpful house rules He wants you to follow. Jesus said, "The one who loves Me will obey My teaching. My Father will love him. We will come to him and live with him" (John 14:23).

Once Jesus moves in with His love, He's not going anywhere. Now, He's asking you to stay with Him.

EVENING

Lord, my house is Your house now. Body and soul,
I am Yours. Use every aspect of my personality to
perform Your will and bring glory to You. I hold
nothing back from You, so please transform me
into the fully new woman You want me to be.

February 25

And thou shalt love the Lord thy God with all thy heart,
and with all thy soul, and with all thy mind, and with
all thy strength: this is the first commandment.

MARK 12:30 KJV

In today's scripture, Jesus summed up the point of humankind's existence: we are meant to love God. Why? Because He loved us enough to sacrifice His only Son so we could be with Him again in perfection. Jesus went all in with His love for us. We are to go all in with our love for Him.

But what does that mean? Imagine a married couple. If the husband isn't fully invested in the marriage, it doesn't matter how faithful the wife is. Commitment is required of both people to make love last. If the husband chooses selfishly to cheat, heartbreak follows.

Jesus doesn't want that kind of heartbreak for us. He's already proved His love by dying for our sins. Now He wants the same level of commitment from us—not only for Himself but for our own good. Are you all in?

EVENING

I am so glad, Jesus, that You went all in for me. I never
have to worry about You leaving or failing me. Help
me now to be fully committed to You. Don't let me be
distracted by the things of this world, Lord. I know that
You are worthy of my full attention and devotion.

MORNING

"The second is equally important: 'Love your neighbor as yourself.' No other commandment is greater than these."

MARK 12:31 NLT

When Jesus went all in with His love for you, He didn't half-fill your love tank. He filled it to overflowing! But what should you do with all that overflowing love? You pass it along to the people around you.

We were made to love God above all else, and one way He feels most loved is when we care for our neighbors, when we provide for the poor, when we take care of widows and orphans, and when we lend our voice to those whom society has refused to hear.

Jesus paid the ultimate price to give you His love. When He paid the cost of sin, your life was made valuable in God's eyes. Now Jesus wants you to ascribe value to others in the same way. Love your neighbor as yourself because Jesus' love overflows from you.

EVENING

Help me, Lord, to be intentional in sharing the love that You have poured into me. As I wind down this day, stir my thoughts toward ways I can spread Your love to others tomorrow. Highlight people in need of Your love so I can show them the worth that You see in them.

February 27

MORNING

> *By this shall all men know that ye are my*
> *disciples, if ye have love one to another.*
> JOHN 13:35 KJV

Uniforms make it easy to identify a person's livelihood. Firefighters wear turnout gear, chefs wear white toques, and professional hockey players wear skates and lots of padding. But when it comes to identifying a person's faith, there is no physical uniform—not even clothing embroidered with a cross or *ichthys* (the "Jesus fish").

Jesus said the world would recognize that we follow Him when we love each other. That love should be visible, wholehearted, and markedly different from the love of the world. The love of Christ enables us to see the needs of others, to meet them sacrificially, and to defer any praise we receive to the One who ultimately deserves it.

If your love for other believers is not as obvious as a firefighter's uniform, it isn't visible enough. Jesus doesn't want you to wear a Christian T-shirt; He wants you to demonstrate His love.

EVENING

> *Jesus, shine through me in such a way that people*
> *around me, from strangers to my best friends, can*
> *see that You live inside me and guide my steps.*
> *Challenge me, more and more each day, to show with*
> *my words and actions that I am Your disciple.*

MORNING

Everything you do should be done in love.
1 CORINTHIANS 16:14 NLV

If love is the identifying trait of Christ-followers, then love should be evident in everything we do. Love isn't something we bring out for special occasions like birthdays and family reunions. It should be present in every mundane task too.

Do the laundry with love. Pay your bills with love. Wash the dishes with love. Greet your neighbors—even the one who doesn't clean up after his dog—with love. Discipline your children with love. Do your job with love. Go to church with love. Do everything with love.

Remember that love is defined as "unselfish loyal and benevolent concern for the good of another." Jesus lived, died, and rose again with love saturating His every action He took. Pray that *you* will be saturated with His overflowing love. Turn your heart and mind and soul and strength to God and to the people around you. And love like Jesus in everything you do.

EVENING

Lord Jesus, I want Your love to permeate everything
I do throughout each day. Nothing is too small to
do with love, so may I be intentional to perform
every task in Your love. In that way, I want to
encourage others and bring glory to You.

March 1

Jesus Christ the same yesterday, and to day, and for ever.
HEBREWS 13:8 KJV

Rebirth. It's a spring thing—and it's beautiful. It wasn't so long ago that all the summer greenery turned orange, red, yellow, or brown. When winter arrived, much of the old growth was dislodged from trees, gardens, and fields by the chill wind. Spring is that blank slate on which Jesus paints brilliant colors all around. He does it every year.

You can get used to the changing of seasons. When spring gives way to summer and summer's end is heralded by the coming of frost, "The grass withereth, the flower fadeth" (Isaiah 40:8). Then you wait again for the coming of spring.

Not all change is as predictable or pleasant. That's why Isaiah 40:8 continues with a beautiful promise: "the word of our God shall stand for ever."

Seasons change all the time. God's Word never does. So enjoy this spring—it's a time of physical rebirth. Jesus offers *spiritual* rebirth. Forever will begin—and never end.

Thank You, Jesus, for the gift of rebirth. You took me once for all from death to life, and now every day You draw me to Yourself in sanctification. May I see in the deadness of winter my old life, and look forward every day to the fresh rebirth of spiritual springtime.

MORNING

To be made new in the attitude of your minds;
and to put on the new self, created to be like
God in true righteousness and holiness.
EPHESIANS 4:23–24 NIV

You can do old-life living without any classroom instruction. This kind of life requires no college degree. *You* make the rules. You follow your heart. You don't feel any obligation to obey anyone at any time for any reason. But when your decisions don't match up with Jesus' plan for you, you'll never find freedom.

For Christians, the old life is a wardrobe we have to get rid of. Jesus planned it that way: "For we know that our old self was crucified with him" (as you give up your past way of living) "so that the body ruled by sin might be done away with, that we should no longer be slaves to sin" (Romans 6:6).

It's impossible to begin new-life living when your old life waits in the closet. Toss it out! Put on Jesus' new wardrobe.

EVENING

Lord, help me to put off my old self and be fully
clothed in Your beautiful perfection. Re-create my
attitudes and actions every day. May Your thoughts
be my thoughts, Your words my words, and Your
deeds my deeds. Help me to look like You, Jesus.

March 3

Put on your new nature, and be renewed as you learn
to know your Creator and become like him.
COLOSSIANS 3:10 NLT

Jesus came so you could be like Him—and you will never look more like Jesus than when you trust Him enough to obey. Even people who don't love Jesus love people who are compassionate like Jesus.

At some point, you will need to rethink your options. You can act like everyone else, and you'll be just like everyone else—or you could change. Jesus called that rebirth, and He's ready to help. He explained, "Humans can reproduce only human life, but the Holy Spirit gives birth to spiritual life" (John 3:6).

Your parents gave you physical life. Jesus gives you abundant spiritual life. You can live for the moment, or you can prepare for eternity. Stay the same or be different.

Change comes to those who ask. You won't be left alone to do the impossible. There will be all kinds of next steps, but Jesus takes each one with you. Keep walking with Him. He knows exactly what You need.

EVENING

Thank You, Lord, for a new nature and abundant
life. I could never truly know You or be like You on
my own. May Your grace draw me into a deeper
relationship with You, creating in me a new nature
that looks nothing like my old sinful life.

March 4

*As Christ was raised from the dead by the great
power of God, so we will have new life also.*
ROMANS 6:4 NLV

God is especially wise. He made sure that many of the things you read in the New Testament had a prequel in the Old Testament. God showed Ezekiel what it would be like for Jesus to rise from the dead. Ezekiel could see physically what God would do spiritually when He brought dead men back to life from a mass of dry bones (Ezekiel 37).

New life means the experience of a fresh beginning. Everyone starts physical life by dying spiritually, but Jesus made sure you had a second chance. He made it very clear how important His offer was when He said, "unless a man is born again, he cannot see the holy nation of God" (John 3:3).

If you haven't accepted this new spiritual life, then you can't really look forward to a home in heaven. Look at it this way: God gave you a limited life on earth—Jesus gives you the opportunity to enjoy a new and forever life in eternity.

EVENING

*Lord Jesus, thank You for seeking me out so that I
could be reborn in You. Your life is so much better
than my experience before I was born again. I know
this life is short, so please help me to use each day to
point others to the saving knowledge of Your love.*

March 5

For they that are after the flesh do mind the things of the flesh;
but they that are after the Spirit the things of the Spirit.

ROMANS 8:5 KJV

We live in a disposable world. Nothing is meant to last, and no one seems even to expect that. Things that were once repaired are now simply replaced. Most of us think repair just isn't worth it.

But Jesus has a different idea, and it seems radical. No one is left without the offer to be made new. This offer isn't self-help, a makeover, or upcycling but an exchange of spiritual components. What you have is failed thinking and a deceptive heart. What you get is new thinking and the gift of God's Spirit, who leads you to all truth. Jesus explained, "I will pray the Father, and he shall give you another Comforter, that he may abide with you for ever; even the Spirit of truth. . .for he dwelleth with you, and shall be in you" (John 14:16–17).

You did not have God's Spirit before you accepted Jesus' offer of rescue. Now? You have a Mentor, Teacher, and Guidance Counselor. You never have to be the same as you were before.

EVENING

Lord, You haven't put fresh makeup over my dirty face—
I am made completely new by Your Spirit.
I can rest assured that each day I have Your
Spirit within, guiding me toward Your will and
transforming me to be more like Jesus.

March 6

MORNING

> *The people were all surprised and wondered. They asked each other, "What is this? Is this a new teaching? He speaks with power even to the demons and they obey Him!"*
>
> MARK 1:27 NLV

Jesus was never like anyone else. He never will be. The most unusual thing about Him was that He never sinned—not even once. He didn't demand that others help Him. Instead, *He* offered help wherever He went. His life was not remembered for the many demands He made on others, but for the burdens He removed from the backs of sinners.

Those who met Jesus marveled at the mercy and power that followed Him. They said, "What is this? A new teaching? He speaks with power." His teaching on a new covenant led to new life. This was where forgiveness was delivered through the sacrifice of Himself—God's only Son. Where grace made you part of God's family. Where eternal life became standard.

Jesus had full authority on earth because He came with the full backing of the God who has always wanted a relationship with you. As a child of God and a co-heir with Jesus, you too have the authority to speak what Your Father has said. You don't have to live under the burden of sin—you can walk in new life with God's authority.

EVENING

> *Lord, I thank You for removing my burden of sin. Don't let me slide back under it. I want my new life to be full of You so I can share Your love.*

March 7

All praise to God, the Father of our Lord Jesus Christ. It is by his great mercy that we have been born again, because God raised Jesus Christ from the dead. Now we live with great expectation.

1 PETER 1:3 NLT

The idea of rebirth would never have been possible without Jesus. People had a date of birth and a date of death, and being right with God in between was impossible because every human who has ever lived has sinned (Romans 3:23). God accepts nothing less than perfection, so everyone is disqualified, early and often.

Satan used that fact to his own advantage. Jesus said, "The thief's purpose is to steal and kill and destroy." You've seen that in action, but Jesus explained why He came to live for a while among humanity: "My purpose is to give them a rich and satisfying life" (John 10:10).

The life Jesus came to give was now and forever. That's rebirth. That's new life. That's something that can belong to you.

Rebirth is yours in three life-changing steps that Jesus exemplified: death, burial, and resurrection. His sacrifice introduced rebirth to people who struggled to believe it was even possible.

Jesus, I know that I have Your promise of eternal life, but please grant me the new life I need on this earth. I want the "rich and satisfying life" You offer, so please help me to find that as I honor and obey You.

MORNING

"This is what I tell you to do: Love each other just as I have loved you."
JOHN 15:12 NLV

This book is called *Jesus Each Day*, and you'll meet Him right here—each day. Oh, there's plenty to talk about, and the Bible doesn't even try to share every bit of His story. John 21:25 says, "There are many other things which Jesus did also. If they were all written down, I do not think the world itself could hold the books that would be written."

You might hear the rest of Jesus' story someday, but the Bible provides everything you need to experience rebirth *today*. It starts with faith. The bare bones of the rebirth process are: (1) you needed rescue, (2) you couldn't rescue yourself, (3) God sent Jesus as His rescue plan, and (4) you choose to accept His rescue.

You don't need to know everything Jesus did to know that He did more than enough. You don't need to know every word He said to know He spoke truth. You don't need to know His every example of compassion to know He loves you.

EVENING

You are enough for Me, Lord. You have forgiven my sin, rescued me, and set Your love to work in my life. I want to love and serve You in return. May my faith in You grow stronger each day.

March 9

Jesus said, Suffer little children, and forbid them not, to come unto me: for of such is the kingdom of heaven.

MATTHEW 19:14 KJV

New life can feel a bit like starting over as a child. . .and that's okay. Children express wonder and delight. They throw themselves into the middle of adventure. They laugh and ask lots of questions. Everything is new and worth discovering. They don't always get things right, but that's to be expected. Jesus once said, "Except ye be converted, and become as little children, ye shall not enter into the kingdom of heaven" (Matthew 18:3).

If you are born for a second time, then you can't expect to be born an adult. You'll have some growing to do. You won't pass every test. You might find yourself with selective hearing. You might even fall. But it's easier to trust when you're a child. New life is the starting line of a new race. It's a journey that has Jesus as a companion.

Don't be too sophisticated to embrace the faith of a child, too stubborn to let go of your past, or too smart to learn God's perspective. Being childlike is being humble and letting Jesus lead.

EVENING

I thank You, Lord, that You invite me to come to You as a little child. I don't need to be "impressive" to enter Your kingdom. May I come to You humbly every day with the anticipation of learning and growing.

MORNING

*Children, obey your parents in the Lord, for this is right.
"Honor your father and mother"—which is the first
commandment with a promise—"so that it may go well
with you and that you may enjoy long life on the earth."*

EPHESIANS 6:1–3 NIV

God's instructions for new life include obedience. You can't follow Jesus if you think the word *follow* is an option—something to take or leave based on your mood or preference.

Jesus wanted children to spend time with Him. They needed to learn. They needed to see love firsthand. It was easier for them to follow. God chose these words for the apostle Paul to write.

These verses could easily be applied to new Christians: "Children, obey the Lord, for this is right. Honor your Father so that it may go well with you and that you may enjoy eternal life." Obedience is what transforms your relationship with God.

Take this new life and take advantage of each opportunity to obey God. When you do, you open your Jesus adventure to even greater satisfaction.

EVENING

*Lord, even as an adult, I need to be reminded to obey.
In those times when I think that I know best, prompt
me to seek Your will first. Remind me that obedience
is the primary way I show my trust in You.*

March 11

> *And so, dear brothers and sisters, I plead with you to give your bodies to God because of all he has done for you. Let them be a living and holy sacrifice—the kind he will find acceptable. This is truly the way to worship him.*
>
> ROMANS 12:1 NLT

Jesus gave His life—perfect and pure. He paid the price for the sin of every human who has ever lived, or ever will. He was raised and it was new life—not just for Him but offered to you.

When you accept that new birth, you get to experience some of what His sacrifice was like. Jesus invites you to use the new life He gave you and sacrifice it for Him as a form of worship. Just to clarify, God is not asking you to kill yourself. . .read carefully: "Let them be a *living* and holy sacrifice" (emphasis added).

New life offers new opportunities to put your old ways to death. Old habits can be traded for new ones. Obedience is now preferred to rebellion. New life is abundant life, and it sacrifices everything that interferes with a life devoted to God.

EVENING

> *Today, Lord, You call me to be a living sacrifice. May I die to my old ways and walk in the new life that You offer me each day. When I am tempted to step back into old habits that do not honor You, help me to give my body to You as a sacrifice. Whatever I give up for You will be generously rewarded.*

MORNING

> *Jesus said to them all, "If anyone wants to follow Me, he must give up himself and his own desires. He must take up his cross everyday and follow Me."*
>
> Luke 9:23 nlv

Before His death on the cross, Jesus invited His disciples to test-drive new life. When He met them they each had their own careers. These men had every reason to believe they would work their jobs for the rest of their lives, but then they saw Jesus. "Come, follow me," Jesus said, "and I will send you out to fish for people" (Matthew 4:19 niv).

They would have a new job. The disciples would learn about the new life coming to humankind and then share what they had learned. People would respond. It was impossible for anyone to know this fantastic news but keep quiet.

Sadly, some who were invited to follow hesitated, gave excuses, or refused. But Jesus offered those people the opportunity just as He does today.

If you have responded affirmatively, you have a new job. Follow Jesus and fish for people. But if you're hesitating, giving excuses, or refusing to follow, consider this: the right choice results in an all-access pass to God's family—forever.

EVENING

> *Lord Jesus, may I never hesitate to publicly and vocally follow You. You have called me to reach the lost and disciple them for Your kingdom. I give up myself and my own desires to follow You—please use me to accomplish Your will.*

March 13

*Let us not be weary in well doing: for in due
season we shall reap, if we faint not.*

GALATIANS 6:9 KJV

Weary? Some days are worse than others, right? You keep waiting for a vacation, the weekend, or sleep. This process isn't fun. It's not productive. Some call it fatigue, and it needs a solution.

This weariness isn't just physical, but a need of the soul. It usually shows up when you try to do things on your own while silently rejecting Jesus' help. Of course, He understands more than you think, and that's why He said, "Come unto me, all ye that labour and are heavy laden, and I will give you rest." Perfect! Then Jesus says, "Take my yoke upon you, and learn of me." A "yoke"? More work? But the promise continues: "and ye shall find rest unto your souls." Why? "My yoke is easy, and my burden is light" (Matthew 11:28–30).

This is more refreshing than iced tea on a hot day, rest after a long week, or an amazing vacation after a hard year. New life knows where to find restoration. . .and that's with Jesus.

*Jesus, thank You for lifting the burden from my
shoulders. You replace my needless striving with Your
light yoke and rest. When I become weary—when I
forget that You are my strength and song—remind me to
return to Your side. Help me to learn of You every day.*

MORNING

> *"Man shall not live on bread alone, but on every word that comes from the mouth of God."*
>
> MATTHEW 4:4 NIV

Rebirth requires a new diet. In our old lives, we feasted on anger, bitterness, and rage, but the benefits of new life are nourished by different "foods."

The Word of God offers every ingredient for a satisfying spiritual meal. Don't ever think scripture is a just nice snack if you have the time. Weak and malnourished believers are the result of this thinking. A steady diet of anything less than God's Word leaves us sick and vulnerable to disease.

God created the physical food your body needs, as well as the spiritual food that is essential to your soul. Even Jesus needed that bread, "every word that comes from the mouth of God." Follow His example and eat well!

EVENING

> *Lord, I want to have a good spiritual diet. Forgive me for the times I have not feasted on Your Word. Give me a deep desire for scripture, and a heart to apply it in serving You. Lead me to Your Word each day and reveal the important truths hidden within it.*

March 15

> *"I am giving you a new commandment: Love each other.*
> *Just as I have loved you, you should love each other."*
>
> JOHN 13:34 NLT

It is human nature to treat others the way they treat you. But this reaction extends no forgiveness and offers no hope to the offender. It simply amplifies a problem, making it even bigger than it should be.

When you are angry over some offense or hurt, a canyon develops between you and another person. And our old, sinful selves devise punishments we believe the other person can't survive—and if they *do* survive, we'll punish them even more. Our world says, "If someone hurts you, return the favor." Jesus, though, has something else in mind: "Do to others whatever you would like them to do to you" (Matthew 7:12).

When we are reborn in Jesus, some things are turned upside down. We'll treat others with kindness when they are rude. Love is the response when hate shows up. Compassion replaces an "I told you so." Living like Christ looks like foolishness to a world that "gives like it gets" but we aren't called to look like the world, we are called to look like Jesus.

EVENING

> *Lord, it's not easy to turn the other cheek and treat an*
> *offender the way I would like to be treated. But You*
> *have forgiven me more than I will ever need to forgive*
> *anyone else. Help me to follow Your example. Let me give*
> *grace upon grace even to those who do not deserve it.*

MORNING

There are many people who belong to Christ. And yet, we are one body which is Christ's. We are all different but we depend on each other.

ROMANS 12:5 NLV

Some people are good at speaking in public or giving a persuasive argument. Some are accomplished singers or painters. Have you wondered why not everyone can do these things with equal skill?

The church of Jesus Christ—what the Bible calls His "body"—would be ineffective if everyone was good at the same thing. You were given a gift that's different from what other Christians have received, and Jesus wants you to use your gift to "go and make followers of all the nations." Take what you learn and share it and "teach them to do all the things I have told you." When that seems hard, remember that Jesus said, "I am with you always, even to the end of the world" (Matthew 28:19–20).

A human body isn't entirely kneecaps. It wouldn't do well if it were solely an earlobe, eyebrow, or philtrum (look it up). New life recognizes God's unique gifts, so instead of wanting to be what you're not, learn to be useful with who you are.

EVENING

Lord, I thank You for creating me with unique gifts that complement Your body. I want to appreciate the differences in those around me and depend on them to be strong in the areas in which I am weak.

March 17

MORNING

*Jesus saith unto him, I am the way, the truth,
and the life: no man cometh unto the Father, but by me.*

JOHN 14:6 KJV

When you began following Jesus, He gave you new life. But this life isn't based on your ability to do better in the future than you did in the past. It isn't a merit system. It isn't a competitive sport. It is trusting that what Jesus did for you was enough to make things right between you and God the Father. It's believing that second chances are for you... if you're willing to admit that God is right, you were wrong, and forgiveness is real.

Jesus didn't come into the world to make things hard for you. He's on your side: "God sent not his Son into the world to condemn the world; but that the world through him might be saved" (John 3:17).

The more you trust Jesus, the more you'll see that He's worth following. Since He's worth following, you'll find yourself wanting to do for others what He's done for you. He brought truth, and you can take that life-changing truth to the people around you.

EVENING

*Jesus, the truth of Your death, burial, and resurrection
is certainly good news. I know that You are the only
way to the Father, the only avenue to eternal life. Please
help me to share this incredible truth with others.*

MORNING

> *"The kingdom of God has come near.*
> *Repent and believe the good news!"*
>
> MARK 1:15 NIV

Jesus once told a story about God's kingdom. He said it was like "yeast that a woman took and mixed into about sixty pounds of flour until it worked all through the dough" (Matthew 13:33).

Like yeast, our new life in Christ becomes larger in the waiting. Just as changes occur in the dough while the baker waits, changes happen within our own lives (and the life of His entire family) as His kingdom grows.

There is wisdom in the waiting. Bread is ruined if the baker doesn't let the dough rise before putting it in the oven. And waiting seems important to God—it's part of what we know as mercy, because God is kind. The kingdom will be filled with people who were rescued from their personal rebellion through the sacrifice of Jesus, in God's perfect time.

While we wait, His kingdom is growing.

EVENING

> *I am glad Your kingdom is growing, Jesus, because*
> *I know people I'd like to see loving You too. As I*
> *wait for Your return, help me to draw closer to You*
> *every day. Then strengthen me with the words and*
> *the courage to approach others in Your name.*

March 19

> *[Jesus] saved us, not because of the righteous things we had done, but because of his mercy. He washed away our sins, giving us a new birth and new life through the Holy Spirit.*
>
> TITUS 3:5 NLT

The jeweler knew that plenty of oysters meant plenty of pearls. He was on the lookout for quality pearls, but perfection was hard to come by—until that day. His trained eye spotted something he'd never seen in a pearl—perfection. He owned lots of things, but selling them off was just a formality. He traded quantity for quality. He had purchased the perfect pearl.

This is a summary of a parable of Jesus comparing the value of what we own with what God offers. The jeweler was convinced that he was making a good deal: "When he discovered a pearl of great value, he sold everything he owned and bought it!" (Matthew 13:46).

Trade what you know for everything Jesus offers. Like the pearl, this trade only increases in value. Missionary Jim Elliot showed that he understood this when he said, "He is no fool who gives what he cannot keep to gain that which he cannot lose."

> *Nothing in this world compares to the value of knowing You, Jesus. Break this world's hold on my imagination, I pray, because the treasure of Your gift of salvation is worth infinitely more than anything on this earth.*

MORNING

> *"I will never turn away anyone who comes to Me."*
> JOHN 6:37 NLV

A landowner needed help in his vineyard. He found workers and invited them to labor for the day. He offered a full day's wage, which many accepted. They went to work.

Because there was a lot of work to be done, the landowner went out three more times from morning to late afternoon to hire new help.

At the end of the day, he paid each worker a full day's wages. This angered those who had started early. After all, the others hadn't worked as long as they had, so they deserved less—or perhaps those who came to work early should receive more. Jesus spoke the words of the owner of the vineyard, "Do I not have the right to do what I want to do with my own money?" (Matthew 20:15).

This is the story of your rescue, your own change from lawbreaker to Christ follower. You might have begun following Jesus decades ago, or maybe yesterday. Either way, you receive *all* of God's love and forgiveness and His eternal kingdom.

EVENING

> *Lord, how can I put a value on knowing You, except to say it's priceless? May I never become jealous of others who have also answered Your call. I can rest knowing that I am no less in Your eyes than someone who has known You longer. Remind me that I am also not better than anyone who is just now coming into Your family. Keep me humble and grateful.*

March 21

*We all have different gifts that God has given to
us by His loving-favor. We are to use them.*
ROMANS 12:6 NLV

Jesus once told His followers about a business owner who was going on a trip. The man gave his three managers some money, hoping they would get busy and make fruitful investments. When he returned, two of the managers had faithfully doubled their money. But the third man said, "I was afraid, and went and hid thy talent in the earth" (Matthew 25:25 KJV). This manager hadn't learned to trust God or invest wisely.

As Christians, the only things we truly own are the choices we make—everything else is a gift from God. New life in Jesus makes us managers of God's resources.

God has always wanted you to use the gifts He gives to make Him famous, to help other people, and to do the things Jesus would do. You can play a role in advancing God's plans! Just be willing to use your new life to benefit those around you.

*Lord, help me to invest in Your kingdom by
faithfully using my gifts to fulfill Your plans. I can
do nothing apart from You, so may I use all of my
gifts and talents for Your glory and not my own.*

Be kind and compassionate to one another, forgiving each other, just as in Christ God forgave you.

EPHESIANS 4:32 NIV

A banker lent money to two customers. When it came time to pay, neither could. One owed about eighteen months' salary, while the other owed about two months' worth. The banker reviewed both files and chose to forgive each man.

Jesus told this story and waited for His Pharisee host, Simon, to respond. Which of the two men felt the most forgiven? Who would have a stronger emotional connection to the banker? Simon replied, "I suppose the one who had the bigger debt forgiven" (Luke 7:43).

This parable was meant for the ears of those who were eating a meal with Jesus. The issue had started when a woman had come into Simon's house. She was a well-known sinner, and she wiped Jesus' feet with her tears. She had poured expensive perfume on Him. And Jesus had forgiven her.

She heard Jesus' words too. This woman would remember this act of forgiveness more than most, and it would introduce her to new life. That is a picture of God's heart. And Jesus is our picture of God Himself.

EVENING

I could never do anything to earn the forgiveness You've provided for me, Jesus. I never want to go back to living in ways that dishonor You. Thank You for Your compassion and forgiveness in forgiving not just some, but all of my sin and shame.

March 23

> *"Be sure of this: I am with you always,*
> *even to the end of the age."*
> MATTHEW 28:20 NLT

You've probably misplaced money at some point. You needed it to pay bills, buy gifts, or purchase groceries. You looked for it, prayed about it, and wondered how you would replace it. Jesus told a story like that.

There was a woman who lost a coin that she couldn't afford to lose. She made sure there was plenty of light for searching and a broom for reaching, and she kept her eyes straining for what was lost. She couldn't imagine doing what needed to be done without that coin. When she found it, she was so grateful she went door to door, sharing her joy with neighbors and friends.

The same Jesus who told this story looked for the lost *you*. He shone His light into darkness, reached into the place where you were, and kept His eyes focused on you. When He found you, all of heaven celebrated: "There is joy in the presence of God's angels when even one sinner repents" (Luke 15:10). This is rebirth. This is new life.

EVENING

Jesus, I thank You for searching for me—and not giving
up until I was found! To think that I am a treasure to You
is amazing. Please remind me, today and every day, that
You are always with me. I need never feel lost or alone.

MORNING

I am sure that God Who began the good work in you will keep on working in you until the day Jesus Christ comes again.

PHILIPPIANS 1:6 NLV

Accepting Jesus is an invitation to lifelong learning. God knows you need to know more than you do—and no one can learn it all at a weekend conference.

So He offers ongoing education. You may want this learning to be a crash course. You may want to pick and choose the classes you'll take. But God doesn't want you to minor in a subject that interests you. He wants you to major in knowing *Him*.

When we find ourselves in the middle of new, we struggle. We remember the past, wrestle with new choices, and sometimes tell ourselves that class attendance is optional.

If you think you already know enough about God, resist any urge to put your Bible aside. Pick it up and read, knowing that Jesus said, "Everyone who listens to the Father and learns from Him comes to Me" (John 6:45).

Learn from God—discover Jesus. Discover Jesus—find new life. Find new life—enjoy fresh hope.

EVENING

There is so much to learn from and about You, Jesus. May I never grow complacent and disregard Your Word. Keep me hungering for more of You each and every day. Let this simple devotion be a starting point for my deeper pursuit of who You are.

March 25

A new heart also will I give you, and a new spirit will I put within you: and I will take away the stony heart out of your flesh, and I will give you an heart of flesh.

EZEKIEL 36:26 KJV

New life. You can't enhance it. You can't improve it. You can't take credit for it. You might want to. You might even feel like you need to do something to earn it. But God owns grace and He created new life. They're His to give. He won't sell at any price. Ephesians 2:8 says, "By grace are ye saved through faith; and that not of yourselves: it is the gift of God."

It's a gift. Of God. It's not a half-and-half deal in which God provides a partial rescue. If new life were something you could half do, you might think that was good enough. . .and miss out on the whole goodness of God. You'd be in a dangerous, half-rescued place, which is no rescue at all.

Broken, jaded, hardened people need full rescue. All of us experience new life we could never manufacture on our own. Jesus offers it all, to you.

EVENING

Lord, You have given me a complete rescue, forgiving me of my sin and offering me new life in Yourself. You completely transformed my hard heart, making it tender before You. Thank You for the fresh start You provide, and the promise of life eternal.

MORNING

> *Everyone born of God overcomes the world. This is the*
> *victory that has overcome the world, even our faith.*
>
> 1 John 5:4 niv

Plenty of philosophies seek to convince us that we don't really need God's rescue. You might hear phrases like, "Do what you want, because this life is all you will ever have." Other voices say God is not real, so there's no reason to trust Him.

But in order to be rescued, you have to believe there is someone who rescues. If you don't believe, you won't accept. The apostle Paul knew people would need clarity on the subject, so he wrote, "For us there is but one God, the Father, from whom all things came and for whom we live; and there is but one Lord, Jesus Christ, through whom all things came and through whom we live" (1 Corinthians 8:6).

Your faith in God and His Son, Jesus, helps you overcome the obstacles that keep you from rebirth. Jesus overcame the philosophies men dreamed up—and when they say He can't save, He just reminds you that He always has.

EVENING

> *I could never be saved on my own, Jesus. My own*
> *strength and self-reliance aren't even enough*
> *for daily needs, let alone eternity. Now, as Your*
> *follower, I trust that You have overcome the*
> *world. My faith will bring me along with You.*

March 27

We are citizens of heaven, where the Lord Jesus Christ lives. And we are eagerly waiting for him to return as our Savior. He will take our weak mortal bodies and change them into glorious bodies like his own.

PHILIPPIANS 3:20–21 NLT

Jesus came. He healed some, fed others, and taught all who would listen. He had been doing all three when He was told that His friend Lazarus was dying. Jesus saw this HELP WANTED sign but delayed long enough that Lazarus died during the waiting.

When Jesus arrived, the dead man's sister Martha asked the Lord why He hadn't come sooner. That's when Lazarus became an object lesson. Jesus told her, "I am the resurrection and the life. Anyone who believes in me will live, even after dying" (John 11:25). This must have confused Martha. She believed Jesus was the Messiah. She believed Jesus could have healed her brother. She didn't expect Jesus to raise her brother from the dead—but that's what Jesus did.

Martha saw new life firsthand. Maybe she needed to see the wonderful truth that the One who could rescue spiritually also had the power to rescue beyond death.

EVENING

Jesus, when my days are sorrowful, help me to trust in Your eternal life—knowing You rescue both here on earth and after death. No person or situation is ever too far gone for You to breathe Your new life into it. Give me faith to live for You as I await Your return from heaven.

MORNING

Even when we were dead because of our sins, He made us alive by what Christ did for us. You have been saved from the punishment of sin by His loving-favor. God raised us up from death when He raised up Christ Jesus. He has given us a place with Christ in the heavens.

EPHESIANS 2:5–6 NLV

Jesus rose from the dead. He raised His friend Lazarus from the dead. And, if you believe in Him, Jesus will raise you from the dead too. "You get what is coming to you when you sin. It is death! But God's free gift is life that lasts forever. It is given to us by our Lord Jesus Christ" (Romans 6:23).

Rebirth brings new life, and that's just what you need—what you've *always* needed. You've tried everything you can to be perfect, but it's never happened. You've been dead spiritually, and there will come a time when you are dead physically. But that's not really the end of the story.

Death is a part of the human experience. But because Jesus wanted you to spend eternity with Him, He offers life—abundant, free, forever life.

EVENING

Lord, I'm amazed when I think that You have raised me, spiritually, from the dead. I couldn't do anything to save myself, but You called me out of my spiritual grave and into Your new life. Thank You for offering me a place with You in the heavens.

MORNING

> *We are his workmanship, created in Christ*
> *Jesus unto good works, which God hath before*
> *ordained that we should walk in them.*
>
> EPHESIANS 2:10 KJV

Have you ever started something new and become an immediate expert? That's just not how things work. Becoming a competent guitar player, singer, baker, or carpenter takes time, patience, and a great handle on the basics. You have to focus on learning, show perseverance, and allow these skills to develop.

In both the physical and spiritual realms, fruit doesn't start fully formed either. It begins as a seed, then grows as it's nurtured and fed. In our Christian lives, Jesus does that through His Spirit. Here's how the apostle Paul described the end result: "The fruit of the Spirit is love, joy, peace, longsuffering, gentleness, goodness, faith, meekness, temperance: against such there is no law" (Galatians 5:22–23).

When you have days where rebirth seems a struggle, remember that Jesus is just getting started. Just as you would have patience with a seed that you've planted, have patience with yourself. Let your roots go down deep into Jesus, who has wonderful plans for you.

EVENING

> *Sometimes it's hard to be patient with myself,*
> *Lord. I want to grow and be strong, not struggling*
> *any longer with the same old things. May I focus*
> *on sending my roots deep into You. Give me the*
> *foundation I need to stand tall and do well.*

MORNING

I am not ashamed of the gospel, because it is the power of God that brings salvation to everyone who believes.

ROMANS 1:16 NIV

If you have new life in Jesus and are living in that new life, then why would you even want to hide it? You probably remember times when you've acted as if Jesus was no big deal or left people thinking He wasn't very important to you. Maybe you've been a bit like Peter, denying that you know Him when it seemed that public opinion was opposed. This is why Jesus said, "Let your light shine before others, that they may see your good deeds and glorify your Father in heaven" (Matthew 5:16).

Jesus is light and He brings you light. He is life and He brings you life. He is love and He brings you love. This is the best news of the day, and it's made for sharing. That's what people with new life do. What can you do today to share this good news?

EVENING

Lord, You don't hold me responsible for how anyone else reacts to Your message—but I am responsible for sharing it. Help me to spread Your incredible good news every day. May I find confidence in the great power of Your salvation.

March 31

> *Those who belong to Christ Jesus have nailed*
> *the passions and desires of their sinful nature*
> *to his cross and crucified them there.*
>
> GALATIANS 5:24 NLT

Today you get one more look at rebirth. The apostle Paul spoke personally when he wrote, "My old self has been crucified with Christ. It is no longer I who live, but Christ lives in me. So I live in this earthly body by trusting in the Son of God, who loved me and gave himself for me" (Galatians 2:20).

Maybe you connect with Paul's words. Maybe you can say, "Every part of who I was has to be set aside daily so I can make the choices God created me to make. Jesus died for me, and I put my past to death so I can live in a broken body with a forever heart. I will trust that Jesus is the only one who can help me live this new life."

You've been given new life. It's important. It has value. Others need to know about it. Acknowledge your imperfections and then introduce your friends and neighbors to a perfect Savior. You can't save others, but you know who can. Make *Him* known.

EVENING

> *I know I'm not perfect, Jesus, but I want others to know*
> *You are. Let my testimony—of being bought with a price,*
> *of coming out of death into life—be a beacon of hope to*
> *others. Put people in my path who need to know You.*

MORNING

God is able to do much more than we ask or
think through His power working in us.
EPHESIANS 3:20 NLV

Today we begin a month dedicated to blessings. The shape or size of the blessing isn't the important thing, but the appreciation of God's generosity and abundance is.

When it comes to blessings, Jesus never shortchanges us. His good friend John spoke of the blessings of Jesus when he wrote, "From Him Who has so much we have all received loving-favor, one loving-favor after another" (John 1:16).

One blessing after another! Benefits that never end! Care that commits to the long haul! This is Jesus. This is a summary of His blessings. They arrive when you least expect them, often don't look like blessings, and nudge you into the center of His path forward.

April is a month dedicated to blessings. One month is not nearly enough, but it's a suitable start. These next few weeks will prove that Jesus loves you. He always has.

EVENING

Thank You, Lord, for all Your blessings. May I
never fail to be thankful for them. Put them on
my heart and in the forefront of my mind each
day. When I begin to doubt or feel self-pity, jog
my memory with what You've done for me.

April 2

*In lowliness of mind let each esteem
other better than themselves.*

PHILIPPIANS 2:3 KJV

Walking toward Jericho, a traveler was ambushed and beaten. What he had was stolen, and he was left injured and alone. The man needed help. It didn't seem like he was in line for a blessing.

Two men who could have helped (and knew they should) refused, walking past without stopping. But a man from Samaria chose to help the injured traveler. They were from different cultures that didn't get along. Normally, they would avoid each other. But this Samaritan reached out to the injured man. In Jesus' words, the Samaritan "set him on his own beast, and brought him to an inn, and took care of him" (Luke 10:34).

This is a story of blessings from unexpected places. The Jewish religious leaders didn't want to hear that God would help anyone other than Jews. Many were surprised that Jesus would speak kindly of people who were considered outcasts.

This blessing story provides a timeless example for all of us. Through Jesus, God cares about everyone. We should do likewise.

EVENING

*Lord, let me be a blessing to those around me,
even those who are outcasts to the rest of society.
Help me not to look past those who think or act
differently than I do. May I see people through
Your eyes and always offer a helping hand.*

MORNING

> *"Seek first his kingdom and his righteousness,*
> *and all these things will be given to you as well."*
>
> MATTHEW 6:33 NIV

Worry inhibits our blessing vision. The more you worry, the less attention you'll pay to the blessings that arrive nonstop. If you don't believe that, it may be beneficial to remember that you're alive. And if you're alive, you're breathing. You can think. And most people can do a lot more than that. God has taken care of you in the past, and He is strong enough to keep providing. If He took a break, nothing would survive.

But God never takes breaks. That's why Jesus said, "Do not worry, saying, 'What shall we eat?' or 'What shall we drink?' or 'What shall we wear?' " Why is this such an issue? Jesus continued, "Your heavenly Father knows that you need them" (Matthew 6:31–32).

You can't use worry as a prayer. It doesn't request, it wonders. It asks questions that become doubt billboards for others to read. Worry admits you aren't sure God's blessings are real.

Count the most visible blessings and keep counting. You will become much more attuned to seeing the blessings in every day, even the very small ones that you may have previously overlooked.

EVENING

> *Lord, You never stop blessing me. I don't need*
> *to worry when I can pray! I ask for every*
> *good thing You're happy to give me.*

April 4

> *[God] has given me a new song to sing, a hymn of praise to our God. Many will see what he has done and be amazed. They will put their trust in the LORD.*
>
> PSALM 40:3 NLT

Psalm 139 indicates God knew you before you were born. Nothing about you is unknown to Him. John 3 indicates He loved you enough to rescue you. Ephesians 1:3 says God has "blessed us with every spiritual blessing in the heavenly realms because we are united with Christ." Your blessing plate is full.

God made you, knows you, loves you, and has blessed you. This combination should lead to praise. Praise is more than being grateful. It includes honor and glory. God is all that you need and more than you could expect. He gives you more than you can ever give Him, yet what He wants most is a place in your life that influences decisions, changes thinking, and offers the best kind of adventures.

If God blesses you and you find it amazing, then say so. When you receive more than you know you deserve—praise Him. By taking time to remember His goodness, you can make His name famous.

EVENING

> *Lord Jesus, I want to praise and worship You—not just for the blessings You've shown me, but simply for who You are. You are amazing and amazingly good to me. You deserve all of my adoration and honor!*

MORNING

*Christ was tempted in every way we are
tempted, but He did not sin.*

HEBREWS 4:15 NLV

It might be easy to pray, "But you just don't understand, God!" And your frustration might be valid if it weren't for the fact that God blessed humankind by sending His Son: "Christ became human flesh and lived among us." Jesus understood the difficulties of being human. But instead of becoming jaded and frustrated, Jesus "was full of loving-favor and truth" (John 1:14).

It would be hard to interact comfortably with a God who doesn't understand you. Therein lies the blessing. God wanted you to understand Him, but you couldn't. His Son became like you so there would be no misunderstanding of the struggles you face. Take this one step further and remember that the God who understands you can help you understand Him. That's relationship. That's blessing.

You may have never thought what a blessing it was, the lengths God took to help you understand Him. Think about it now! Let this truth sink deep into your soul: you'll never face anything that Jesus can't understand.

EVENING

*Thank You for becoming human, Jesus—even facing
the temptation of sin. I know that You understand how
hard my life can be even when it feels like I'm alone in my
struggles. Help me to seek You when I'm tempted, and
provide a way of escape so I can still honor Your name.*

April 6

Let your conversation be without covetousness; and be content with such things as ye have: for he hath said, I will never leave thee, nor forsake thee.

HEBREWS 13:5 KJV

Some say that God wants you to choose poverty. Others argue that God wants you to seek wealth. Jesus did say, "Blessed be ye poor: for yours is the kingdom of God" (Luke 6:20). But this verse describes a spiritual condition, not a socioeconomic status.

You can be physically poor yet rich in spirit. You can be rich in the world's eyes yet poor in spirit. But you can also be poor in both ways, as you can be rich in both ways. If that seems confusing, then know this: the biggest tests we face are less about money and more about contentment. Will you still seek God if you have a better income? Will you despise God because you didn't get a raise?

When you know that your bank account means nothing compared to what you have in Jesus, you can begin to understand Luke 6:20.

Being poor can be a blessing. Being rich can be a blessing. Being content puts those blessings in perspective.

EVENING

Jesus, financial gifts are wonderful, but nothing compares to the blessing of knowing You. Please help me to find contentment in knowing You. The greatest blessing of all is the new life You offer me by faith.

MORNING

> *Jesus declared, "I am the bread of life. Whoever comes to me will never go hungry, and whoever believes in me will never be thirsty."*
>
> JOHN 6:35 NIV

It's never fun to do without something you really want. It's worse when you can't see the sacrifice as simply seasonal or view the deprivation as a blessing. Jesus said, "Blessed are you who hunger now, for you will be satisfied" (Luke 6:21).

Think of this as something more than physical hunger. It could be hunger for a relationship, a better job, or a nicer house. It could be hunger for fame, influence, and legacy. Just remember that blessings often arrive looking something less than ideal. God's timing may differ—a lot—from our own. So if you don't check off your whole list of personal goals, and your hunger for achievement remains strong, know that when you "hunger and thirst for righteousness," something happens. You "will be filled" (Matthew 5:6).

When you hunger for the things God wants, you'll ultimately find satisfaction—and it will be a supersized blessing.

EVENING

> *I know that You can see the end from the beginning, Lord. What You are doing in me is a lifelong learning process on my part. Teach me to hunger and thirst for the righteousness that comes from being closely related to You. I want my life to reflect those things that matter most to You.*

April 8

All praise to God, the Father of our Lord Jesus Christ. God is our merciful Father and the source of all comfort. He comforts us in all our troubles so that we can comfort others. When they are troubled, we will be able to give them the same comfort God has given us.

2 CORINTHIANS 1:3–4 NLT

You will mourn. There will be moments of profound grief. You may be experiencing a great sense of loss right now. Mourn because it hurts. Cry because you've experienced loss. But this common path can lead to blessings. Jesus said, "God blesses those who mourn, for they will be comforted" (Matthew 5:4).

The losses you suffer reassign your limited, personal comfort sources to the God of all knowledge and power, the God who knows how to care for the brokenhearted.

He is not in the business of making you sad. But God can take your sadness and use it to help you know Him even better. Don't forget—Jesus was a "man of sorrows" Himself (Isaiah 53:3).

EVENING

Lord, You know when I hurt and how much I want the pain to go away. Please use it all for Your kingdom purpose, so that none of my experience is in vain. As I lie down this evening, remind me that You are with me even in the longest and darkest of nights. Give me faith to believe that You offer joy and new mercies every morning.

MORNING

> *"Those who show loving-kindness are happy, because they will have loving-kindness shown to them."*
> MATTHEW 5:7 NLV

A kind and compassionate response looks like Jesus. He is always our example, and He said, "Give, and it will be given to you. You will have more than enough." Then He discussed the measuring cup of kindness: "The way you give to others is the way you will receive in return" (Luke 6:38).

You'll notice that Jesus left the giving column wide open. He didn't say "give money," He just said, "give." That could be time to a worthy cause, resources to an organization you believe in, or a helping hand to someone who really needs it.

You are blessed when you show kindness, and you are blessed when someone receives your kindness. And if you wonder whether giving really results in being blessed, don't worry. Jesus will ultimately say, "Well done," even when no one else seems grateful for your help. No matter what anyone else thinks, God is the ultimate judge. And you're obeying the One who blesses those who are kind.

EVENING

> *Jesus, remind me to be kind even when no one else is watching. Giving to those in need will always make me look more like You, and that is a great goal. I know that You're pleased when I live out the commands You've given me. Enable me to be a blessing to others.*

April 10

Follow righteousness, faith, charity, peace, with them that call on the Lord out of a pure heart.
2 Timothy 2:22 kjv

If you want to be as close to God as you possibly can, you need to learn the value of obedience. If a pure heart is one that follows righteousness, it is free from blemishes and imperfections. And while it is impossible to be both *perfect* and *human*, it is possible to make obedience your best response. If you wonder why a pure heart is so important, Jesus said this: "Blessed are the pure in heart: for they shall see God" (Matthew 5:8)

The goal of following is not to see how far away you can get and still detect God. It's to be as close as you can. It's recognizing Jesus' footprints in your affairs. This approach to your Christian life is a blessing because obedience doesn't require correction or time-outs. It makes you faithful now so you can be faithful again. It doesn't require the attention of other humans. It doesn't ask for a competition. It's a blessing because Jesus said it was a blessing.

EVENING

Lord, I want to follow You as closely as I possibly can. May I never try to push the boundaries of being a true disciple. Give me a pure heart and a desire to follow faithfully after righteousness, faith, love, and peace. Show me how to obey You in all my words and actions.

MORNING

"Take my yoke upon you and learn from me, for I am gentle and humble in heart, and you will find rest for your souls."

MATTHEW 11:29 NIV

You want to appear strong. That's understandable. Being strong seems to give you an advantage and power seems practical. There are lots of things you can't do if you're weak. But *weak* is not the word Jesus used when He said, "Blessed are the *meek*, for they will inherit the earth" (Matthew 5:5, emphasis added).

Let's try this description for meekness: people who are meek are first disciples. These individuals choose to follow the example of Jesus and use the strength God gives through the power of His Spirit. They have a controlled strength. There's no need to be bossy. This kind of woman becomes wise without wanting people to think she is the smartest person in the room. These are the people in line for the inheritance Jesus spoke of.

Be strong in the power of God's Spirit. Then? Be meek in the presence of Jesus, the servant leader who blesses in ways we can't even imagine.

EVENING

In Your yoke of meekness, Lord Jesus, I will find the blessing of strength. Help me to be meek, not weak. When I trust You to be my shield and protector, I don't have to fear what the enemy will do to me. I can be meek and humble and let You take care of the rest.

April 12

> *Do all that you can to live in peace with everyone.*
> ROMANS 12:18 NLT

Some Bible translations refer to the person who helps to stop arguments as a "peacemaker," but there may be more to it than that. Jesus said, "God blesses those who work for peace, for they will be called the children of God" (Matthew 5:9).

God's family members are defined as people who are willing to seek peace. That can mean that you love another person enough not to fight about things that ultimately don't matter. It may mean knowing that arguments place a wedge between people. It may mean knowing that any argument with another might result in the need for long-term repair.

Jesus said things that needed to be said, and because He was God's Son, those things were always correct. This was a blessing, because people didn't have to guess what Jesus was thinking. We don't have all the answers ourselves, but we know the One who does. So when people want to argue, let them argue with God. He will always win. And when He wins, so will they. So will you.

EVENING

> *Lord Jesus, help me to be a person of peace. I don't*
> *want to bicker or contend with people over unnecessary*
> *things. Remind me to be humble and to seek to make*
> *peace when I can. And if anyone else refuses to live*
> *peacefully with me, I ask You to change their heart.*

MORNING

> *"If the world hates you, you know it
> hated Me before it hated you."*
>
> JOHN 15:18 NLV

In a perfect world, people would be celebrated for doing the right thing. But we don't live in a perfect world. Many times, people gain bragging rights by what they believe they got away with. This can be disheartening when *you* make it a priority to do the right thing—and God always wants you to do the right thing. No matter what the world thinks, you should never be ashamed for doing the right thing.

Jesus calls the desire to do good a blessing. He knew there would be times when it would be tough to do the right thing: "Those who have it very hard for doing right are happy, because the holy nation of heaven is theirs" (Matthew 5:10).

Some people experience physical harm for following Jesus—yet Jesus still calls them blessed. Why? The right thing is the right thing no matter what argument anyone else might use. And if there are moments of injustice for Christians, there is still eternity, without pain, without tears, without injustice.

EVENING

*Jesus, it is a blessing to suffer for You, even if that
suffering is simply a rude comment or an eye roll. You
were absolutely perfect and many hated You—why
should I expect to be loved by this world? Give me
the courage to always stand up for Your honor.*

April 14

All scripture is given by inspiration of God,
and is profitable for doctrine, for reproof, for
correction, for instruction in righteousness.

2 TIMOTHY 3:16 KJV

Whether you call it an attitude adjustment, a time-out, or a situational realignment, being corrected is no fun. It's no fun for children and even less fun for adults. When we are not allowed to do the things we want to do, it can seem unfair.

True correction, though, is less about punishment and more about course readjustment. God's Word recognizes both the struggle and the blessing of correction: "No chastening for the present seemeth to be joyous, but grievous: nevertheless afterward it yieldeth the peaceable fruit of righteousness unto them which are exercised thereby" (Hebrews 12:11).

You weren't born knowing everything, and you might end your life feeling as if you didn't learn all the stuff you should have. Between those mile markers, however, Jesus can teach, guide, and correct you when you get off track. Accept the blessing of training, retraining, and exchanging your thinking for His instruction. To do anything less wastes time and short-circuits the positive impact you could have on those around you.

EVENING

It is difficult to be corrected, Lord. It makes me feel
like a failure. Please remind me that Your correction
is done in love and is always for my good and
Your glory. Correct me so that I can learn from
my mistakes and walk more closely with You.

MORNING

I urge, then, first of all, that petitions, prayers, intercession and thanksgiving be made for all people—for kings and all those in authority, that we may live peaceful and quiet lives in all godliness and holiness.

1 TIMOTHY 2:1–2 NIV

In the United States, it's time for Tax Day. That's generally not thought of as a day to celebrate—but it could be. Think of the blessing behind these words from Jesus: "Give back to Caesar what is Caesar's, and to God what is God's" (Matthew 22:21).

Perhaps that sounds like you *have* to pay taxes and you *owe* God things you might prefer to keep. But Jesus' words are a blessing when you consider that God gives you the skills and strength to do things that are taxable by the government. On the other hand, you may have been given enough from God that you want to give back in gratitude. You could grumble about taxes, or you could just tell God, "Thanks."

You aren't blessed by obeying some compulsory duty. You're already blessed by God. . .and acknowledging that only adds to the blessing.

EVENING

Lord Jesus, when I feel like I am losing by paying taxes, remind me that everything I have came by Your generous blessing anyway. Thank You for giving me more than I need so I can return to You the tithes and offerings that help to advance Your kingdom.

April 16

Those who trust in the Lord will find new strength.
They will soar high on wings like eagles. They will run
and not grow weary. They will walk and not faint.
ISAIAH 40:31 NLT

The disciples were confused. And who could blame them? Jesus had said how difficult it will be for some people to see their need for rescue. Some won't accept that truth at all. So, Jesus' followers asked if *anyone* could be saved. Jesus told them, "Humanly speaking, it is impossible. But with God everything is possible" (Matthew 19:26).

Salvation is a blessing because it's a free gift. You can't aid in your own rescue. If you could rescue yourself, you would have already done that. But you can't. Jesus can.

His gift of rescue is not possibility or probability—it's certainty. Your trust invites the strength of Jesus, the adventure of God, and the endurance of God's Spirit. Each contributes value-added blessings that are yours when you trust Jesus. He made this impossibility possible. That's a blessing.

EVENING

I believe in today's scripture, Jesus—I will be renewed
when I trust in You. Even when it becomes difficult,
overwhelming, or tiresome to press on in pursuit
of righteousness, I know that You will lift me up
and strengthen me with Your power and love.

MORNING

*Try to understand other people. Forgive each other.
If you have something against someone, forgive
him. That is the way the Lord forgave you.*

COLOSSIANS 3:13 NLV

It is a blessing to be a blessing.

Don't think so? Jesus said. "Love those who work against you. Do good to those who hate you." *Whoa, hold on a minute. . .*this sounds like the Golden Rule at full volume, right? You understand that God wants you to treat people with the same kindness you want for yourself, but isn't this too much? Jesus continued, "Respect and give thanks for those who try to bring bad to you. Pray for those who make it very hard for you" (Luke 6:27–28).

Blessing others who don't deserve it can be very hard. But it can become an incredible personal blessing. You might get a front-row seat to a life change. You might see walls come down that had been erected years earlier. You might find that your own attitude changes in the midst of doing what God knows you can do with His help.

Bless others—discover blessings in return.

EVENING

*Lord Jesus, You taught me to treat others as I'd like
to be treated. Help me to be a blessing—and to find
blessing in return. Still, remind me that receiving a
blessing can't be my motivation. . .it's pleasing You.*

April 18

Every good gift and every perfect gift is from above,
and cometh down from the Father of lights, with whom
is no variableness, neither shadow of turning.

JAMES 1:17 KJV

John called himself the "disciple Jesus loved." He felt the encouragement and blessings of the only One who could rescue his soul, and he learned the value of blessing others because Jesus had blessed him. You can read about this blessing for yourself: "I wish above all things that thou mayest prosper and be in health, even as thy soul prospereth" (3 John 2). Short, sweet, and to the point, this blessing is proof that John wanted for others what Jesus wanted for him.

If you think the blessing was primarily about health and money, you're always welcome to read the verse again. Whatever we think we most need comes after (or alongside) a God-enriched soul. Jesus knew that when your soul is rich—when you seek Him most—whatever you receive from Him will be plenty.

The blessing you can pass on to others reflects the recognition that you have been abundantly blessed. You have been.

EVENING

I have received so many blessings, but none can
compare to the greatest blessing of all—having You in
my life, Jesus. The eternal life and hope that I find in
You far exceeds any earthly gift. I thank You for each
gift You give me, in this life and in the life to come.

MORNING

*Let us consider how we may spur one another
on toward love and good deeds.*

HEBREWS 10:24 NIV

You'd probably be okay with a little honor today, right? You do something good for someone and you're hoping the press release is issued, the photo op is well timed and complimentary, and that the celebration to name that street after you wouldn't be too over the top. Okay, so maybe that's not exactly how you feel, but some recognition for your good deeds would be nice.

Jesus said, "When you give to the needy, do not let your left hand know what your right hand is doing." The idea is, don't make a big deal out of it to be noticed by others. Why? Because "Your Father, who sees what is done in secret, will reward you" (Matthew 6:3–4). The One who counts most notices what you do.

Remember, you were made to bless others by being a blessing, not the grand marshal of a personal parade. When you try to bless, who are you really seeking to honor?

EVENING

*Lord Jesus, You are the one who should be honored.
May I give You all the glory You deserve, knowing that
I am simply Your servant. Humble me if I ever begin
to think that I can do good things on my own. I know
that I need Your Spirit's power to help me please You.*

April 20

> *Pursue righteousness and a godly life, along with*
> *faith, love, perseverance, and gentleness.*
> 1 TIMOTHY 6:11 NLT

Set your sights on something and you might find it runs away from you faster than you can chase it. If you can't catch it one way, you might try coming at it from another angle. But some things refuse to be caught.

Of course, the Bible has some guidance on such issues. You know how Jesus taught the apostle Paul, who later taught a young minister named Timothy. First Timothy 6:11 is Paul's advice to help his protégé know what to chase. Chase these things and you'll find that God helps you catch them. It's a way He blesses you and then helps you use what you pursued to bless others.

Imagine how much you can bless others when you are full of "love, joy, peace, patience, kindness, goodness, faithfulness, gentleness, and self-control" (Galatians 5:22–23). Let the chase begin.

EVENING

> *Lord Jesus, I want to chase the right things in my life.*
> *Help me to avoid pursuing unimportant and unholy*
> *things. Teach me how to follow after righteousness so*
> *that my life will honor You first and foremost. I want*
> *the blessing of a God-honoring life so that I can also*
> *bless others with the fruit You are producing in me.*

MORNING

"You have done well. You are a good and faithful servant."
MATTHEW 25:23 NLV

Jesus was and is faithful, right? He kept the promises He made, right? Yes, and yes. This, too, is a blessing. First Thessalonians 5:24 says, "The One Who called you is faithful and will do what He promised."

Promises kept are blessings. In keeping His promises, Jesus assures you that He can be trusted. You don't feel blessed when someone lets you down. They've done it before, and they'll disappoint you again.

But you shouldn't take your cues from people who break promises. You take your cue from Jesus. Don't follow those people who disappoint you—follow the One who will never let you down.

It's easy to look at other people's lives and think their promise-breaking gives you permission to do the same. God's blessing, through the example of Jesus Christ, should dismiss that thought immediately. Don't you want to hear Him acknowledge *you* for being a faithful blessing to others?

EVENING

*You are so faithful to keep all of Your promises,
Jesus. You have never let me down, and I can
trust that You never will. Let me be a blessing to
others by being faithful to my promises—to be
a woman of my word each and every day.*

April 22

> *My God shall supply all your need according*
> *to his riches in glory by Christ Jesus.*
> PHILIPPIANS 4:19 KJV

You follow Jesus, say you love Him, and try to do what He says. So if you expect God to bless you but withhold blessings from unbelievers, you might be disappointed. Jesus said that God "maketh his sun to rise on the evil and on the good, and sendeth rain on the just and on the unjust" (Matthew 5:45).

Everyone experiences something they call a blessing, and God doesn't discriminate when choosing who gets those blessings. But blessings like sunshine and rain are different from the specific, tangible blessings reserved for God's children. Things like faith, hope, and love take on fresh meaning for the rescued.

Those who don't follow Jesus don't have faith in God, so their hope is misplaced. Their perception of love is something with strings attached. Does that sound like a blessing to you?

Jesus said that some blessings are for everyone. But the Bible makes it clear that other blessings—the really important ones—are only for God's family.

EVENING

> *Lord Jesus, I know You have special blessings in mind*
> *for me, and I am glad. Help me both to enjoy them and*
> *to share them with others. I remember my life before*
> *You, when I could enjoy many of the good things of*
> *life—but now, as a believer, I can enjoy them even more!*

MORNING

"Peace I leave with you; my peace I give you. I do not give to you as the world gives. Do not let your hearts be troubled and do not be afraid."

JOHN 14:27 NIV

Blessings are not one-time events. Jesus continually blesses you, so don't think that blessing others is something you place on your to-do list and then check off, never to return to it again. You wouldn't expect that from Jesus, and you shouldn't allow it of yourself.

The Bible says in 1 Thessalonians 5:11, "Encourage one another and build each other up, just as in fact you are doing." The people of Thessalonica *were* blessing each other and speaking life into those around them. And they were encouraged to never stop.

One of the most profound observations about blessing is that God the Father and Jesus the Son always bless first, before they ask you to go against human nature and bless others.

You need reminders that God is good, that His peace is perfect, and that He will provide everything you need to live here and love forever. Reread Jesus' words above. Don't be afraid.

EVENING

I need never fear when I am following You, Lord. Give me Your peace as I step out of my comfort zone to bless others. Remind me that You first blessed me. Now it is my privilege to reflect that blessing to others.

April 24

> *"May the LORD bless you and protect you. May the
> LORD smile on you and be gracious to you. May the
> LORD show you his favor and give you his peace."*
>
> NUMBERS 6:24–26 NLT

You have been blessed, and you can bless others through prayer. When Jesus prayed, He was able to focus on the blessings His disciples would receive. He said, "I have revealed you to them, and I will continue to do so. Then your love for me will be in them, and I will be in them" (John 17:26). You could use these words in your own prayers, asking God to use you to bless others by revealing Him. Pray that God's love would fill others and change their lives.

There are many passages that can be transformed into prayers that ask God to bless others. They could be for a spouse, a child, other family, friends, neighbors, and even strangers.

When you ask God to bless others by using His own words, don't be surprised if something changes within you. Go ahead—use the verse above to begin a season of blessing prayers.

EVENING

*Jesus, show me verses from Your Word that I can
pray over friends, family members, coworkers,
and even strangers. May my prayers bless them
as I speak to You about their needs. And may
I enjoy spending more time with You as I pray
these prayers of blessing over other people.*

MORNING

I pray that because of the riches of His shining-greatness, He will make you strong with power in your hearts through the Holy Spirit.

EPHESIANS 3:16 NLV

Can you imagine what a blessing it was for the disciples to walk with Jesus, in the flesh and by His side? There would be all kinds of things they could share about their time with Him—and they did. But Jesus continued to prove that He came to bless. He spoke to many people after He rose from the dead. He prayed with His disciples, "And while He was praying that good would come to them, He went from them (and was taken up to heaven and they worshiped Him). Then they went back to Jerusalem with great joy" (Luke 24:51–52).

The blessings Jesus makes available did not end with His sacrifice on the cross. He continues to bring good to those who love Him. His blessings bring joy.

You see that in Luke 24. Jesus' grace was sufficient, and His mercy was personal. And they still are today.

EVENING

Lord Jesus, I thank You for still being a blessing-giver. You continue to increase my faith when I focus on Your sacrifice and the blessings that You give me daily. I am so grateful for Your infinite and yet personal mercy and grace.

April 26

Ye have heard that it hath been said, Thou shalt love thy neighbour, and hate thine enemy. But I say unto you, Love your enemies, bless them that curse you, do good to them that hate you, and pray for them which despitefully use you, and persecute you.

MATTHEW 5:43–44 KJV

The life of Jesus is worth reading about. . .and reading about again. His healings were blessings. His miracles were blessings. His teaching and compassion were blessings. He came for sinners and blessed them by offering new life. Many seemed willing to follow Him for such generous blessings, but then He gave instructions few wanted to hear: He told them not only to love their enemies, but to bless those who cursed them. Finally, Jesus took it a step further when He said, "Do good to them that hate you, and pray for them which despitefully use you, and persecute you."

Bless the persecutor? Pray for those who use you? Love those who never prove to be a friend? Love and help those who hate you? *Yes!*

We might think it's no problem to follow Jesus—but what He's asking in this verse is just too much. *He doesn't understand how hard this is. He's asking the impossible.* But it's not impossible. It's exactly what He's done—for you (Romans 5:8). He can help you do what you can't do on your own. That's blessing.

EVENING

Jesus, I know that only You can empower me to love and bless my enemies. It is not in my nature to help those who hurt me, but I know that I can follow Your example. Your Spirit will empower me to treat others as You treated all people, with love and compassion.

MORNING

Do your best to present yourself to God as one approved, a worker who does not need to be ashamed and who correctly handles the word of truth.

2 TIMOTHY 2:15 NIV

Jesus was on a mission. He came to save humankind. In the process of rescue, He experienced everything humankind experiences every day. In the sacrifice, He experienced the physical and mental pain of people's sin. Despite all He went through, He never wavered on the idea of blessing. He would ask all who followed Him to bless others in the way He blessed them.

Jesus lived the life He was meant to live. He died the death that saved humankind. He rose to new life to defeat the stronghold of death. And because of this, His gifts brought new life to unlikely people. The vicious persecutor Saul would learn of Jesus' love and follow even when no one believed he had really changed. As the apostle Paul, he would say, "Brothers and sisters, stand firm. Let nothing move you. Always give yourselves fully to the work of the Lord, because you know that your labor in the Lord is not in vain" (1 Corinthians 15:58).

Be blessed, be a blessing, keep blessing.

EVENING

Lord, when I am walking with You, I have no reason to ever stop blessing others. I have been blessed to be a blessing, so please remind me of this call to action when I grow weary of serving others.

April 28

The LORD is my strength and shield. I trust him with all my heart. He helps me, and my heart is filled with joy. I burst out in songs of thanksgiving.
PSALM 28:7 NLT

Every human who has ever lived could be compared pretty equally with a sheep. Descriptive words might include *confused*, *misguided*, *anxious*, *fearful*, and *weak*. You can look over a crowd and have thoughts that suggest you are better or worse off than the people you see, but in reality, in most ways, you're very much like the others.

You may see needs in other people but for various reasons feel unable or unwilling to help. But when Jesus saw a crowd, "he had compassion on them because they were confused and helpless, like sheep without a shepherd" (Matthew 9:36).

The greatest need humankind will ever have is to know Jesus. When you follow His example of blessing others, it becomes a statement. You believe Jesus can be trusted, that He is who He says He is, and that He has the power to help. Now *that's* saying something—and that message is a blessing.

EVENING

Lord Jesus, when I feel afraid, confused, or anxious, bless me with Your compassion. I cannot compare myself to anyone else because all people are lost without You. I thank You that I have been brought into Your flock. Remind me to bless others and show them the way to You as the Shepherd.

MORNING

*God kept us from what looked like sure death and He is
keeping us. As we trust Him, He will keep us in the future.*

2 CORINTHIANS 1:10 NLV

A full array of blessing is seen in the Bible. The source of blessing is
God. The One who delivered God's eternal blessing was Jesus. Understanding blessings means understanding God. Understanding God
means accepting His Son. God doesn't shortchange anyone when it
comes to understanding how and why He blesses: "Everything that
was written in the Holy Writings long ago was written to teach us.
By not giving up, God's Word gives us strength and hope" (Romans
15:4). You've learned by now that there are actual attitudes and
behaviors that God blesses. What you do matters. What God does
is a promise fulfilled.

The rescue Jesus offers comes with the promise of eternal life.
This isn't just the ability to live forever, but to live eternally *with God.*
It means face-to-face encounters, heart-to-heart conversations, and
old-life-for-new transformations. And Jesus will be with you until
His eternity becomes your reality.

EVENING

*You are my blessing, Lord Jesus. The new life You've
given me, the transformation of my mind and
heart, and the daily blessings I see are all gifts. You
are worthy of all of my praise and adoration.*

April 30

> *God is able to make all grace abound toward*
> *you; that ye, always having all sufficiency in all*
> *things, may abound to every good work.*
>
> 2 CORINTHIANS 9:8 KJV

Many of the Old Testament prophecies about Jesus—from His arrival on earth to His death—are found in the Psalms. Mixed in between are blessings extending beyond this month's readings. Spend some final moments this month marveling at the depth of the blessings in store for followers of Jesus:

The blessing of trust: "Blessed are all they that put their trust in him" (Psalm 2:12).

The blessing of faithfully following: "Blessed are they that dwell in thy house: they will be still praising thee" (Psalm 84:4).

The blessing of living in God's strength: "Blessed is the man whose strength is in thee" (Psalm 84:5).

The blessing of righteous living: "Blessed are they that keep judgment, and he that doeth righteousness at all times" (Psalm 106:3).

The blessing of continually following: "Blessed are the undefiled in the way, who walk in the law of the LORD" (Psalm 119:1).

The blessing of the seeker: "Blessed are they that keep his testimonies, and that seek him with the whole heart" (Psalm 119:2).

EVENING

> *Lord Jesus, help me to seek Your truth, live*
> *in Your strength and righteousness, and*
> *faithfully follow You all the days of my life.*

MORNING

*Don't be misled—you cannot mock the justice of
God. You will always harvest what you plant.*

GALATIANS 6:7 NLT

How are you at growing things? Maybe your thumb is more grey than green, but that doesn't mean you can't cultivate something beautiful. . .with the help of the Master Gardener.

Jesus used many gardening illustrations to help people understand His teaching. And the law of "sowing and reaping," which the apostle Paul referenced in Galatians, was something the Lord's audience understood well. You harvest what you plant. That's true in the natural world, and it's true in the spiritual world. If you plant and tend peas, you'll harvest peas. If you plant doubt and worry in your heart, that's exactly what you'll reap.

Jesus wants to plant good things in the soil of your heart. If you allow Him to work, you'll harvest in ways you could never have imagined. Paul wrote of that harvest: "The Holy Spirit produces this kind of fruit in our lives: love, joy, peace, patience, kindness, goodness, faithfulness, gentleness, and self-control" (Galatians 5:22–23).

Let's dig into growth this month.

EVENING

*Jesus, I can't sow weeds and harvest wheat. Teach me to
plant Your good seeds and reap Your good harvest. When
I begin to sow doubt, worry, or complacency, remind me
to replace them with the seeds of the fruit of Your Spirit.*

May 2

*"I am the Vine and you are the branches. Get your
life from Me. Then I will live in you and you will give
much fruit. You can do nothing without Me."*

You don't need to be an accomplished gardener to know that different plants tend to grow better in particular climates and soils—settings where other plants won't thrive. For example, pineapple does great in the warm, wet climate of a place like Hawaii, but it'll wilt and die in cooler, drier places—where a crop like wheat will produce a big yield.

Thankfully, Jesus knows exactly what we need to grow in our relationship with Him—no matter where He's "planted" us. There is no guesswork involved. He doesn't have to bring in a specialist to decipher growing problems or send samples away to a lab. That's because Jesus Himself is our strong and healthy vine. We are the branches that grow from Him. His very life inside us is all we need. Invite Him in and ask Him to grow His spiritual fruit in your life.

*Lord Jesus, You've planted me in a specific place
and time for my good and Your glory. You know
what fruit is needed in my life to lead others into
Your kingdom. Teach me to abide on Your vine
and to receive all that I need from You alone.*

MORNING

"Every tree that does not have good fruit is cut down and thrown into the fire. So you will know them by their fruit."
MATTHEW 7:19–20 NLV

The Bible talks a lot about fruit—*spiritual* fruit. When Jesus is Lord over our lives, His presence within starts to transform us, enabling us to produce fresh spiritual fruit as we grow ever more like Him.

In Matthew 7:20, Jesus said we can recognize people by the fruit their lives produce—that is, we can tell which people are letting Jesus live out His life through them by seeing the good fruit in their lives. Selfish people produce bad fruit, but those who live in and for Jesus produce the best stuff.

What kind of fruit are you producing? Allow Jesus to be your personal fruit inspector. Do parts of your life need more pruning? Is there an area that requires tending? A place that isn't growing at all? Give yourself entirely to Jesus, and He will gladly grow good in your life.

EVENING

How can I grow better fruit for you, Lord Jesus? Whatever You need to change in my life, I humbly accept. I know that You are the Master Gardener and You know much better than I do what is needed from my life. Prune me and tend me according to Your will.

May 4

But anyone who does not love does not know God, for God is love.

1 John 4:8 nlt

In the famous and beloved "Fruit of the Spirit" passage (Galatians 5:22–23), the first quality mentioned is love. People tend to think of love as a feeling, but true biblical love is more than simple emotion. This kind of love is a choice, meaning you can decide to love another person even when you don't feel like it. That's the kind of love God calls His followers to demonstrate.

The apostle Paul told us more about true love: "Love is patient and kind. Love is not jealous or boastful or proud or rude. It does not demand its own way. It is not irritable, and it keeps no record of being wronged. It does not rejoice about injustice but rejoices whenever the truth wins out. Love never gives up, never loses faith, is always hopeful, and endures through every circumstance" (1 Corinthians 13:4–7).

Love like that isn't possible apart from Jesus living and working inside you. But it's the kind of love that will fill your heart as you faithfully follow Him.

EVENING

*Lord Jesus, You work in me to produce love for others.
Fill me with Your love and allow me to see myself and
others the way that You do. Teach me what real, selfless
love looks like and convict me to live it out each day.*

MORNING

> *For the Kingdom of God is not a matter of what*
> *we eat or drink, but of living a life of goodness*
> *and peace and joy in the Holy Spirit.*
>
> ROMANS 14:17 NLT

How can we be blessed and feel God's joy inside? Blessing and joy are byproducts of being with Jesus. Joy is a fruit of the Spirit who lives in every follower of Christ, and that joy applies both to the good and bad times of life. Even when things are going wrong, we can have joy. Why? Because of this promise to all who follow Jesus: "We know that God causes everything to work together for the good of those who love God and are called according to his purpose for them" (Romans 8:28).

Just as an apple or a pear or an orange must develop over time, so will our spiritual fruit. Joy grows as we realize that God is with us, working everything out for our good. How could it be otherwise, considering He sent Jesus to die for our sins (Romans 5:8)?

EVENING

> *Thank You for the joy You put in my life, Lord.*
> *May I never lose focus on living well for You.*
> *You work all things out for my good, so it is my*
> *pleasure to live a life that honors You. Continue*
> *to fill me with Your goodness, peace, and joy!*

May 6

> *The peace of God is much greater than the human*
> *mind can understand. This peace will keep your*
> *hearts and minds through Christ Jesus.*
>
> PHILIPPIANS 4:7 NLV

The peace of God gives you a supernatural ability to remain calm in the midst of anything. It's been said that "peace isn't the absence of trouble, but the presence of God in the midst of the trouble." Peace is a deep assurance that God always has His eye on you, and He is at work in your circumstances.

Divine peace is beyond our ability to fully understand. We don't create it ourselves—God has to grow this spiritual fruit in our hearts.

Our heavenly Father wants us to take our worries to Him in prayer... read the rest of Philippians 4. When we tell Him what's on our minds, thanking Him for what He has already done for us, we'll sense a growing confidence in what He *will* do. And this peace comes through our Lord Jesus Christ.

EVENING

> *I thank You for giving me peace, Jesus. I bring all of my*
> *worries and cares to You now and allow You to lift them*
> *off my shoulders. Please take all my anxiety so that I can*
> *go through my day tomorrow with calm and confidence.*

MORNING

*Since God chose you to be the holy people he loves,
you must clothe yourselves with tenderhearted mercy,
kindness, humility, gentleness, and patience.*

COLOSSIANS 3:12 NLT

Patience can be a tricky fruit to grow, but it's one that Jesus wants us to have. Check out these verses:

- "And not only so, but we glory in tribulations also: knowing that tribulation worketh patience" (Romans 5:3 KJV).
- "Always be humble and gentle. Be patient with each other, making allowance for each other's faults because of your love" (Ephesians 4:2).
- "Brothers and sisters, we urge you to warn those who are lazy. Encourage those who are timid. Take tender care of those who are weak. Be patient with everyone" (1 Thessalonians 5:14).

If you've had trouble growing the fruit of patience, go to God in the name of Jesus and ask for help. The only perfect Person in human history will be glad to help you develop this beautiful quality.

EVENING

*Lord, patience can be a challenge. I thank You for being
patient with me as I experience my daily struggles.
Sometimes it's difficult to humble myself and be patient
with others. Please grow this spiritual fruit in me today.*

May 8

The Lord came to us from far away, saying, "I have loved you with a love that lasts forever. So I have helped you come to Me with loving-kindness."

JEREMIAH 31:3 NLV

God is kind, and all His ways are kind. The Bible is filled with examples of His loving-kindness. Scripture tells us that He draws us to Himself through kindness (Romans 2:3–4).

God showed His great kindness by offering salvation to all through Jesus. When we know Jesus, we must allow Him to grow that spiritual fruit of kindness in our lives. So many people misunderstand God, so it's our job as Christians to show them who He really is.

Jesus said He came to provide an abundant life (John 10:10). Part of that abundance is the true kindness that God's Spirit grows in us. As we allow that fruit to develop, others will see Jesus—the kindest man who ever lived—in us. And, we hope and pray, they will be drawn to salvation through Him.

EVENING

Lord Jesus, You have been so kind to me. I know that it is Your kindness that draws people to repentance, and repentance leads to a relationship with You that lasts for eternity. May others see You in how I live and be drawn to You in salvation.

MORNING

Trust in the LORD and do good. Then you will
live safely in the land and prosper.
PSALM 37:3 NLT

It's hard to do the right thing all the time, especially when people around you are not. That's why we need God's help in growing the spiritual fruit of goodness.

First John 5:18 says: "We know that God's children do not make a practice of sinning, for God's Son holds them securely, and the evil one cannot touch them." We can stay away from sin and make right choices because Jesus Himself protects us. And His Spirit will grow goodness in our lives when we turn to Him for help with our choices.

We all make mistakes. We all sin. But when that happens, God wants us to run *to* Him, not *from* Him. You can always go to God with confidence because you are covered in the righteousness of Jesus. You don't need to hide from Him because of the shame of Your sin—He sees it anyway! Go to Him in humility and confession and you will be forgiven immediately. Trust in the Lord and do good.

EVENING

Oh, Jesus, I often feel ashamed and embarrassed when
I sin. Remind me that You see my entire life anyway,
and that You have already provided forgiveness
by Your sacrifice on the cross. Please forgive my
sins and cause me to walk in Your goodness.

May 10

"His owner said to him, 'You have done well. You are a good and faithful servant. You have been faithful over a few things. I will put many things in your care. Come and share my joy.'"

MATTHEW 25:21 NLV

As you draw closer to Jesus, faithfulness is another fruit the Holy Spirit will grow in your life. God has given us all work to do on this earth as we wait for Jesus to return. Each of us has gifts and talents to use as we serve God and share the good news of Jesus with others. The Spirit provides the desire, the energy, and the ability to pour out these gifts in productive ways.

In His parable of the talents, Jesus taught that human faithfulness begins with God (He gives responsibility to His children), continues with us (we use the ability He's given), and circles back to God again (He gives us even more ability and responsibility). We work with God to grow the fruit of faithfulness in our lives. Note: We cannot just sit back and expect to become faithful; growing faithfulness requires effort on our part.

EVENING

Forgive me, Lord, for my moments of unfaithfulness. Reveal to my heart any areas in which I am not being faithful with my very best efforts to honor You. May my life be a holy and acceptable sacrifice to You, faithful and fruitful.

MORNING

Let your gentleness be evident to all. The Lord is near.

PHILIPPIANS 4:5 NIV

Are you generally gentle with the people around you? Are you gentle with yourself?

When life becomes busy and stressful, it's easy to forget about gentleness. Sometimes we say whatever we're thinking, not giving a thought to anyone else's feelings. And we can be hard on ourselves, too, thinking negative and unhelpful things that bring us down even further.

But our gentle Lord doesn't want us to live that way. Jesus, who welcomed little children, the sick and lame and blind, and the outcasts of society, wants us to allow His Spirit to grow the fruit of gentleness within us. According to the apostle Paul, we should be gentle because "the Lord is near."

Jesus is coming soon. When He comes, may He find a healthy, fully developed crop of gentleness within His people.

EVENING

Jesus, I know that You plan to return for a bride that is pure and holy. Grow gentleness in me so that my first response to a stressful or frustrating situation isn't anger or harsh words. Help me to cultivate gentleness in such a way that people know whose I am.

May 12

For this very reason, make every effort to add to your faith goodness; and to goodness, knowledge; and to knowledge, self-control; and to self-control, perseverance; and to perseverance, godliness; and to godliness, mutual affection; and to mutual affection, love.

2 PETER 1:5–7 NIV

Today's scripture passage is quite a list! How in the world can we manage all of that?

The apostle Peter gave the answer just a few verses earlier: God's "divine power has given us everything we need for a godly life through our knowledge of him who called us by his own glory and goodness" (2 Peter 1:3).

We don't have to grow these godly characteristics in our own strength. It is "divine power" at work inside of us that makes all good things happen. As the fruit of God's Spirit grows inside us (Galatians 5:22–23), the virtues listed above will come along too. As we die to ourselves every day, allowing God's power to work inside us, we'll have more and more of the qualities of 2 Peter 1:5–7. We'll look more and more like Jesus.

In my own power, Lord, I can't make good things happen. Draw me closer to You, so that the fruit of Your Spirit will develop naturally. Help me to spend time in Your Word. Help me to worship You each day. May I never neglect our important time together.

MORNING

*And this is my prayer: I pray that your love will grow more
and more. I pray that you will have better understanding
and be wise in all things. . . . And I pray that you will
be filled with the fruits of right living. These come
from Jesus Christ, with honor and thanks to God.*

PHILIPPIANS 1:9, 11 NLV

As the Spirit of God works in your heart, spiritual fruits begin to
grow. Are they growing within you? Take a quick inventory: love,
joy, peace, patience, kindness, goodness, faithfulness, gentleness,
self-control. Are these taking root and developing in your heart?

If you recognize that some of these qualities aren't growing inside
you, take your concern to Jesus. Ask Him to clear the weeds out of
your heart, making room for the good things He wants to grow there.

We're all sinful human beings, so there's no shame in asking. The
real problem would be to pretend you're okay! The "fruits of right
living" come from Jesus Himself. He is your source of growth. He
wants to prepare your heart to bear real fruit.

EVENING

*Lord Jesus, help me to do an honest inventory
of my heart. Am I demonstrating each of these
fruits in my life? Convict me in the areas where
I fall short and give me direction as to how I can
do better. You are my only source of growth.*

May 14

> *Let us run with perseverance the race marked out for us,*
> *fixing our eyes on Jesus, the pioneer and perfecter of faith.*
> *For the joy set before him he endured the cross, scorning its*
> *shame, and sat down at the right hand of the throne of God.*
>
> HEBREWS 12:1–2 NIV

Have you ever beaten yourself up for messing up? For struggling with the same sin over and over? This can happen when we try to grow spiritual fruit in our own strength. If so, may this passage encourage you.

As the "pioneer and perfecter," Jesus starts and finishes our faith. It was His endurance of the shame of the cross that led to our salvation, so all we must now do is accept His work. Jesus' goodness covers our badness! There is nothing we have to do to earn salvation. We simply accept His grace and walk in renewed life, fixing our eyes on Him.

Jesus gives us all His strength to rise again and keep on going—and growing. He is with you, and He is at work in you. Don't give up.

EVENING

> *Lord, help me to "never, never, never give up," or to*
> *beat myself up for failures. I'm turning each failure*
> *over to You, asking You to grow good fruit in my life.*
> *As I wind down this day, please give me Your grace and*
> *forgiveness and refocus my eyes on the finish line.*

MORNING

*For God is the one who provides seed for the farmer and then
bread to eat. In the same way, he will provide and increase your
resources and then produce a great harvest of generosity in you.*

2 CORINTHIANS 9:10 NLT

Gardening is a beautiful—and accurate—illustration of the spiritual life. The seed comes from the hand of God. It is planted in the ground, and as the gardener tends to it, it sprouts and grows, eventually producing an abundant harvest that feeds the gardener and his family, often with abundance to share.

When we follow Jesus, we become part of God's garden. He plants His "seed" of kindness and compassion within us, and then makes sure there is ultimately "a great harvest of generosity."

Just as God loved the world so much that He gave Jesus (John 3:16), we as followers of Christ should overflow in our giving. Everything starts with God anyway, so why not be open-handed? Always remember that Jesus laid down His life for His friends (John 15:13).

EVENING

*Lord, I want my life to overflow with a good harvest
that I can share with others. You have given me
more than I could ever ask or imagine. Help me to
be unselfish with all that I've been given. I want
to be radically generous in giving to others.*

May 16

MORNING

We can rejoice, too, when we run into problems and trials, for we know that they help us develop endurance. And endurance develops strength of character, and character strengthens our confident hope of salvation. And this hope will not lead to disappointment. For we know how dearly God loves us, because he has given us the Holy Spirit to fill our hearts with his love.

ROMANS 5:3–5 NLT

Life on earth is like a pendulum: happiness and disappointment, wonder and heartache, breathtaking highs and overwhelming lows. But these tensions help us to grow.

Can you imagine watching a movie in which nothing but good things happened, where there was no struggle and nothing to overcome? That sounds boring. You'd probably move on to a story with a little more excitement.

The best adventures have highs and lows. And the adventure of the Christian life will too. But with Jesus always at our side, and His Holy Spirit filling our hearts with love, we can rejoice in all things. Through Jesus, we have the hope of eternal salvation. . .and we will not be disappointed.

EVENING

Lord Jesus, sometimes I dream of a life of ease. But I know that's not realistic. In this world I will have troubles, but I can take heart because You have overcome the world. Help me to see the lessons I can learn from each disappointment, heartache, and trial.

MORNING

*But grow in the grace and knowledge of our Lord and Savior
Jesus Christ. To him be glory both now and forever! Amen.*

2 PETER 3:18 NIV

Jesus was "full of grace and truth" (John 1:14). As His followers, we are to "grow in the grace and knowledge of our Lord and Savior." If truth is the seed, then grace is the rich soil that allows it to bloom into a garden of love. You know how important love is: "Now these three remain: faith, hope and love. But the greatest of these is love" (1 Corinthians 13:13).

You can grow in truth, obtaining more and more knowledge . . .but if this is not seasoned with love, the apostle Paul says it means nothing (1 Corinthians 13:2). That's a big deal.

Love is the most important thing. If you're growing in the knowledge of Jesus but not in grace and love, you'll accomplish nothing for the kingdom of God. You don't want to just be a clanging symbol, making noise about the Bible without having a heart of grace and love behind your words. Ask Jesus to align your heart with His.

EVENING

*Lord, I don't want to miss out on the greater calling
by focusing solely on facts and details of Your Word.
Please help me to live out Your command to love You
first and then others as myself. Let my knowledge
of Your Word grow me into a woman of grace.*

May 18

*And now, just as you accepted Christ Jesus as your
Lord, you must continue to follow him. Let your roots
grow down into him, and let your lives be built on him.
Then your faith will grow strong in the truth you were
taught, and you will overflow with thankfulness.*

COLOSSIANS 2:6–7 NLT

A tree with deep roots is far less likely to topple when storms come. It's strongly attached to the earth. And it is more able to find the water it needs to stay healthy.

The Bible tells us to let our roots grow down deep into Jesus Himself. We are to build our lives on Him. So, how are your roots? Are you firmly planted in the Word? Is your faith strong enough to keep you upright during life's storms? Healthy in times of drought?

You can grow deep roots fast. Spend time—quantity and quality time—with Jesus. Be present with Him in every moment, and you'll find yourself strong for the challenges of life. You'll even find yourself overflowing with thankfulness.

EVENING

*Thank You, Jesus, for giving me roots as well as
branches. When my roots are deep in You, my limbs
reach out into life's challenges and remain strong,
no matter what storms may come. My history with
You, Lord, gives me confidence in my future.*

MORNING

"And the seeds that fell on the good soil represent honest, good-hearted people who hear God's word, cling to it, and patiently produce a huge harvest."

LUKE 8:15 NLT

Jesus' parable in Luke 8 describes a farmer who scattered seeds. Some fell on the pathway, some on the rocks, and some in the thorns. But some seeds landed on good soil. The only seeds that grew and produced a crop were those that fell on the good soil.

Jesus later explained the parable: the seed that produced the good crop stood for people who heard God's Word and followed through—they made a decision for Jesus and continued following Him no matter what. They patiently trusted God for all things. . .and He blessed them for it.

Read the rest of Luke 8 to understand the other kinds of soil. Which describes you? If your soil type is poor, ask Jesus to break up the hard surface, carry away the rocks, or root out the weeds. He'll be happy to clear out the land so His fruit can grow.

EVENING

Jesus, work the soil of my heart so that it is good enough to produce the fruit of Your Spirit. Clear away anything that might choke out my enthusiasm for You. Show me the rocky spots that might cause me to doubt. Strengthen me to trust You all the more during the difficult seasons of my life.

May 20

So we have not stopped praying for you since we first heard about you. We ask God to give you complete knowledge of his will and to give you spiritual wisdom and understanding. Then the way you live will always honor and please the Lord, and your lives will produce every kind of good fruit. All the while, you will grow as you learn to know God better and better.

COLOSSIANS 1:9–10 NLT

Can you work for God without God? Yes, you can. Many Christians do. They spend years gaining biblical knowledge and pursuing ministry endeavors. But doing "Christian" things doesn't mean they are growing in Christ. Many times, less is more—less doing means more real listening to God.

Jesus is the source of all knowledge and wisdom and understanding. You grow in your faith and produce good fruit for Him when you ask Him to lead and guide you.

EVENING

I need Your wisdom and understanding, Jesus, so I can serve You well. Lead and guide me in the work You've laid before me. May I never fall into the trap of "doing" instead of "being." Whatever work I do for You, I want to do with You.

MORNING

> *The man who is right and good will grow like the palm tree.*
> *He will grow like a tall tree in Lebanon. Planted in the house of*
> *the Lord, they will grow well in the home of our God. They will still*
> *give fruit when they are old. They will be full of life and strength.*
>
> PSALM 92:12–14 NLV

An apple tree can live up to eighty years, producing an abundance of fruit throughout its lifetime. Blueberry plants can produce fruit for up to fifty years. And citrus trees can live and produce fruit for more than fifty years. Notice the word *can*: all of these plants depend on careful tending for their health and longevity. It's much the same with people.

Today's scripture says that "the man who is right and good will grow." Other versions say "the godly" or "the righteous" will flourish. As Christians, we know that we are only righteous—considered clean in God's sight—because of Jesus (Philippians 3:9). As we allow Him to tend to us, we continue to grow. As we root ourselves deeply in Him, we will produce fruit all the days of our lives. . .whether that's fifty or eighty years, or even longer.

EVENING

> *Lord Jesus, I want to grow like a flourishing tree in*
> *Your orchard, giving good fruit all my days. I know*
> *that is nothing I could do on my own, so I welcome*
> *Your tending and making me into a good, righteous*
> *woman because of Your forgiveness and mercy.*

May 22

MORNING

*Oh, the joys of those who do not follow the advice of the wicked,
or stand around with sinners, or join in with mockers. But they
delight in the law of the Lord, meditating on it day and night.
They are like trees planted along the riverbank, bearing fruit each
season. Their leaves never wither, and they prosper in all they do.*

PSALM 1:1–3 NLT

Have you canoed on a river? If so, you might have noticed that the trees growing along the banks are usually big and healthy. That's because they are planted by a source of life. In John 7:38 Jesus said, "Anyone who believes in me may come and drink! For the Scriptures declare, 'Rivers of living water will flow from his heart.' "

When we are firmly planted and rooted in Christ, the living water—Jesus Himself—will flow from within us. We have the very source of life itself alive and at work in us! You can stop striving to make things work out on your own. Simply rest in the fact that the source of life Himself will help you grow like a tree on a riverbank.

EVENING

*Lord, plant me by Your living water. I want to
drink deeply of You and feel Your life permeating
my own. I trust that as I stay close to You, You'll
give me all I need to live a life that pleases You.*

May 23

MORNING

> *Don't copy the behavior and customs of this world, but let God transform you into a new person by changing the way you think. Then you will learn to know God's will for you, which is good and pleasing and perfect.*
>
> ROMANS 12:2 NLT

The life of Jesus within you is bringing about transformation. But transformation isn't always easy. Think about the butterfly. Before that beautiful creature appears, a caterpillar has to stop eating, hang itself upside down, and spin a cocoon where the transformation will take place. This metamorphosis changes the lowly crawler into a colorful flyer—which is akin to the growth in human beings when they come to Jesus. His life changes us into all that He wants us to be, polishing and perfecting our own personal gifts, abilities, and desires.

When you change the way you think—when you consciously turn your thoughts to Jesus—you will grow. You will understand God's pleasing and perfect will. And you'll help to change the world for good.

EVENING

> *Jesus, I thank You for the transformative work You are doing in my life each and every day. Show me Your pleasing and perfect will for my life. Keep changing the way I think to become more and more like You, Lord.*

May 24

> *"Oh, that we might know the Lord! Let us press on to know him. He will respond to us as surely as the arrival of dawn or the coming of rains in early spring."*
>
> Hosea 6:3 nlt

The Lord wants you to know Him personally. Isn't that amazing? He is not playing hide-and-seek. He is not leading you down some path to ultimate disappointment. No—God is good, and He has your best interest at heart.

Don't forget that Jesus came looking for you first: "For the Son of Man came to seek and save those who are lost" (Luke 19:10). *He* was looking, but He wanted *you* to find Him.

Are you "pressing on" to know Jesus? The apostle Paul used those words to describe the work he did to know and grow: "I have not achieved it, but I focus on this one thing: Forgetting what is past and looking forward to what lies ahead, I press on to reach the end of the race and receive the heavenly prize for which God, through Christ Jesus, is calling us" (Philippians 3:13–14).

EVENING

> *Lord Jesus, I thank You for seeking me when I wasn't looking for You. Now I want to press on to know You more deeply. It is my privilege to seek out Your truths.*

May 25

MORNING

Jesus said to her, "I am the resurrection and the life. The one who believes in me will live, even though they die; and whoever lives by believing in me will never die. Do you believe this?"

JOHN 11:25–26 NIV

New life begins the moment we begin our walk with Jesus, but the rate at which we grow and change is different for each person. Christians experience Jesus in many different ways. Some have a "come to Jesus" moment and are instantly changed, miraculously transformed from a former way of life. Many others begin the walk of faith and then grow gradually as the Holy Spirit teaches and trains them in the ways of Jesus.

It's important to have grace for yourself—and for others—as you journey through this life with Jesus. We humans will never get everything right, all the time. Every journey is different. Enjoy the growth process with great hope for the future. When you believe in Jesus, you will live and never die!

EVENING

Give me grace for myself and others, Lord Jesus, as we all walk with You. My walk does not, and will not, look exactly like anyone else's. May I never forget what a privilege it is to walk with You, now and for all eternity.

May 26

> *Now you are the body of Christ,*
> *and each one of you is a part of it.*
> 1 CORINTHIANS 12:27 NIV

Once you know Jesus, once you believe what He has said about Himself, once you understand who you are because of Him, everything changes. Jesus is alive, and He's helping you grow in your relationship with Him. Now you are free to live the life God created you to live, no matter what anyone else thinks or what's going on around you.

As a believer, you are part of Jesus' body here on earth. You belong because God says you belong. Nothing and no one can change that. You can love and be loved no matter what. As you grow and mature in Christ, you grasp this truth ever more firmly.

There's no need for insecurity or any feeling that you don't belong. You are who you are and where you are for a reason, and you can now partner with Jesus on His mission of extending the Father's kingdom. And as you grow individually, you build up the body of Christ.

EVENING

> *Thank You, Lord, for letting me belong to You, for*
> *making a place in Your family for me. Grant me*
> *confidence and courage to help build Your kingdom.*
> *I never need to doubt my place in Your family because*
> *You have chosen and equipped me for Your service.*

MORNING

When I was a child, I talked like a child, I thought like a child, I reasoned like a child. When I became a man, I put the ways of childhood behind me.

1 CORINTHIANS 13:11 NIV

Have you ever seen a child throwing a temper tantrum? It's uncomfortable to watch, but we understand how it happens: children are immature. Have you ever seen an *adult* throw a temper tantrum? That is far more uncomfortable, because we expect grown-ups to act like grown-ups.

Today's scripture is smack-dab in the middle of 1 Corinthians 13, also known as "the Love Chapter." Why would a verse about childishness be included there? Because growing up in Jesus means putting away our youthful ideas and desires, and learning to love our fellow Christians. The way we love is actually the measure of our maturity in Christ. Jesus Himself said, "By this everyone will know that you are my disciples, if you love one another" (John 13:35).

EVENING

Jesus, I am grateful that You didn't leave me in my childish state. It is immature to live a life that only serves my own interests. Thank You for showing me the way to grow up, to love You and others selflessly.

May 28

> *Then we will no longer be immature like children. We won't be tossed and blown about by every wind of new teaching. We will not be influenced when people try to trick us with lies so clever they sound like the truth. Instead, we will speak the truth in love, growing in every way more and more like Christ, who is the head of his body, the church.*
>
> EPHESIANS 4:14–15 NLT

Though the devil is often portrayed in horns and a red cape, he doesn't really show up that way. He would be too easily noticed! No, Satan typically masquerades as something good—maybe even as that one thing you've always wanted. The devil is tricky, so tricky that Jesus called him the father of lies (John 8:44).

When we're young, we're more easily tricked. But as we get older, we're not as easily fooled. . .or at least that's the way it should be. The important thing is growth. In the spiritual realm, are we spending time in God's Word? Are we praying in the Spirit? Are we patterning our lives after the perfect life of our Lord, Jesus Christ? May this always be true of us, so we won't be tossed by every wind of new teaching.

EVENING

> *Lord Jesus, I don't want to be fooled by the evil one. Please help me to grow spiritually as I spend time in Your Word. I know that the enemy will often masquerade as something I desire, so remind me that nothing I want can compare with You.*

MORNING

*Be sure to use the gift God gave you. The leaders saw
this in you when they laid their hands on you and said
what you should do. Think about all this. Work at it so
everyone may see you are growing as a Christian.*

1 Timothy 4:14–15 nlv

In Matthew 5:16, Jesus said, "Let your light shine in front of men. Then they will see the good things you do and will honor your Father Who is in heaven." He wanted His followers to consistently model kindness, forgiveness, and good behavior. The apostle Paul, in today's scripture, urged his protégé Timothy to "think about" and "work at" his Christian life. Then everyone can see that "you are growing as a Christian." Of course, we don't earn our salvation—but when we live out our relationship with Christ by modeling His character, we are proving our faith goes deep in our hearts.

God has given each of us particular spiritual gifts. The faithful development and use of our gifts will bring honor to both the Father and the Son, and might even draw unbelievers into God's family. Our growth in grace is for God's glory and other people's benefit. So, as Paul said, "work at it."

EVENING

*Thank You for the growth I've experienced as I walk
with You, Lord Jesus. Help me to develop every one
of Your gifts for the advancement of Your kingdom.
I want to honor You in the way that I live out my faith.*

May 30

Remember this: Whoever sows sparingly will also reap sparingly,
and whoever sows generously will also reap generously.

2 Corinthians 9:6 niv

Serious gardeners take notes, tracking their progress throughout the season as well as their harvest. They want to learn from both their mistakes and their successes. Of course, depending on the climate and locale, what works for one gardener may not work for another. In many ways, that's true of our spiritual lives too. Don't compare your own growth with anyone else's. You have your own garden . . .and a good and loving Master Gardener helping you tend it.

Take a moment to inventory your growth. Is the fruit of the Spirit sprouting and growing in your life? How are you doing with love? Joy? Peace? Patience? Ask Jesus to help you build on the successes and correct the mistakes. He is all about your ultimate success—not in terms of wealth and fame, but your growth in grace and likeness to Him.

EVENING

Jesus, I don't need to compare myself to other
Christians, but I do need to measure my growth
against Your Word. Please help me to see where You
want me to grow or where I've gone astray. And
when I get off track, bring me back to Your way.

MORNING

> *"The holy nation of God is like a man who plants seed in the ground. . . . The earth gives fruit by itself. . . . And last, the grain is ready to gather. As soon as the grain is ready, he cuts it. The time of gathering the grain has come."*
>
> MARK 4:26, 28–29 NLV

Imagine a farmer spending countless hours planning and preparing his land, anticipating a great return. The farmer works hard all season, cultivating the soil, pulling weeds, tending each plant carefully. Then, as the autumn arrives, he walks away without his harvest.

Who would do that? Certainly not God, the Master Gardener, who has a vested interest in growing His spiritual fruit in you. He sent Jesus to earth to provide the salvation you needed, and He will absolutely not leave you on your own. The responsibility to grow and prosper is not all on your shoulders.

Your part is to stay faithful. In the meantime, Jesus will be praying for you (Hebrews 7:25). He will nourish you with His living water. He will finish the job He started in your life the day you were born again.

EVENING

Lord, I thank You for Your continued work in the garden of my life. I am so grateful that You never leave me to grow and produce fruit on my own. Please help me to abide in You, as a branch connected to the Vine.

June 1

*The angel said to them, "Do not be afraid. I bring you good news
that will cause great joy for all the people. Today in the town of
David a Savior has been born to you; he is the Messiah, the Lord."*

LUKE 2:10–11 NIV

For many of us, the beginning of summer is a highly anticipated time.
June and *joy* even start with the same letter. But today, let's take a
quick look back at the Christmas season.

Before that angel appeared, announcing the birth of the Messiah,
joy probably wasn't an emotion the shepherds around Bethlehem
felt. They were up late, as always, keeping a sharp eye out for trouble
among their smelly, silly charges.

But God chose this particular group of shepherds to hear the best
news humankind has ever heard: God had come in the flesh to save
people from their sin. No wonder the angel said the news would
"cause great joy for all the people."

Here's a special reminder, on June 1, of the incredible, miraculous,
truly life-changing birth of Jesus in Bethlehem. Does the news make
your heart leap for joy? A Savior has been born to you.

EVENING

*Lord Jesus, the great joy of Your message has made such
a difference in my life. Thank You! May I be mindful of
Your saving grace all year round. I can find joy each day
in the good news of Your birth. It isn't just for Christmas.*

June 2

*The seventy-two returned with joy and said, "Lord,
even the demons submit to us in your name."*
LUKE 10:17 NIV

When you think of spiritual warfare, *joy* is probably not the first word
that comes to mind. But after Jesus sent out seventy-two followers
to tell others of the coming kingdom of God, they returned with
great joy because demons were submitting to His name. Notice that
these disciples didn't rejoice in their own power, but in the power
of their Lord.

That was a good perspective on their part, but Jesus took things
a step further. "I have given you authority to trample on snakes and
scorpions and to overcome all the power of the enemy," He told
them. "Nothing will harm you." But even better than that, He said,
"Rejoice that your names are written in heaven" (Luke 10:19–20).

You never need to fear what's happening in the world. You have
the joy of the Lord! What could be better than that?

EVENING

*Jesus, I can be joyful even in trials and spiritual
battles because Your joy is available to me!
Please exchange my fears and worries for Your
confidence and hope. Nothing in this world can
compare to Your goodness and power, Lord.*

June 3

> *While he was blessing them, he left them and was*
> *taken up to heaven. So they worshiped him and then*
> *returned to Jerusalem filled with great joy.*
>
> LUKE 24:51–52 NLT

Jesus' disciples—the twelve He specifically selected and the other men and women who followed Him regularly—got to experience some amazing things. They saw Him heal the sick, raise the dead, calm a storm, walk on water. And, after He'd miraculously come back from the dead Himself, they watched Him ascend into heaven! After all the emotion of the previous weeks, little wonder that they were "filled with great joy."

We have not seen Jesus with our eyes, heard Him with our ears, or touched Him with our hands. But we have the written Word of God—the unchanging, powerful scriptures—that tell us everything we need to know about Him.

One thing we know is that He promised to return to heaven and prepare a place for us (John 14:2). Just thinking of that ought to fill our hearts with joy.

> *Jesus, I know the miracles of Your time on earth*
> *through Your Word. But I have experienced the*
> *miracle of Your salvation. As I rejoice in Your*
> *promise of heaven, please help me to live my life in*
> *a way that honors You and points others to You.*

MORNING

> *Go, eat your food with gladness, and drink your wine with a*
> *joyful heart, for God has already approved what you do.*
> ECCLESIASTES 9:7 NIV

Do you realize that God wants His children to enjoy the simple plea-sures of this life? Ecclesiastes 9 mentions things like food, drink, and the love of a spouse. We don't have to wonder whether these are good, since God tells us to partake of them with a joyful heart.

Jesus said that He came to bring His followers life "to the full" (John 10:10). That doesn't necessarily mean physical abundance, but it certainly indicates spiritual growth, blessings, and ultimately eternal life. What could be better?

When you consider today's scripture and John 10:10 together, it's safe to conclude that Jesus intends for us to enjoy our life on this earth—while continuing to grow in grace, knowing that heaven draws nearer each day. With the proper perspective, we'll find that our hearts are full of joy over what we have now *and* what we'll experience in the future.

EVENING

> *Lord Jesus, all financial considerations apart,*
> *I have abundance in You. Thank You for giving me*
> *the most important things. Keep my heart and mind*
> *focused on heaven and let me find the joy in all of*
> *the things You have given me here on earth.*

June 5

> *"When you obey my commandments, you remain in*
> *my love, just as I obey my Father's commandments and*
> *remain in his love. I have told you these things so that you*
> *will be filled with my joy. Yes, your joy will overflow!"*
>
> JOHN 15:10–11 NLT

Many people react negatively to the word *obedience*. They think that implies a restriction of their freedoms. But as followers of Jesus, we find joy in obeying everything He commanded. Obeying our Lord is an honor.

That's why missionaries in third-world countries get so excited when they talk about ministering to orphans. And that's why Christians who work in prison ministry can exit with a smile. But you don't have to be called to some specific ministry to find such joy. As you share the Word of God with a friend or offer a hot meal to a person in need, your spirit will rejoice. You will find that You don't miss out on anything by obeying.

You know what Jesus taught. Look for ways to live out His commands as you go about your day. Joy will overflow as you obey.

> *Obedience brings me joy, Jesus, as I see the blessing*
> *of following Your will. When my old desires rise*
> *up inside, remind me that I don't miss out on*
> *anything by denying myself and serving You.*

MORNING

You make known to me the path of life; you will fill me with joy
in your presence, with eternal pleasures at your right hand.

PSALM 16:11 NIV

Motivational speakers make careers out of helping people find the path they should travel. The question is, is their wisdom sound? Are they directing people toward the right path? Do the people listening ultimately find true joy?

Long before Jesus' birth, the psalmist David had knowledge—under the inspiration of the Holy Spirit—of the Messiah's characteristics, and he penned the words of today's scripture. In the New Testament, in Acts 2:25–28, Peter referenced this psalm, saying it was indeed about Jesus—the One who makes known the right path and fills people with joy in God's presence.

Don't overlook that last phrase: we find *joy* in the presence of God—the Father, Jesus the Son, and the Holy Spirit. When the troubles of life begin to chip away your joy, the remedy is Jesus. Spend time in His presence.

EVENING

Lord Jesus, I need to spend time with You. Allow
me to soak up Your presence and delight in all that
You are. I find the fullness of joy in Your presence
where all my fear, doubt, and worry melt away.
Thank You for the pleasure of knowing You.

June 7

*"But now I come to You, Father. I say these
things while I am in the world. In this way,
My followers may have My joy in their hearts."*

JOHN 17:13 NLV

John 17 captures a long prayer of Jesus. He prayed for His followers, including those who would believe because of the disciple's message. (That includes you!) And what did Jesus pray? That they would all have joy in their hearts.

This world will hate and reject us as Christians. Jesus Himself promised that (Mark 13:13; Luke 21:17). But we can still find tremendous joy in everything He's done for us—dying for our sins, conquering death, preparing an eternal home for us, interceding for us in heaven. It's true—Jesus is still praying for us, there at God's right hand, whispering our names into the Father's ear (Romans 8:34).

Does that fill you with joy? It should. And it's a direct answer to Jesus' prayer in John 17.

EVENING

*Thank You for praying for me, Jesus. When the world
rejects me, I want to find joy in Your perfect love for me.
Teach me how to pray for others like You pray for me.*

June 8

MORNING

*The jailer brought them into his house and set a meal
before them; he was filled with joy because he had come
to believe in God—he and his whole household.*

ACTS 16:34 NIV

After Paul and Silas shared the gospel with the Philippian jailer,
the man and his family came to faith in Christ. In joy and gratitude,
the jailer set a meal before the two missionaries. We can only imagine their conversation.

Do you recall the day you began your new life in Christ? Was
there a joy you had never before experienced? You'd been washed as
white as snow, and you actually felt clean before the Lord. Those who
were saved as young children may not have experienced a major life
change—but there have certainly been moments since when they
recognized Jesus' mercy and responded with the same joy as the
Philippian jailer. These are moments that forever mark the life of a
believer and impact the course of her testimony to others.

May we never lose our sense of joy and wonder at salvation.
Jesus has changed our lives forever!

EVENING

*Lord, I thank You for the joy of Your salvation. You
have washed me clean, changing my life forever and
promising me eternity. Remind me of the joy I felt when
You first brought me into Your family, the moment
when You forever changed the course of my life.*

June 9

> *Rejoice in our confident hope. Be patient*
> *in trouble, and keep on praying.*
> ROMANS 12:12 NLT

Human beings hope for many things. Some hope for a promotion or a better paying job. Others hope their family stays safe. Some even hope for thinner thighs. But none of these things are guaranteed.

Today's scripture, though, says we can find joy in our "confident hope"—that is, the good news of Jesus Christ and our assurance of heaven. No matter how difficult, no matter how uncertain our current circumstances, we can rejoice in two things: what Jesus has done and what is yet to come as a result of His finished work.

It's fine to have earthly hopes. We can still hope for health, happiness, and financial security in this life. However, nothing in this world compares to our confident hope in the next. One fades, the other endures. Now that's something to rejoice over!

EVENING

> *Lord Jesus, help me to keep my priorities straight*
> *regarding the things I hope in. You know the desires*
> *of my heart and what I'd like in this life—but keep my*
> *real focus on You. As the eternal God, You can give*
> *me hope that outlasts everything in this world.*

MORNING

For the kingdom of God is not meat and drink;
but righteousness, and peace, and joy in the Holy Ghost.
ROMANS 14:17 KJV

How often in scripture do we see Jesus partaking of meals? At the home of Simon in Bethany, after calling Matthew to be a disciple, at the Last Supper. He even ate a piece of broiled fish after His resurrection. Food, while a physical necessity, is also one of life's great joys, given by God Himself.

But there's a much greater blessing for us as believers. . .the righteousness, peace, and joy that come through the Holy Spirit. Yes, Jesus Himself enjoyed sharing food with His friends. . .sometimes as many as five thousand of them (Mark 6:30–44)! But we as His followers don't live on "bread alone," as Jesus told Satan in the wilderness, "but by every word that proceedeth out of the mouth of God" (Matthew 4:4).

Dining with those we love provides an hour or two of pleasure. We find eternal joy when we take in God's Word to know our Lord.

EVENING

A good meal is certainly a joy, Lord, but it passes
quickly. Help me to feast on Your righteousness,
peace, and joy, which never fade away. Remind
me each day that Your Word is the main thing that
I should consume as the true source of life!

June 11

The precepts of the LORD are right, giving joy to the heart.
The commands of the LORD are radiant, giving light to the eyes.

PSALM 19:8 NIV

Turn on the TV and you'll be told that satisfaction can be found in a nicer vehicle, a bigger home, faster phone service, or some miracle drug. But we know from experience that the shine on these things quickly fades. Culture even has a term for when the pleasure of a purchase evaporates: buyer's remorse.

But God's Word offers a different sort of satisfaction, one that will never disappoint. Following "the precepts of the LORD" brings joy. Nothing the world has to offer can do that. But once we've accepted the life, work, and teaching of Jesus, we can actually pursue pleasures that last, happiness that satisfies, real joy that brings "light to the eyes."

The power that raised Jesus from the dead now enables you to walk in obedience to His commands. And in doing so, your heart finds joy.

EVENING

Lord Jesus, when this life seems disappointing, I can
always seek encouragement in Your Word. I know that,
as I follow Your precepts, You will never disappoint me.
You have never failed me, and I know that You never will.

MORNING

*May the God of hope fill you with all joy and peace
as you trust in him, so that you may overflow
with hope by the power of the Holy Spirit.*

ROMANS 15:13 NIV

Sometimes pastors pray Numbers 6:24–26 over their congregations: "The LORD bless you and keep you; the LORD make his face shine on you and be gracious to you; the LORD turn his face toward you and give you peace."

The apostle Paul prayed a similar prayer in today's scripture—asking God to fill followers of Jesus with "all joy." Why? Perhaps because we are so prone to bogging down in the here and now that we forget the blessing of all that Jesus has done for us. Or maybe because Paul recognized that once a believer fully realizes the joy of the Lord, he or she can face anything.

Knowing Jesus changes your entire life. Knowing His joy changes your daily experience. If you're struggling to find that joy, don't hesitate to ask. God loves to answer such prayers.

EVENING

*I am truly blessed when I am filled with Your joy,
Jesus. May I never forget Your many blessings;
remind me to celebrate Your joy in my life. Give me
Your peace as I wrap up this day, and may Your
power and hope overflow in my life tomorrow.*

June 13

> *In the midst of a very severe trial, [the Macedonian churches'] overflowing joy and their extreme poverty welled up in rich generosity.*
>
> 2 CORINTHIANS 8:2 NIV

The Macedonian churches were poor. They had undergone intense persecution. Even so, they gave of themselves and their possessions for the advancement of God's kingdom—and they did so out of an overflowing joy for Jesus' blessings.

Wouldn't it be great to be known as a Christian whose joy overflows? But how do you get to that point? Those Macedonian believers would probably say their own joy overflowed *because of* their trials and poverty. In other words, their hardships gave them an opportunity to show their appreciation for their Savior's gifts, some of which would be known only in eternity. What could be a better representation of the faith?

Nobody seeks hardship. But when it comes—as it surely will—it's the perfect opportunity for us to show the world that we love Jesus. And that may ultimately cause others to follow Him too.

EVENING

> *Lord, I would like to avoid trials, but I know they are part of the testing that helps me grow. May every trial show forth the love You've placed in my heart and draw more souls to You. Let me not waste any opportunity— even a hardship—that can draw me closer to You.*

MORNING

You followed our way of life and the life of the Lord.
You suffered from others because of listening to us.
But you had the joy that came from the Holy Spirit.

1 THESSALONIANS 1:6 NLV

Sometimes believers suffer for following Jesus Christ. Mockery and persecution come to those who defend the unborn or stand for biblical sexuality or simply choose to live their lives differently than the culture around them. But in many cases, these Christians are unfazed. They graciously accept such trials as a byproduct of following the Lord.

As today's scripture indicates, following Jesus often leads to suffering. But it also generates a joy that comes from the Holy Spirit. What's your first response when the world criticizes your faith? Defensiveness comes from the flesh, but joy is a fruit of the Spirit. This type of joy realizes that trials are temporary, but the love of Jesus Christ is eternal.

Such joy can't be manufactured. But it can be enjoyed by anyone who commits to the Lord Jesus. He will reward you in ways you can't even imagine.

EVENING

I can't create my own joy, Lord, but You provide it through Your Spirit. In this troubled world, please help me to respond with the joy that comes from knowing You are still in charge. Your Holy Spirit gives me joy that goes far beyond the passing circumstances of this world.

June 15

"Where were you when I laid the earth's foundation. . .while the morning stars sang together and all the angels shouted for joy?"

JOB 38:4, 7 NIV

Creation was a time of joy, and it was Jesus Himself who made it happen: "The Son is the image of the invisible God, the firstborn over all creation. For in him all things were created: things in heaven and on earth, visible and invisible, whether thrones or powers or rulers or authorities; all things have been created through him and for him. He is before all things, and in him all things hold together" (Colossians 1:15–17).

The morning stars sang together, the angels were shouting for joy, all in honor of their incredible Creator. Can we do any less? It doesn't matter if you lack a certain vocal quality. . .it's the quality of Jesus that matters supremely.

EVENING

Lord Jesus, I rejoice in You as my Creator. Thank You for making me so specially—and holding me together every day. Help me to find joy in even the smallest aspects of Your creation. May I marvel in Your incredible wisdom, power, and creativity.

MORNING

*You suffered along with those in prison and joyfully accepted
the confiscation of your property, because you knew that
you yourselves had better and lasting possessions.*

HEBREWS 10:34 NIV

Sometimes we read a scripture passage and see it as hyperbole. No doubt, the Bible contains some of that. But today's scripture isn't an example of exaggeration to make a point. The writer wanted to remind early Christians of a time when they actually had joy when their goods were plundered. Why? Because they felt honored to be considered worthy of suffering for Jesus. And they knew that their heavenly reward would far outweigh anything that could be taken from them on earth.

There are times to stand up for your rights; the apostle Paul did so as a Roman citizen when he was unjustly incarcerated (Acts 16:37). But there are also times to view losses through spiritual eyes, knowing that Jesus gave up so much more for you. . .that losing something for His sake means the world sees you as His true follower.

You can "joyfully accept" any hardship when you suffer for Jesus' sake.

EVENING

*Lord Jesus, I can rejoice in suffering that comes because
I love You. May I never forget the pain You experienced
so I could have better and lasting possessions in
Your kingdom. You made the ultimate sacrifice to
bring me into Your family. Nothing that I could ever
give up compares to what You did on the cross.*

June 17

> *Though you have not seen [Jesus], you love him; and even though you do not see him now, you believe in him and are filled with an inexpressible and glorious joy, for you are receiving the end result of your faith, the salvation of your souls.*
>
> 1 PETER 1:8–9 NIV

First Peter 2:9 calls us as Christians "a chosen people, a royal priesthood, a holy nation, God's special possession." We are these things that we "may declare the praises of him who called [us] out of darkness into his wonderful light." Christians are very different from other people—not better in some boastful sense, but specially chosen to honor the Lord.

We cannot see Jesus, but we can observe His presence in the form of changed lives—including our own. We have trusted Him with our souls, and if we can do that, we can trust Him with everything else, even our trials.

Our world is filled with trouble, and we as Christians can't escape it. But as we consider who we are in Christ, we can have an inexpressible joy. In and through Jesus, we receive the end result of our faith—the salvation of our souls.

> *Though I haven't seen You with my eyes, Jesus, my heart sees you clearly. Thank You for the joy I have in knowing You. I rest in the comfort of knowing that I am saved and can never be plucked from Your hand.*

MORNING

Nehemiah said, "Go and enjoy choice food and sweet drinks, and send some to those who have nothing prepared. This day is holy to our Lord. Do not grieve, for the joy of the Lord is your strength."

NEHEMIAH 8:10 NIV

Pop culture loves to portray Christians as dour, angry, and mean. At times, the overall church—and each of us individually—have probably poured fuel on that fire. We're not yet perfect, just forgiven.

But our default position should be joy, God's own joy that gives us strength. Jesus "endured the cross" (now that's strength!) "for the joy set before him" (Hebrews 12:2). He was "full of joy through the Holy Spirit" (Luke 10:21) and praised His Father. He taught His disciples to obey His commands, "so that my joy may be in you and that your joy may be complete" (John 15:11).

Three steps to Jesus' joy: Look ahead to the reward, praise God, and obey His commands. We serve a Lord of joy who wants us to be joyful too.

EVENING

Where else can I find true joy, Lord? Help me to praise You, obey Your Word each day, and look to Your reward. You are the giver of joy, so I have no reason to be sour or critical. Please give me Your unspeakable joy!

June 19

MORNING

That which we have seen and heard declare we unto you, that
ye also may have fellowship with us: and truly our fellowship
is with the Father, and with his Son Jesus Christ. And these
things write we unto you, that your joy may be full.

1 John 1:3–4 kjv

In recent years, health experts have concluded that loneliness is a big risk, with one study asserting it may be as damaging as smoking fifteen cigarettes a day. With more than a quarter of the American population living by themselves, the dangers of loneliness are magnified. Researchers identify a simple solution to this problem: friendship.

Scripture also highlights the importance of friendship, and our most vital relationship is the one we have with Jesus Himself. That is one aspect of a circle of friendship also involving God the Father and our fellow believers.

This is the perfect solution for the problem of loneliness. It's how our joy is made full.

EVENING

Thank You, Jesus, for being my best Friend. And I
thank You for my other friends who are also part
of Your family and share Your joy with me. When
I feel lonely or out of place, remind me that You
are the closest friend I could ever have. Please stir
other friends to support me in my walk with You.

MORNING

Now all glory to God, who is able to keep you from falling away and will bring you with great joy into his glorious presence without a single fault. All glory to him who alone is God, our Savior through Jesus Christ our Lord.

JUDE 24–25 NLT

Have you ever felt smothered by some sin you've committed? Perhaps you've wondered if you could ever be pure enough to enter heaven. If so, today's scripture offers invaluable encouragement.

Jesus Christ, who is your righteousness, will bring you—without a single fault and with great joy—into the presence of His Father. And why wouldn't you have joy? You will no longer know sorrow, sin, or death.

But you don't have to wait for heaven to experience joy in Jesus' finished work. Romans 5:20 says, "God's law was given so that all people could see how sinful they were. But as people sinned more and more, God's wonderful grace became more abundant." The blood of Jesus has covered your sin. His grace has set you free. Rejoice!

EVENING

Jesus, it's hard to imagine being perfectly free from sin, but I look forward to that day with joy. You are able to keep me from falling away into sin by convicting me through Your Holy Spirit. I thank You for the abundant grace that draws me back to You each day, no matter how badly I may have failed.

June 21

The women ran quickly from the tomb. They were very frightened but also filled with great joy, and they rushed to give the disciples the angel's message.

MATTHEW 28:8 NLT

When you attend a committed Christian's funeral, it truly is a celebration. Yes, there is sadness for the loss, but the message of the ceremony is centered on the hope that person had in Jesus Christ. You might even leave the service feeling uplifted—even joyful.

That is similar to what we see in today's passage. The women who went to visit Jesus' grave had just encountered an angel who told them the Lord had risen from the dead. And more than that, they would see Him in Galilee. Even in their stunned state, the women were filled with great joy.

By His resurrection, Jesus conquered death. On the last day, just like Him, we will rise again. We need not fear the grave! Knowing that Jesus has defanged death fills us with joy.

EVENING

Lord Jesus, You have removed the human being's greatest fear—the fear of death. I am so happy that one day I will share in Your resurrection to eternal life. You have already proven Your victory over the grave. Let me look forward to eternity with joy, while living my life here on earth well.

MORNING

Blessed are ye, when men shall hate you, and when they shall separate you from their company, and shall reproach you, and cast out your name as evil, for the Son of man's sake. Rejoice ye in that day, and leap for joy: for, behold, your reward is great in heaven.

LUKE 6:22–23 KJV

When is the last time you leaped for joy? Probably as a little girl? You don't see a lot of adults leaping as a sign of happiness. We are inhibited by societal norms, so we don't actually jump over a larger-than-expected tax refund or a new job we've been praying for.

If we don't act like that for exciting, happy things, would we ever leap for joy over trouble and persecution? That's exactly what Jesus told us to do. If you're hated for His sake, criticized for following Him, or cast out of "polite society" for faith in Him? According to Jesus, "Rejoice ye in that day, and leap for joy."

It sounds impossible, and, humanly speaking, it is. But "with God all things are possible" (Matthew 19:26). The key is to put all those troubles into perspective. . .they are absolute trifles compared to your great reward in heaven.

EVENING

Lord, it's against my human nature to celebrate when I'm insulted or hated for following You. Please help me to find joy in knowing that I am receiving the same treatment You did—that I am actually sharing in Your suffering.

June 23

Hitherto have ye asked nothing in my name:
ask, and ye shall receive, that your joy may be full.
JOHN 16:24 KJV

A prayerless Christian is a joyless Christian. That's one takeaway of what Jesus says in today's scripture. Maybe you've experienced this lack of joy at times. Famed British pastor Charles Spurgeon offers the remedy:

> *Prayer is the natural outgushing of a soul in communion with Jesus. Just as the leaf and the fruit will come out of the vine-branch without any conscious effort on the part of the branch, but simply because of its living union with the stem, so prayer buds, and blossoms, and fruits out of souls abiding in Jesus.*

Plug in to Jesus today. Make your requests known to Him. Worship Him. Confess your sins, knowing that He's ready to forgive and cleanse you. Thank Him for what He's already done in your life. Pray for the needs of others and yourself. As you wait expectantly for His answer, your joy will increase.

EVENING

May my joy in knowing You, Jesus, rush out of me in
prayer. I praise You for Your salvation and the work
You're doing in my life. Let me not put other things
before prayer in my life. Nothing is more important
than spending time with You in prayer. Please give me
Your joy, and use me to help others find joy as well.

June 24

Paul and Barnabas shook the dust off from their feet against [the Jews in Antioch who made them leave the city] and went to the city of Iconium. The missionaries were filled with joy and with the Holy Spirit.

ACTS 13:51–52 NLV

When we experience opposition to our witness for Jesus, it is cause for joy. Why? Because that opposition means Satan recognizes our work and wants to thwart it in any way he can. Even when the enemy appears to be successful (as in today's scripture), the truth is that God's kingdom continues to grow steadily. Satan lacks the power to stop it.

When your love for Jesus creates spiritual opposition, "shake the dust off your feet" and move on. To Satan's utter disgust, the message you leave behind may take root long after you're gone.

Believers engaged in kingdom work, regardless of the immediate outcome, experience a joy the world cannot understand. Live for Jesus today and get a taste of heaven.

Lord Jesus, even when my mission for You seems to have failed, I know Satan cannot stop Your will. I rejoice that You can bring joy even out of opposition to Your gospel. Encourage me when I begin to doubt if my efforts are producing any fruit. Remind me that planting seeds is what I'm called to do.

June 25

> *But none of these things move me, neither count I my*
> *life dear unto myself, so that I might finish my course*
> *with joy, and the ministry, which I have received of the*
> *Lord Jesus, to testify the gospel of the grace of God.*
> ACTS 20:24 KJV

As the apostle Paul neared the end of his ministry—and ultimately his life—his thoughts were of finishing well. That meant offering up his life as a "living sacrifice" for the sake of the gospel. Paul relinquished his right to himself and his own desires, and by doing so he found joy.

Living that way is countercultural. The world encourages us to chase money and status and other things we want. It tells us to "look out for number one." And it scoffs at anyone who chooses a different path, pursuits that will last beyond this life.

Jesus told us to lay down our life to find it, to die to ourselves daily, and to pick up our cross (an instrument of death) and follow Him. As we do, we find purpose and joy—not because of what we have accomplished, but due to what Jesus does in and through us.

EVENING

> *Lord Jesus, I don't want to live like a selfish culture*
> *that doesn't rejoice in You. May I stand strong*
> *for You, and even lay down my life if need be.*

June 26

*But the fruit of the Spirit is love, joy, peace, forbearance,
kindness, goodness, faithfulness, gentleness and self-control.*

GALATIANS 5:22–23 NIV

When you think about the fruit of the Spirit, does joy get its proper due? Many of us focus on love, peace, and self-control. But the entire list is important, the result of God's Spirit working in us.

Joyless Christianity is not contagious. But when the world sees us living in Jesus' joy—no matter the circumstances—we become the ambassadors He's called us to be. We become magnets who draw others to Him.

If you find yourself lacking in joy, it's an indicator that you need to spend more time with Jesus. You can't manufacture the fruit of the Spirit in your own strength, no matter how hard you try. The fruit simply develops on us as branches, as we are grafted into Jesus, our vine. He is the source of all good.

*Jesus, as I spend time with You, please fill me with
a joy that I cannot manufacture on my own. I can't
fake the peace and ease that knowing You gives me.
Please give me a pleasant night's rest and fill tomorrow
with joy as I consciously stay in Your presence.*

June 27

> *After all, what gives us hope and joy, and what will be our*
> *proud reward and crown as we stand before our Lord Jesus*
> *when he returns? It is you! Yes, you are our pride and joy.*
> 1 THESSALONIANS 2:19–20 NLT

Jesus so closely aligns Himself with His church that when a Pharisee named Saul was persecuting Christians, Christ asked him, "Saul! Saul! Why are you persecuting *me*?" (Acts 9:4, emphasis added).

After his dramatic conversion to faith in Jesus, Saul (later known as the apostle Paul) developed such close bonds with fellow believers that he considered his converts his "pride and joy." God had flipped the script. Paul became so close to his spiritual brothers and sisters that he felt joy when he thought of them standing before Jesus on the final day.

Look for Jesus in your fellow believers. When you seek Him, you will find Him there. . .and all of your joy will increase.

> *Lord, I want to be close to You and to my brothers*
> *and sisters in the faith. Keep me from finding fault*
> *and being unnecessarily critical of Your church,*
> *Jesus. Let me see You in Your people. Together we*
> *will worship You, on earth and in eternity.*

June 28

MORNING

> *Always be joyful. Never stop praying.*
> *Be thankful in all circumstances, for this is God's*
> *will for you who belong to Christ Jesus.*
>
> 1 Thessalonians 5:16–18 nlt

God's will can seem mysterious at times. But scripture tells us many aspects of His will for every believer, as we see in today's scripture.

The apostle Paul offered a threefold prescription for living within God's will: (1) Always be joyful. (2) Never stop praying. (3) Be thankful in all circumstances. But how do we do these things? And how does joy, our topic for this month, relate to prayer and thankfulness?

We don't whip up feelings of joy—real joy overflows from a prayerful heart. John Wesley said it this way: "Unceasing prayer is the fruit of always rejoicing in the Lord, and thankfulness is the fruit of both the former."

When you find your joy tank running low, pray. Thank God first of all for your salvation in Jesus Christ, then for everything He does for you in good times and bad. Joy will follow.

EVENING

> *Jesus, may I always draw near to You in prayer so my*
> *joy can overflow. Thank You for standing with me, no*
> *matter what's happening in my life. I come to You with*
> *rejoicing today, because You hear my prayers. Thank You*
> *for always giving me more than I could ask or imagine!*

June 29

Consider it pure joy, my brothers and sisters, whenever you face trials of many kinds, because you know that the testing of your faith produces perseverance. Let perseverance finish its work so that you may be mature and complete, not lacking anything.

JAMES 1:2–4 NIV

Have you ever known a Christian who handles adversity well—even to the point of being joyful within it? What is her secret?

If you want to impact the world for Jesus, make spiritual maturity your aim. But know that maturity only occurs after you've persevered through trials of many kinds, challenges that test your faith. That's why James calls us to consider it "pure joy" when we do indeed face trials.

What circumstance is testing your faith now? You'd probably prefer that things were different, right? But what you really need is a new perspective. Tough situations are simply an opportunity to learn perseverance, which leads to maturity, which makes you more like Jesus. That makes every trial a potential source of joy.

EVENING

Help me to see my trials from the proper perspective, Lord Jesus, as something to make me more like You. I want to experience real joy even in the midst of hardships. You bring joy to even the darkest of situations.

MORNING

> *Submit to God's royal son, or he will become angry,*
> *and you will be destroyed in the midst of all your*
> *activities—for his anger flares up in an instant.*
> *But what joy for all who take refuge in him!*
>
> PSALM 2:12 NLT

Psalm 2 is a messianic psalm, meaning it points to Jesus Christ. Today's scripture was written with kings and leaders in mind, showing the supremacy of Jesus as King of kings and Lord of lords. This verse calls us to submit to Him. When we do, we find joy.

In our modern culture, submission of any form is often viewed as a weakness. Most people demand the right to make their own decisions without any interference. As so many of our fellow humans are asserting autonomy from God, we as followers of Jesus know the folly of such a mind-set. We seek refuge in the Lord.

As the world falls apart, you can find joy in the safe, loving arms of Jesus. Remember, He's the one who "existed before anything else, and he holds all creation together" (Colossians 1:17). He can handle anything.

EVENING

> *Jesus, it can be tough submitting to other people—*
> *but I know I can always submit to You without*
> *worry. You only want the very best for me, so I*
> *commit to doing exactly what You call me to do.*

July 1

I will walk about in freedom, for I have sought out your precepts.
PSALM 119:45 NIV

Both Christians and nonbelievers claim to walk in freedom. Non-Christians throw off all restraints and live by their own moral code. Sadly, they don't realize that they are enslaved to sin. Christians live by a higher code: God's Word.

Even believers will struggle against the flesh, and never walk in perfect freedom. But Jesus has thrown open our prison doors. He has sent His Holy Spirit to help us walk through them. And He has blessed us with His Word to lead and guide us.

To walk in true freedom, seek the Lord's precepts. They are found in the Bible. Spend time and energy on that book and, without fail, you'll hear Jesus speak. Obey what He says—and He will make you free.

EVENING

I want to walk in Your freedom, Lord, not my own will. Only then can I be truly free. Help me to spend my time and energy on the truths of Your Word. Fill me with Your Holy Spirit and the freedom that You offer through obedience.

July 2

It is for freedom that Christ has set us free. Stand firm, then, and do not let yourselves be burdened again by a yoke of slavery.

GALATIANS 5:1 NIV

When Jesus forgave our sins, He set us free—not only from patterns of sin but also from trying to make ourselves right with God through some religious ritual. The earliest Christians were often at odds with the Jewish religious leaders, who wanted believers in Jesus to be holy by adhering to Old Testament ceremonial laws. What they didn't realize was that Jesus *fulfilled* the ceremonial law. We are made holy in Jesus alone.

Our issue today isn't so much the ceremonial laws as some other form of religious ritual. Most of them aren't bad in and of themselves, but they cannot set us free from sin. We can never attend enough church services or log enough hours of community service to sanctify ourselves. They do not make us holy. Jesus does. Today, thank Him for setting you free from the bondage of sin, and for enabling you to walk in the newness of life.

EVENING

Thank You, Jesus, for setting me free from sin and making me holy. I want to walk in a way that glorifies You. I could never earn the righteousness that You freely give me for simply believing.

July 3

The Spirit of the Sovereign LORD is upon me, for the LORD
has anointed me to bring good news to the poor. He has
sent me to comfort the brokenhearted and to proclaim that
captives will be released and prisoners will be freed.

ISAIAH 61:1 NLT

Imagine being held captive in a foreign land. You don't speak the language and have no friends or support team. You've been bound with ropes and tossed into a dingy cell. With only a minimal amount of food and water, you've been left to rot. After months, then years, without rescue, you've lost all hope. You fully expect to die without ever seeing the light of day again.

Then one day, beyond the prison door, you hear a voice saying your name. It speaks with authority, demanding that you be set free. And, after years of hopelessness, you are!

This is what Jesus has done for you. He has set you free, and you are free indeed (John 8:36). Now walk every day in the fresh air and sunshine of His love. . .and tell everyone you can how to find freedom too.

Lord Jesus, You have freed me from sin and doubt,
ending my hopelessness. Help me to walk in Your light
and share Your good news. I want to carry Your comfort
to the brokenhearted and bring the same freedom to the
captives that You offered me when I lived in darkness.

MORNING

*Though I am free and belong to no one, I have made myself
a slave to everyone, to win as many as possible.*

1 Corinthians 9:19 niv

On the day the United States celebrates its freedom, every Christian can pause to thank God for the liberty He offers through Jesus Christ.

But in today's scripture, the apostle Paul said he was using his freedom to become a slave! Only mature believers can understand this. Paul made himself a slave to others to break down the barriers that might otherwise separate him from them. When he was around people who followed the old covenant law, he followed it too. . .but always with an eye toward sharing the message of salvation through Jesus. And when he was around non-Jews, Paul *didn't* practice the old covenant rites—for the same reason.

In Jesus Christ, you are free! Now use your freedom to become a slave like Paul. . .and break the chains of the people around you.

EVENING

*I don't want to misuse the freedom You paid such a great
price for, Jesus. Show me how I can serve others and be
a picture of Your salvation. Give me daily opportunities
to put others first and draw them into Your kingdom.*

July 5

> *"Now a slave has no permanent place in the*
> *family, but a son belongs to it forever. So if the*
> *Son sets you free, you will be free indeed."*
>
> JOHN 8:35–36 NIV

Adoption is special. It means parents have consciously chosen to bring a child into the family, and the adoptee's place cannot be taken away. No matter how difficult the previous situation, the child is part of its new family forever. The same can be said for us as Christians.

Before you trusted Jesus for your salvation, your future was dark. In fact, you were bound for eternal separation from God. But after you came to Jesus, eternity became crystal clear. You were adopted into the family of God, sealed by the Holy Spirit, and bound for heaven, where Jesus has gone to prepare a place for you.

You are now a rightful heir of God, a co-heir with Jesus, a child of the promise (Romans 8:17). Why not take a moment today to thank God for your freedom in Christ? It's *great* news!

EVENING

Lord Jesus, I praise You for making me part of Your
family. I thank You both for freedom from sin and
the permanent place I have in Your heart. You have
grafted me into Your vine where I can abide forever
without fear of losing my place in Your family.

MORNING

*All things are lawful for me, but all things are not expedient:
all things are lawful for me, but all things edify not.*

1 CORINTHIANS 10:23 KJV

One of the key tenets of the Christian faith is that believers are free in Christ. We are bound by the scriptures and our consciences, not by anyone else's rules and regulations.

Of course, there are believers who seem bound up in rule keeping. It's easy to think that by pursuing or avoiding certain activities (and often insisting that others do the same), they'll "earn" God's favor.

In today's scripture, however, the apostle Paul tells us that unless God specifically calls something sin, it is allowable ("lawful") for us as Christians. The other side of the coin, though, is that not every allowable thing builds us up in our life with Jesus. Part of our freedom is knowing which things are "expedient" and which aren't.

That takes Bible study and prayer. And Jesus will be happy to guide you.

EVENING

Lord, I'm grateful that I don't need to follow a man-made list of rules—but I know that I need to study Your Word and follow its commands. Show me the things I should avoid and keep me on Your path of blessing. Continue to convict my heart and weed out anything that doesn't belong in my life.

July 7

*Sin is no longer your master, for you no longer
live under the requirements of the law. Instead,
you live under the freedom of God's grace.*

ROMANS 6:14 NLT

The Christian life is full of paradoxes. We gain our lives by losing them (Matthew 10:39). To be first, we must become last (Mark 9:35). We are slaves of God, yet free (Romans 6:16).

The apostle Paul taught that our sinful selves must be crucified along with Jesus so that "sin might lose its power in our lives"; then we will be "no longer slaves to sin" (Romans 6:6). If we stay slaves to sin, we find death. If we choose to obey God, we live righteously. We are *His* slaves, which is really the freest way to live.

Jesus breaks the power of our fears, our addictions, and our discontentment. In Him, we "live under the freedom of God's grace." Drop the old sin chains and tie yourself to Jesus with "ropes of kindness and love" (Hosea 11:4). Jesus promises that when you take on His yoke, the burden is easy and light—there is freedom in being obedient to Him alone.

EVENING

*By becoming Your slave, Jesus, I am free
indeed. It's hard to fully understand, but I am
thankful for the ease of Your yoke. Help me to
drop my sin chains and live freely in You.*

*Now the Lord is the Spirit, and where the
Spirit of the Lord is, there is freedom.*

2 CORINTHIANS 3:17 NIV

You've probably known Christians who try to live by "the letter of
the law." Their intentions are good, but they've missed an important
truth: since Jesus paid the price for our sins, the Holy Spirit lives
inside of believers and frees us from burdensome regulations.

Of course, we still obey God's moral laws, the Ten Commandment–type rules against murder and adultery and dishonesty. But we
need not worry over ceremonial rules or man-made regulations. As the
apostle Paul said, "where the Spirit of the Lord is, there is freedom"!

Be grateful for the freedom Jesus won for you—it's a glorious
thing. But when the Spirit inside you speaks, listen and obey. Be
ready to go where He leads and do what He wants you to do. Christian freedom is much better than a total lack of restrictions. . .it's
the ability to do what is right.

*Lord, I don't want to endanger my freedom in You
with unnecessary rules. Please help me follow Your
biblical path by listening to Your Spirit. Thank You
for Your new covenant of grace and freedom.*

July 9

*In [Christ] and through faith in him we may
approach God with freedom and confidence.*

Ephesians 3:12 niv

Adam and Eve's sin had huge ramifications. Not only did they feel a
need to hide from God, but He also separated Himself from them—by
ejecting them from the Garden of Eden. Later, during the history of
His nation Israel, God only met with the high priests, who sacrificed
to atone for the people's sin. Common people didn't dare approach
God's Holy of Holies.

But the heavy temple curtain that separated God and humanity
was torn in two when Jesus died. Suddenly, there was access to God
for everyone who would believe in Jesus' sacrificial work.

When we sin, we don't have to hide like Adam and Eve. We can
drag our ugly, embarrassing misbehavior into the light and confess
it to God in total confidence. We know He will forgive us based on
Jesus' work. This is freedom.

EVENING

*Jesus, I am so glad that salvation removed the
space between us. Help me to confess any sin that
is interfering with our relationship and grant me
freedom for my soul. I don't have to be ashamed or
embarrassed to bring my sin before You, since You
have already offered forgiveness and grace for it.*

MORNING

It is God's will that your honorable lives should silence
those ignorant people who make foolish accusations
against you. For you are free, yet you are God's slaves,
so don't use your freedom as an excuse to do evil.

1 PETER 2:15–16 NLT

Freedom always comes with responsibility. No matter how free your nation, there are always certain restrictions—speed limits, noise ordinances, tax requirements, and the like. These restrictions are for our own good, as well as the good of others.

In today's scripture, the apostle Peter described a similar situation for Christians. In Jesus, we have been set free from our sin, period. But we should not use our freedom as an excuse to do evil. To do so would dishonor our Lord.

Jesus freed us from the ultimate penalty of our sin—eternal separation from God. Now we live for Him as slaves. While that is not a popular concept, know that God is nothing like a human slaveowner. He always treats His people fairly, and He loves us beyond our ability to comprehend. We are free to voluntarily serve out of love.

EVENING

Now that I know You and have been forgiven, Jesus,
I want to serve You well. Help me to use the freedom
You offer to serve Your kingdom, not myself. May I never
use Your grace as an excuse to sin or hurt others.

July 11

> *Jesus said to the people who believed in him, "You are truly*
> *my disciples if you remain faithful to my teachings. And*
> *you will know the truth, and the truth will set you free."*
>
> JOHN 8:31–32 NLT

Even non-Christians say, "The truth will set you free." In a sense, that is accurate: anytime truth prevails, it brings a degree of freedom. But that's not necessarily what Jesus meant in today's scripture. He was telling His followers that remaining faithful to Him and His teachings would free them from their own corrupted motivations and passions.

Hopefully, at some point in our Christian walk, we all experience this truth. Maybe you stopped to pray for an enemy when your natural reaction would be to fight. Perhaps you gave generously, beyond what you thought you could, because you felt it was what Jesus wanted. This freedom from selfish, worldly behavior develops as we remain faithful to Jesus' teachings. Only believers can understand this freedom because it is so contrary to normal human instinct. Jesus' words are the truths that truly set us free.

EVENING

> *Lord, Your idea of freedom can be very different*
> *from mine. Help me to see that Your teaching and*
> *example are the truths that will finally break the*
> *power of my sinful nature. I can live within this*
> *beautiful freedom by staying faithful to Your Word.*

July 12

"I have indeed seen the oppression of my people in Egypt. I have heard their groaning and have come down to set them free."

ACTS 7:34 NIV

God has always been personal with His people. Even under the old covenant—in the days of the Old Testament—He heard the cry of His oppressed people in Egypt, and He arranged for their freedom. Their journey to the land of promise wasn't an easy one, but God provided for them every step of the way.

At some point, God heard *your* cry for help—a cry that begged His forgiveness. Like the Israelites in Egypt, you were oppressed—not by a foreign nation but by the power of sin. God arranged for your freedom by coming to earth in the form of Jesus Christ, who lived a perfect, sinless life before offering Himself as the once-for-all sacrifice for sin.

Never forget that God is for you. Jesus died to save you from sin. Even when you struggle to obey, keep talking to God. He will hear your groaning.

EVENING

Thank You, Lord Jesus, for hearing my every cry and providing the freedom I need. You came to earth to live as a man and die as the sacrifice to set me free. I know that You are always for me, even when no one else seems to be.

July 13

> *"Through [Jesus] everyone who believes is set free from every sin, a justification you were not able to obtain under the law of Moses."*
>
> ACTS 13:39 NIV

Some say that any religion or belief system can lead to God. As long as you believe sincerely and are a "good person," you'll enjoy a positive afterlife. But that's far from what the Bible teaches. If all roads lead to heaven, why would Jesus die on a cross to free us from sin?

Jesus' exclusive claim to be the way, the truth, and the life—His assertion that no one comes to the Father apart from Him (John 14:6)—stands in contrast to other religions. They demand that people work their way to heaven. Jesus has already done the work for us.

Praise God, Jesus stepped into humanity and did what no religion could ever do: He lived a sinless life and died in our place, offering us freedom from the power and consequences of sin. . .forever. We never have to doubt or worry if we are living up to the price of salvation, which we could never pay anyway. Jesus did it all.

EVENING

> *Lord Jesus, You have done what no one else could do—and I am awed by Your willingness to suffer for me. Now I want to live for You. Give me the strength to live out that sacrifice of praise.*

MORNING

He gives justice to the oppressed and food to the
hungry. The LORD frees the prisoners.

PSALM 146:7 NLT

God hates injustice. When His people face it, He hears their cries. Sometimes God delivers them quickly; at other times He calls them to endure for a while. Either way, His justice will eventually win the day.

In a broken, sinful world, we'll all face injustices. They might be daily, minor irritations or massive, life-changing upheavals. But He is always aware, always compassionate, and always on your side. His answer will come, though it will be in His own time and way.

Don't forget that Jesus, the perfect man, faced terrible injustice through His betrayal, arrest, and crucifixion. And though He prayed for His Father to "take this cup of suffering away from me," God said no (Luke 22:42). But God said no so others could be saved, and that Jesus would ultimately be "elevated. . .to the place of highest honor" (Philippians 2:9).

As a follower of Jesus, you'll be there with Him, forever.

EVENING

Oh, Jesus, how happy I am that You are aware
of every injustice and will respond at the perfect
time. Remind me that You will win in the end, even
when I feel as if Your justice is taking too long.
I know that Your timing is always perfect.

July 15

MORNING

> *We know that our old sinful selves were crucified with*
> *Christ so that sin might lose its power in our lives.*
> *We are no longer slaves to sin. For when we died with*
> *Christ we were set free from the power of sin.*
>
> ROMANS 6:6–7 NLT

The Bible paints a vivid word picture of what happens when we come to Jesus for salvation: our pre-conversion lives are described as "the old man" or "our old sinful selves." That person was crucified with Christ, though we still carry that sinful self in the form of our flesh. At times, it weighs us down and trips us up. But we are no longer slaves to our old sin nature.

Jesus has given us a new life, one that sets us free from the power of sin. Practically speaking, that means reminding "the old man" (or "old woman")—who tries to influence us—of that *death*. And it means keeping the dead one in the grave by choosing to walk in the Spirit.

Whenever temptation comes, pause, pray, and obey God. You are free to do right because your "old woman" was crucified with Jesus.

EVENING

> *Lord, I thank You that the "old woman" is gone*
> *and that I can now live in Your Spirit. When my*
> *old sin nature tries to rise up in my moments of*
> *weakness, remind me that I am not a slave to sin*
> *any longer. I choose to be Your slave, Jesus.*

MORNING

And ye shall hallow the fiftieth year, and proclaim liberty throughout all the land unto all the inhabitants thereof: it shall be a jubile unto you; and ye shall return every man unto his possession, and ye shall return every man unto his family.

LEVITICUS 25:10 KJV

Under the old covenant, every fifty years on the Day of Atonement, a trumpet was to be sounded. That particular year was set aside as holy. Everyone in servitude was to be set free and all land that had been purchased was to be returned to its original owner. It was like hitting a reset button: everything and everyone was redeemed and made right.

This practice was a shadow of things to come under the new covenant. The moment Jesus died for our sins, humankind no longer needed a "day of atonement." Jesus *was* the atonement, the once-for-all-time sacrifice for all who would believe. He proclaimed liberty throughout the land as His blood covered all our sins.

Now that we've been redeemed, we can carry forward the gospel message and proclaim liberty to anyone who will listen.

EVENING

As I reflect on this day, Lord Jesus, I want to remember all that You've done for me. I thank You for atoning for me, once and for all. Now help me to share that freedom with someone who is still in bondage.

July 17

> *How can I know all the sins lurking in my heart?*
> *Cleanse me from these hidden faults. Keep your servant*
> *from deliberate sins! Don't let them control me. Then*
> *I will be free of guilt and innocent of great sin.*
>
> PSALM 19:12–13 NLT

Though David was a man after God's own heart (1 Samuel 13:14), he was also a great sinner. In a rather bold prayer recorded in Psalm 19, he addressed both his hidden sins (the ones lurking in his heart) and his deliberate sins, asking for cleansing so he could be free.

We can all relate. We have both hidden and deliberate sins—too many to number—and no chance of eradicating them on our own. But God didn't leave us to fight this battle on our own. Jesus came to set captives free. His blood covers your every sin, even the hidden ones.

Jesus' death on the cross doesn't give us a license to sin. It frees us from sin, giving us hearts full of joy that want to worship Him. Let's celebrate everything He's done for us.

EVENING

> *Lord, sometimes it's hard to be honest with myself*
> *about my hidden sins. But I need to acknowledge every*
> *one—You already know them! Forgive me and make*
> *me new each day. I thank You for Your unfailing mercy*
> *that convicts me of sin and doesn't let me linger in it.*

MORNING

> *I prayed to the LORD, and he answered me.*
> *He freed me from all my fears.*
>
> PSALM 34:4 NLT

As Christians, we know that fear doesn't come from God (1 John 4:16–18). But as humans, we aren't immune to feeling fear. David certainly did before he penned the words of today's scripture. He was running from King Saul and ended up in enemy territory, where he was found out. David turned to God in prayer, and the Lord freed him from all his fears.

What frightens you? Money issues? Health concerns? Relationship troubles? Here's the bad news: you often cannot control your circumstances, and that can lead to fear. Now the good news: Jesus is not only in control of your circumstances, but He can also set you free from your fear—even when the Father allows you to continue in your difficulty.

Whatever you fear today, offer it up to Jesus. Then leave it in His very capable hands.

EVENING

> *Lord Jesus, here are all my fears. Take them into Your*
> *own strong hands and give me the peace that passes*
> *all understanding. I want to walk confidently each*
> *day by faith in You. I thank You for being my refuge!*

July 19

"Come to me, all you who are weary and burdened, and I will give you rest. Take my yoke upon you and learn from me, for I am gentle and humble in heart, and you will find rest for your souls. For my yoke is easy and my burden is light."

MATTHEW 11:28–30 NIV

The Jews of Jesus' day were weighed down by the Mosaic law. And their religious leaders created even more burdens by adding other rules. Jesus wanted people to be free from such stress. He said people could find rest for their souls if they followed the lead of this gentle, humble Servant.

Human nature hasn't changed much since Jesus' time. Even the most well-meaning Christians and churches can fall into the trap of the old-time Jewish leaders, creating rules and expectations that go beyond the perfect demands of God's Word.

Jesus would tell us the same thing He told His friends and neighbors, "You can be free from all the man-made burdens by simply following Me." He perfectly obeyed every law the Father had issued, then died in your place to pay for the times you fall short.

You are absolutely free in Jesus Christ!

EVENING

Thank You, Lord, for the absolute freedom You offer. May I never misuse it. I don't want to be like the old-time Pharisees, consumed by striving and picky rules. I want to rest completely in Your freedom.

MORNING

*I will walk in freedom, for I have devoted
myself to your commandments.*

PSALM 119:45 NLT

Too many people follow the ways of the world and not Jesus' teachings. The Lord's commands are far from their minds, and they insist on doing life their own way. They call it freedom, but they are really bound by the chains of sin.

The writer of Psalm 119 offers a stark contrast to this worldly thinking, connecting his desire to walk in freedom with his commitment to following God's commandments. Placing God first, honoring your parents, staying faithful to your spouse, and avoiding lying or coveting or stealing are all examples of living for something beyond yourself—beyond your own sinful cravings. That is what freedom in Jesus really looks like.

Jesus empowers us to turn our backs on sin and instead pursue Him. If some stubborn sin is troubling you, recommit yourself to Jesus and His command to love God and love others. When you do that, you'll be truly free.

EVENING

*How thankful I am, Jesus, that You make it possible
to live in the freedom of divine law. Help me to turn my
back on sin each day and walk according to Your Word.
I know that requires a daily commitment to the life You've
called me to live. I am making that commitment now.*

July 21

Be sure of this: The wicked will not go unpunished,
but those who are righteous will go free.
PROVERBS 11:21 NIV

Have you ever seen people who seem to get away with everything? People who steal or lie or cheat but never face consequences? Maybe you've even talked to God about them—especially if they have victimized *you*. You wonder, *Why doesn't God punish wicked people on the spot?*

Of course, we wouldn't want swift justice for our own sins, would we? Thankfully, God is slow to anger and quick to forgive. That's His nature. He gives human beings far more time and opportunity than we deserve to repent. But today's scripture reminds us that a day will come when the wicked will be punished. . .and the righteous will go free. Their righteousness is perfect because it's based on what Jesus did.

This is a wonderful truth, and it should change the way you view sinful people. You once were among the wicked, but you were transformed when you joined God's family. Pray for those who are still living in sin, separated from God, and thank Him for the freedom Jesus has secured for you.

EVENING

Oh, Jesus, I pray for the sinful people in my life—
including myself. I'm grateful for Your patience.
Teach me to be slow to anger and quick to forgive,
just as You are. I know that You will ultimately bring
justice, so help me to wait on Your perfect timing.

July 22

> *"I have swept away your sins like a cloud. I have scattered your offenses like the morning mist. Oh, return to me, for I have paid the price to set you free."*
>
> Isaiah 44:22 NLT

Revelation 20:12 indicates the dead will be judged according to what they had done as recorded in "the books." Ecclesiastes 12:14 says God will bring every evil deed into judgment, and Jesus added that people will give an account for every empty word they have spoken (Matthew 12:36).

Imagine how many evil deeds you've committed and empty words you've spoken. They would be too many to count, but each of them is recorded and waiting for you on the day of judgment—or at least they *were* waiting. Jesus' death prompted God to sweep away your sins, to scatter them as the wind disperses a mist. The moment you called on Jesus' name for salvation, you were freed. God no longer remembers your sins or holds them against you.

A breathtaking reality, wouldn't you say? It should move you to praise Jesus right now.

EVENING

> *I praise You, Lord Jesus, for sweeping away my sins so they are no longer remembered. How can I hold others' sins against them, when You've been so generous to me? Lead me to forgive in the same manner in which I have been forgiven. I know that love keeps no record of wrongs, so help me to wipe the slate clean for others.*

July 23

*"But as for me, I know that the One Who bought me
and made me free from sin lives, and that He will
stand upon the earth in the end. Even after my skin
is destroyed, yet in my flesh I will see God."*

JOB 19:25–26 NLV

It's hard to imagine Job's pain, how he must have felt after losing so much. It's even worse when you consider the trials were through no fault of his own. In a single day, Job lost his livestock, his servants, and worst of all his ten children. And in the midst of such unbearable grief, he experienced little human support. Job's own wife wanted him to "curse God and die" (Job 2:9), and three friends who came to console him eventually accused him of secret sin. But Job knew that he had been redeemed. . .and that knowledge got him through an awful situation.

Whatever has troubled, is troubling, or will trouble you is covered by your own Redeemer. Unlike Job, we know His name: Jesus, who has freed you from the power of sin. One day, you will see Him in person, and you will worship.

EVENING

*In You, Lord Jesus, my sin is completely covered.
May I ask Your forgiveness, then never hold my
failures against myself. Your redemption never
changes. To the day You return in glory—and forever
afterward—I am free from my past sin and shame!*

MORNING

Jesus realized that power had gone out from him. He turned around in the crowd and asked, "Who touched my clothes?" . . . The woman, knowing what had happened to her, came and fell at his feet and, trembling with fear, told him the whole truth. He said to her, "Daughter, your faith has healed you. Go in peace and be freed from your suffering."

MARK 5:30, 33–34 NIV

There's a big, overarching aspect to Christian freedom, namely the breaking of our bonds of sin. When we believe and receive Jesus, we are no longer enslaved and bound for hell. That freedom is worth more than anything else in this life.

But Jesus provides smaller, day-to-day freedoms as well. In the story of a woman who had suffered from bleeding for twelve years, the Lord honored her desperate, unspoken prayer-by-touch by saying, "Be freed from your suffering." What the was the key? "Daughter, your *faith* has healed you."

Faith is what pleases God (Hebrews 11:6). Faith is what unlocks our salvation (Romans 3:22). Faith is the precursor to freedom.

EVENING

Lord Jesus, with Your gentle words, this woman was healed completely. Remind me that my faith unlocks salvation and that You are willing to help with any affliction I face. Give me the courage to boldly seek You out, and answer my prayers for freedom from everything that keeps me in chains.

July 25

"The Son of Man came not to be cared for. He came to care for others. He came to give His life so that many could be bought by His blood and made free from the punishment of sin."

MATTHEW 20:28 NLV

Has anyone ever cared for you when nobody else did? Maybe it was your mother or grandmother. Looking back now, you realize how that person sacrificed personal hopes and dreams to make sure you had everything you needed—and probably many things you wanted.

Mothers and grandmothers live for their offspring. They'll do anything for them, to the point of giving up their own lives if a situation calls for it. But as inspiring as that is, no other person can do what Jesus did. The second Person of the Trinity, God Himself took on flesh for the purpose of dying on the cross, paying the price for human sin so we could be freed from the prospect of hell.

"Because of this, those who belong to Christ will not suffer the punishment of sin" (Romans 8:1). How can you express your gratitude to Jesus today?

EVENING

*Lord, You have done so much for me. How could I
ever thank You enough? You did not come to earth
to be cared for, but to care for all of Your people.
Thank You for the sacrifice You made to offer
me freedom. Let me thank You with my life.*

MORNING

> *"Then they will see the Son of Man coming in the clouds with power and much greatness. When these things begin to happen, lift up your heads because you have been bought by the blood of Christ and will soon be free."*
>
> LUKE 21:27–28 NLV

Do you ever wonder if Jesus will return in your lifetime? Have you considered how you might react if that were the case? Today's scripture indicates that if we are indeed the generation to see Jesus' return, we will have a brief moment to lift our heads and see that our ultimate freedom is upon us.

If Jesus were to return today, we would never again have to worry about the devastating effects of sin—our own or anybody else's. Our battles will be over. Our countenances will change from those of weary travelers to joyful victors, as we realize we are about to be whisked away to a place where we will never again know pain or sorrow or injustice.

That day is coming, and it may be sooner than you think. Jesus is near!

EVENING

*Lord Jesus, come quickly. I look forward to the day
You return to set things right. But please remind me
to live with others' eternity in mind. May I never
be so focused on Your return that I forget to share the
good news of salvation with the people around me.*

July 27

*"God raised [Jesus] from the dead, freeing him
from the agony of death, because it was impossible
for death to keep its hold on him."*

ACTS 2:24 NIV

Unbelievers have a difficult time understanding why Christians focus so much on the death, burial, and resurrection of Jesus. But the Bible teaches that Jesus' death on the cross made it possible for us to be forgiven of sin. It also says that our faith would be in vain if Jesus hadn't come back from death, because then we'd be without hope of resurrection ourselves (1 Corinthians 15:17).

It was impossible for death to keep its hold on Jesus. Even when the enemy thought he'd had the last laugh, Jesus proved Himself victor over death and the grave. He was destined to die in our place and then conquer death, giving those of us who follow Him the ultimate hope: everlasting life.

No matter what troubles you face today, Jesus has freed you from the fear of death. You get to live with Him forever! You will either meet Him in the air or He will call you forth from the grave. Either way, you can't go wrong.

EVENING

*Death couldn't keep its hold on You, Jesus. And
because of that, death will not hold on to me either.
I thank You for the eternal life You promise to all
who follow You. I am free to walk in the newness
of life that You've given me, without fear.*

MORNING

> *"The Spirit of the Lord is on me, because he has anointed me to proclaim good news to the poor. He has sent me to proclaim freedom for the prisoners."*
>
> LUKE 4:18 NIV

In one form or fashion, everyone is a prisoner. Some people languish in actual jail cells. Others are imprisoned by anger or lust or fear or greed. And even if none of these descriptions apply to you, you're still living on a broken earth, among sinful people, in a dying body. Prisoners we are, every one of us.

Until, that is, Jesus comes into our lives. As He said to His Nazarene neighbors, reading from the prophecy of Isaiah, He had come "to proclaim freedom for the prisoners."

No shackles can survive Jesus' proclamation. No anger or lust or fear or greed need restrain us any longer. This broken earth and its sinful people and our dying bodies will be dealt with—perfectly, justly, and eternally—by the Lord Himself. The freedom for prisoners that He announced has been partially fulfilled already and will be completely understood soon enough. In the meantime, live like the free person you are!

EVENING

Lord, I thank You for freeing me from the prison of sin. Help me never to live as if I were still in bondage. I remember the chains I wore as a slave to sin, and I never want to return to that way of life. I praise You for true freedom!

July 29

> *O Israel, return unto the LORD thy God; for thou hast fallen*
> *by thine iniquity. . . . I will heal their backsliding, I will love*
> *them freely: for mine anger is turned away from him.*
>
> HOSEA 14:1, 4 KJV

Israel had a history of backsliding. One generation would walk with the Lord, then several successive generations would not. It's almost shocking to read what those wandering generations did wrong. Yet God stood at the ready to heal His people, to turn His anger away from them because He loved them so freely.

Think about your own life. Have there been times when you played the part of a Christian, but your heart was far from Jesus? Sometimes we consciously walk away from Him for a season. But because He loves you so much, Jesus stands at the ready, willing to forgive you and heal your soul.

Our mistakes (and even our willful disobedience) are not the final word in our lives. Through Jesus, we always enjoy the freedom of returning to God. He may send discipline to bring us back to Himself, but that's just another sign of His love. It's never too late to return to the Lord.

EVENING

> *Jesus, I'm grateful for a freeing love that remains*
> *steadfast even when I've failed. Help me to confess my*
> *sins to You and enjoy Your freedom to its greatest extent.*

MORNING

My soul is in great suffering. But You, O Lord,
how long? Return, O Lord. Set my soul free.
Save me because of Your loving-kindness.

PSALM 6:3–4 NLV

Sin causes suffering. From the time of Adam and Eve's failure, every human being has felt the pain of their own bad choices and the failures of others. It is an inescapable part of the human condition.

The psalm writer David was experiencing that struggle when he penned the words of today's scripture. He longed to be set free, based on the righteousness of God. David knew his own failures and shortcomings, but he also knew that God could offer the freedom that would save his soul.

As followers of Jesus, we have all known suffering, to some extent or another, related to our own sin. We may even call out like David, asking God how long it will be until we're free.

But Jesus has already set you free. Even if you've chosen to walk back into the prison of sin, Jesus has unlocked your cell door once and for all. Leave the jail behind and walk in His freedom.

EVENING

Lord, I have suffered from sin and eagerly await the
day when it will no longer influence my life. May I
live in Your freedom as much as I can here on earth
as I look forward to complete holiness in heaven.

July 31

O Lord, in You I have found a safe place. Let me never be ashamed. Set me free, because You do what is right and good.

PSALM 31:1 NLV

The world offers us many "escapes," and many of them aren't inherently wrong. Movies and music and activities may help us forget our responsibilities for a while. But if we rely too heavily on these things, we quickly find that they never really set us free. . .they just distract us for a time.

In Psalm 31, David declared that the Lord was his escape—and not just a temporary distraction from trouble, but a truly safe place. There is no shame in wanting or pursuing God in that way. When we seek refuge in God, we find a safe place where we can be truly free.

As Christians, we know that we come to God the Father through His Son, Jesus Christ. The one who "was tempted in every way we are tempted, but. . .did not sin" (Hebrews 4:15) is a loving and sympathetic "safe place." He offers freedom and rest.

EVENING

Lord Jesus, I delight in You as my safe place and praise You for Your kindness in offering freedom and rest. May I always find my refuge in You and never be afraid to turn to You in my weakness. You are absolutely what is right and good for me.

MORNING

"That joy is mine, and it is now complete. He must become greater; I must become less."

JOHN 3:29–30 NIV

August has arrived, and with it the "dog days of summer." This is a month for persevering.

To achieve our goal, we must keep focus. We can't charge at every task like an easily distracted squirrel. John the Baptist sure didn't. He was serious—deathly serious—about his goal, and everything we know about him says he focused, persevered, and succeeded.

John's task was to go ahead of Jesus, baptizing followers to receive the "Lamb of God" (John 1:29). He never stopped, refused to waver, and moved ever closer to victory. He began with the end in sight.

Today, let's consider the way John did his job and see our own task as the same thing—finding a thousand different ways to accomplish the one purpose of leading people to Jesus. Let's make sure that whatever we do shows Jesus to someone, every single day. It will take effort, but it will be worth it.

EVENING

May all of my life be a gospel message to others who need to know You, Lord. May my every word and deed persistently reflect Your love. I want my life to be a witness to Your unfailing mercy and grace, so let me honor You with my perseverance.

August 2

> *After this Jesus went out and saw a man who gathered*
> *taxes. His name was Levi (Matthew). Levi was sitting*
> *at his work. Jesus said to him, "Follow Me." Levi*
> *got up, left everything and followed Jesus.*
> LUKE 5:27–28 NLV

The excitement of new adventures dances in our hearts and gives a kick to our souls. We're eager to rejoice, share, love. That's what Matthew did after Jesus stunned all of Capernaum.

Jesus demonstrated His divinity by healing a crippled man and forgiving his sins. Then He demonstrated His humanity by turning to another man everyone mistrusted to request his help. When Jesus asked, Matthew responded in faith and then threw a party—"a big supper for Jesus in his house" (Luke 5:29).

Matthew was an eager servant, committed to his Savior and blind to his future. We know now the treacherous road Matthew started on, and we know he never left it. Maybe, when he was hurting, afraid, tired, and discouraged, he remembered those early days with Jesus and found joy and strength to keep going in the tough days that followed.

We can too. Jesus delights in helping His own.

> *Lord, I want to enter new adventures with You with*
> *a spirit of joy. Please help me to hold on to my initial*
> *eagerness and be persistent in the work You have*
> *for me. You've saved me out of a life of misery and*
> *put me in the middle of an adventure with You!*

MORNING

Whatever work you do, do it with all your heart.
Do it for the Lord and not for men.
COLOSSIANS 3:23 NLV

Our days are busy. We never have enough time, talent, or inclination for everything, and we feel defeated, frustrated, unable to control the ever-growing list of things to do. But it's not our *what* that's off—it's our *why*.

No one had more to do than Jesus, and we know what framed His every choice. His answer was always "yes" when He had the opportunity to make someone's life better. He didn't look down at a list, He looked through to a heart. He always chose to love, help, forgive, and share. He did only what the Father told Him to do, and that was to show compassion and grace to all who needed Him.

Everything Jesus did came from the right place, for the right reasons. What are our reasons for the things we do. . .or don't do? If our goal is reflecting Jesus to those around us, we'll frame our choices the way He did. We'll find strength to continue the journey. When we know *why* we're carrying on, we have the *will* to carry on.

EVENING

Lord Jesus, help me to focus on those things that
reflect You to the world—and then do them well.
Give me a good sense of priorities and the strength
I need to accomplish them. Help me to do only
what You call me to do, and then do it well.

August 4

*Because Jesus did these things on the Day of Rest, the Jews
made it very hard for Him. Jesus said to them, "My Father
is still working all the time so I am working also."*
JOHN 5:16–17 NLV

Jesus walked and taught, helped and healed, mindful always of the needs of others. A man lame for thirty-eight years craved help and happened to meet Jesus on a Sabbath. Jesus not only healed the man's bones but his heart as well. Those who saw responded with judgment instead of jubilation—they missed the end by focusing on the means. And they complained.

Sometimes the good work we do will bother people, regardless of our intent or God's resulting blessings. Jesus experienced that, but He didn't care. He continued.

Sometimes we'll have to work around unbelievers. Sometimes we'll have to explain our motives or our methods. But if we're following Jesus—who followed God—we need only God's blessing. So if your work looks unconventional, do it anyway. If it requires boldness and courage, do it anyway. You're in good company.

EVENING

*I know, Jesus, that some people will make life
difficult because I'm serving You. Please give me the
courage to move forward anyway—Yours is the only
approval I need. Remind me that I am working to
hear You say, "Well done, good and faithful servant."
I don't need anyone else's pat on the back.*

MORNING

When Jesus reached the spot, he looked up and said to him,
"Zacchaeus, come down immediately. I must stay at your house
today." So he came down at once and welcomed him gladly.

LUKE 19:5–6 NIV

The story of Jesus and Zacchaeus is pure and perfect, full of the possibility of loss but ending in rewarded perseverance instead.

As Jesus passed through Jericho, Zacchaeus wanted to see Him. "But because he was short he could not see over the crowd. So he ran ahead and climbed a sycamore-fig tree to see him" (Luke 19:3–4). And Zacchaeus did see Jesus—more importantly, Jesus saw him. Jesus talked to him, stayed with him, saved him.

If we stop at the "but" without getting to the "so," we'll miss Jesus looking at us too. Seeing Jesus and having Him see us means finding the tree. Jesus will be at that spot because He's already arranged the answer to our obstacle. He's ready to meet us there.

EVENING

Jesus, if Zacchaeus could climb a tree to see You,
I want to do whatever I can. May I never let
anything keep me from seeing You face to face. Let
me not be ashamed of my limitations but work to
overcome them so that I can see You more clearly.

August 6

> *Do not allow anyone to change your mind. Always*
> *do your work well for the Lord. You know that*
> *whatever you do for Him will not be wasted.*
> 1 Corinthians 15:58 nlv

Are we tenacious, or just stubborn? When we won't quit, is it annoying or admirable? The answer to these questions depends on our reasons for perseverance. If we just want our own way, that's a problem. If you're intent on completing the job God assigned, more power to you!

The apostle Paul wrote to the church in Corinth about grace—the grace through Jesus that, besides giving us eternal life, helps us through our work here and now. When our work is God's work, we can't let anything or anyone change our minds.

Yes, there will be obstacles, and they'll be challenging. But in Christ, we can walk over them, knock them down, or plow through them to get where we need to be. Every bit of work we do is making God's way, clearing the path He's chosen for us—that path that ultimately leads us, and others, into Jesus' presence.

> *Lord, show me the difference between godly*
> *tenacity and selfish stubbornness. I want to honor*
> *You by doing the right thing in the right way.*
> *You've given me much to accomplish—please*
> *help me to do it in a way that honors You.*

MORNING

Then Jesus said to Simon, "Don't be afraid;
from now on you will fish for people."
LUKE 5:10 NIV

Simon Peter was tired, frustrated, and ready to quit—staring at his empty nets after fishing all night. We all know that feeling of fatigue and doubt and, like Peter, we have two choices. He chose wisely.

We don't have to know where the fish are. But we can always believe that our best move is to do exactly what Jesus says—don't give up. Peter chose belief over doubt, taking fishing advice from a carpenter: "Master, we've worked hard all night and haven't caught anything. But because you say so, I will let down the nets" (Luke 5:5).

If we let down our nets because Jesus says so, even if the timing seems odd and the odds are against us, Jesus will fill them. If we keep fishing because of our belief and trust, Jesus will help us complete the work we see and then lead us to amazing work we can't even imagine seeing. If Jesus says so, it's because He'll have more to say to us as we go. There is never any lack in Him. Fish are everywhere.

EVENING

Lord Jesus, Your will hasn't always made perfect
sense to me, but I've seen how Your will is best.
Show me where to put down my nets so that
I can bring many to Your saving grace.

August 8

*For this very reason, make every effort to add to your
faith goodness; and to goodness, knowledge; and to
knowledge, self-control; and to self-control, perseverance;
and to perseverance, godliness; and to godliness,
mutual affection; and to mutual affection, love.*

2 PETER 1:5–7 NIV

Corruption, deceit, unrest, lies, personal attacks—they defined the apostle Peter's world just as much as they do ours. Peter knew every follower of Jesus would have to battle long and hard, so he taught us how to be effective and productive no matter what.

In today's scripture, faith and love bracket all the other factors that help you fight on. Peter told us all to learn, remember, trust, push onward. . .and keep hold of Jesus.

When we work with Jesus to grow these qualities in our lives every day, we welcome even the hardships of this world, because we know we can make a difference in another person's life. We know the deep joy of becoming a little more like Jesus. . .if we "make every effort."

*Thank You, Jesus, for the encouragement to
grow in my faith in You. Remind me to work at
it, to make the effort to grow in my walk with
You every day. Please make me more like You so
that I can make a difference in this world.*

MORNING

All these many people who have had faith in God are around us like a cloud. Let us put every thing out of our lives that keeps us from doing what we should. Let us keep running in the race that God has planned for us.

HEBREWS 12:1 NLV

When you think about the day ahead, do you see a path lined with new and budding growth, leading to heights you know and others you want to? Or is it cluttered with debris and discards that drag you down?

In fear or pain, it's easy to get distracted, but our work remains. Abraham, Sarah, Isaac, and others of great faith stayed focused regardless of their circumstances. Jesus did too: He did not give up when He had to suffer shame and die on a cross, because He knew of the joy that would later be His (Hebrews 12:2). All that would hurt was pushed aside to allow more faith, and that meant going forward. It's the same for us.

We can give up and become curators of clutter, or we can push that stuff aside and move ahead. It's a daily choice of faith lived out in action.

EVENING

Lord Jesus, help me to put the nonessentials out of my life and freely run the race You have set before me. This world can be so distracting, and sometimes even fellow believers confuse things. Keep me focused on You, for the joy that lies ahead.

August 10

So do not throw away this confident trust in the Lord. Remember the great reward it brings you! Patient endurance is what you need now, so that you will continue to do God's will. Then you will receive all that he has promised.

HEBREWS 10:35–36 NLT

Keeping our faith in focus when distractions mount is tough. But changing our thinking can help. The foundation of the past—what we've survived, achieved, and enjoyed—supports our future and keeps us going with confidence.

The tough work today and the unknowns of the future can cause us to stumble. But if we call on what we know—our history with Jesus—we'll continue strong and assured. We can keep doing today's work because we remember how we did it yesterday.

Every victory with Jesus leads to another. What He's done with us, for us, and through us becomes a part of us. Remembering means repeating with assurance every faithful step. The confidence we have in Jesus now is the same confidence He'll give tomorrow.

EVENING

Oh, Jesus, remind me of my past just enough to see what You have done in and through me to this point. May I build on the positives with new victories of faith in You. I believe that You will do even greater things in my life than I've seen yet.

MORNING

*For we are God's handiwork, created in Christ Jesus to do
good works, which God prepared in advance for us to do.*

EPHESIANS 2:10 NIV

Do you believe that God knows what He's doing? That's not a trick
question. It's a comfort. God finishes what He starts, preparing
ahead of time for everything for all time. But He doesn't do it alone.
He could do it all without our limited, flawed, human contribution.
But He never has, and He won't start now.

Knowing all, God chooses to do it the hard way, through us, knowing that we'll find a way to get scared, make a mess, and complain.
That's okay, He decided, and declares good work for us anyway—lots
of it—thought out by Him long before we would ever touch it.

We don't see the end yet, but Jesus does. It is our blessing simply
to accept what He's planned. Let's just approach today's tasks, do
them with love and obedience, and believe they're part of all the
good that is to come.

EVENING

*You made me, Lord, for good works, not selfish,
sinful ones. Thank You for turning my imperfect life
into one that can accomplish great things through
love and obedience to You. I am certainly not
qualified in my own right, but You have chosen and
equipped me for Your service and Your purpose.*

August 12

Let us help each other to love others and to do good.

HEBREWS 10:24 NLV

The work God prepared for you is yours, different from that of others but still the same. Fellow believers can be inspired when they see you giving your best for God and those He loves. It makes them want to do it too. That's what is the same.

When we see others push through difficulties, continuing despite disappointments, we know they must have a good reason. When we see them love and do good even when it's hard—*especially* when it's hard—we know they don't do it for themselves. We know they go with Jesus in their hearts.

Watch those around you who treat each day like the gift it is. Watch them overcome anything in their way to be a little more like Jesus. Follow their example. When we act and react in love no matter what, those around us will learn to do the same.

EVENING

*Jesus, I thank You for giving me work that You
prepared just for me to do. May I be faithful in it,
despite every challenge. Help me to be aware of the
work that others do for You despite the difficulties.
I want to support them with encouragement.*

MORNING

> *He said to his disciples, "The harvest is great, but the*
> *workers are few. So pray to the Lord who is in charge of the*
> *harvest; ask him to send more workers into his fields."*
> MATTHEW 9:37–38 NLT

We've all behaved like "sheep without a shepherd," as Jesus described it (Matthew 9:36). He knows the many ways we feel lost and alone, burdened and overwhelmed—and He knows we're not at our best then. So He sends helpers.

Our helpers have been parents or children, spouses or strangers. They come to help us so that we can help others. What we learn in the big, dark pastures are the skills and grace that help us keep going, that comfort us so we can learn the lesson of today. And then we can pass it on.

Touching others with the compassion of Jesus becomes a magnificent part of our job. Treasuring the help we've received from others means being Jesus' helpers when He puts us with those whose pain we understand. We are blessed so that we can be part of the blessing going forward.

EVENING

> *Thank You, Lord, that I need not take on the harvest*
> *alone. You use many people in bringing souls to Yourself.*
> *Guide me to be a good part of the team and help*
> *others who are in need, just as I have been helped.*

August 14

So let us come boldly to the throne of our gracious God. There we will receive his mercy, and we will find grace to help us when we need it most.

HEBREWS 4:16 NLT

Jesus knows our weaknesses better than we ourselves do. And He's not ashamed of us. The reality is that Jesus is exceedingly able and, more important, *willing*, to help us. What is our part? Get in front of Him and ask.

Jesus is never annoyed with our pleas. We need to believe that He hears us and sees us and will have an answer for us—a way for us to keep going when we don't think we can. When we're weak or hurting or exhausted or embarrassed, His grace is waiting. He's there when we realize He is our only source, our only way to carry on.

Whenever all we see is the long road ahead, we need to look up to the One who's at the beginning, middle, and end. . .the One who overlooks our stumbles, as long as we continue. Our strength comes from boldly and confidently asking.

EVENING

Lord, I know I'm weak and I need Your help. I often stumble through my walk of faith, but I know that You are gracious. Help me to walk boldly with You, to come before Your throne to receive Your mercy. Thank You for being so kind and helpful.

MORNING

> *Blessed is the one who perseveres under trial because,*
> *having stood the test, that person will receive the crown of*
> *life that the Lord has promised to those who love him.*
>
> JAMES 1:12 NIV

Getting through a tough day at work is hard, but since we know the end is coming, we push through to finish our job. Some of our life struggles, though, seem to have no end. It doesn't matter. The same choice applies.

We can quit or we can continue, trusting daily grace to get us through a little at a time. The completion of one day of the work Jesus has given us will lead to another beginning. Today's work done becomes one part of the whole.

As we keep on, we receive a two-fold blessing. We're living and loving Jesus through every hard thing we do *and* showing others what that means. And with every testimony, every victory, every time we hold on when it gets hard, Jesus is rooted ever more deeply in our hearts. We can't share His love without some of it spilling out onto us, growing faith anew. He promises grace, and we receive it to share it.

EVENING

> *Lord, I look to You for the crown of life you promised.*
> *In all of my trials, help me to always trust in Your*
> *grace. Help me to hold tightly to You, and bless*
> *me when I persevere through the hardships.*

August 16

Then Jesus stood up again and said to the woman, "Where are your accusers? Didn't even one of them condemn you?" "No, Lord," she said. And Jesus said, "Neither do I. Go and sin no more."

John 8:10–12 NLT

Mistakes derail us. The embarrassing moments of our lives interrupt our work and threaten our growth. Sometimes we just want to stop—ashamed, defeated, lost. But Jesus has a better response.

When an angry crowd wanted to stone a woman to death for adultery, Jesus didn't join the attack on her obvious sin. Nor did He sanction those who ridiculed the woman. He recognized that they were all the same—that *we're* all the same.

At any moment, any of us could be caught doing something that would make us stop, give up, and shrink away. But Jesus chooses not to focus on the past, or even the present. He's thinking of our future. Nothing we do changes the plans He has for us.

Everybody keep going, He says. *Learn from this mistake. Examine your motives. Change your behavior. Just don't stop. Follow Me. Let's go.*

I thank You, Jesus, that You encourage me instead of condemning my faults. You call me out of my sin and shame into Your marvelous light. The condemnation of others cannot derail me, because I know that You have called me Your own.

MORNING

*"I have put wisdom in the hearts of all who are wise,
so they may make all that I have told you."*

EXODUS 31:6 NLV

Ever feel overwhelmed by your responsibilities? Maybe not up for the job? Unable to do what God says you should? Relax. You are perfectly equipped, just as the Israelites were thousands of years ago.

After escaping their slavery in Egypt, on the long, hard march to their homeland, God told Moses to oversee construction of the tabernacle and its many detailed furnishings. It was a job of massive scope and importance, something that had never been attempted before. Moses had nothing to go by except God's word. . .but that was plenty.

Today, we have Jesus, who is "the Word" (John 1:1). Through Him, we are equipped and empowered for every task, no matter what challenges line our way. By His power, we can overcome sin, stand firm in battle, and point others to heaven. Let's get to it.

EVENING

*Lord, I am not up for the job You've given me for Your
kingdom, unless I trust in You. Equip and empower me
for the task before me. Send others to help me when I
feel like giving up. Above all, I need You to help me when
I want to throw in the towel. You are forever faithful.*

August 18

> *"This is life that lasts forever. It is to know You, the only
> true God, and to know Jesus Christ Whom You have sent.
> I honored You on earth. I did the work You gave Me to do."*
>
> JOHN 17:3–4 NLV

Before He was arrested for being who He was, the Son of God, Jesus prayed. He prayed for those closest to Him, the men who were charged with carrying on His work in a hostile time. He prayed for those of us who would believe in Him for all time. He talked with His Father about His job—to save us and give us "life that lasts forever."

Jesus wasn't there to teach the disciples how to build tents or dig wells. He isn't in our hearts to help us balance our checkbooks or change tires. He came to love us into understanding who God is. He came to offer us the peace and grace we can't manufacture for ourselves.

Jesus left no catalog of inventions or body of writings, but He did everything the Father sent Him to do. He did not stop one moment too soon. Jesus finished His work, and He set ours in motion.

EVENING

> *Lord Jesus, thank You for helping me understand
> the Father's love. I praise You for pursuing Your
> work until it was finished. Help me not to grow
> weary of the work that You've called me to do.*

MORNING

"Let your light shine in front of men. Then they will see the good things you do and will honor your Father Who is in heaven."

MATTHEW 5:16 NLV

When Jesus walked this earth, people were drawn to Him. They followed Him, listened to Him teach, knew that He was different from everyone and everything else in this world. In all that He did, the pure love of God shone through—and those who were lost, ashamed, afraid, or confused accepted that love and experienced new life.

Jesus is not physically walking our streets today, but He's here. He's still reaching out to people, teaching and helping, loving and healing. . . through you and everyone else who follows Him. So how do we carry out this work with His same compassion, mercy, and love?

Let us greet each new day with this thought: *What will I do that shows Jesus to someone else?* That challenge, purpose, and privilege is why we continue to pick up where He left off, why we're still drawn to follow Him. Work that comes from a heart full of Jesus helps others fill their hearts with Him too.

EVENING

Jesus, may my heart be full of You today. Help me to show Your love to others by demonstrating compassion, mercy, and kindness. Let my life cause others to seek You!

August 20

> *"I have prayed that your faith will be strong and that you will not give up. When you return, you must help to make your brothers strong."*
>
> LUKE 22:32 NLV

Our failures, our weaknesses, our episodes of abandonment are no surprise to Jesus. He lived a human life, so He understands our fears and lapses. And He prays for us. He prayed for Peter, whom He knew would get scared and deny even knowing his Savior. But Jesus also knew Peter would overcome that horrible misstep, that he would remember his faith and get back to work.

That's what we have to remember too. Jesus sees our troubling times, our weakness of faith and dearth of perseverance, long before we experience them. And He's always ready to help us to return to what we know. What we learn during those failures will serve us well as we carry on.

When we start again after we've tripped up, backed away, or lost our confidence, we go with more gratitude, more purpose, more strength. And we lend our own lives as examples.

Our failures should be commas, not periods. Start again and keep going.

> *I know I'm going to fail, Jesus, but I don't want any failure to stop me. Help me to overcome in Your love and strength because I know I can't be good on my own. When I stumble, strengthen me to pick up the pieces and start again.*

MORNING

> *When Jesus heard this, he was amazed. Turning to those who were following him, he said, "I tell you the truth, I haven't seen faith like this in all Israel!"*
>
> MATTHEW 8:10 NLT

In the story of a Roman officer's faith and action, even Jesus was amazed. The officer believed that Christ could do all He claimed for anyone who believed, and he claimed Jesus' unlimited power and grace for himself.

The officer traveled to meet Jesus, to ask for healing for his young servant. Jesus, in His compassion, agreed. The officer knew he needed no physical proximity for what Jesus was guaranteeing. "Just say the word from where you are, and my servant will be healed," the soldier said (Matthew 8:8). And that's what happened.

The officer knew what to do and did not stop until he did it. He went to Jesus in faith, plainly asked for help, and believed Jesus would listen. Faith said the Lord would not withhold His willingness and power to finish the work. Let's follow this soldier's bold and confident lead. He did his part and trusted Jesus to do His. That's how God's work gets done.

EVENING

> *Lord Jesus, I want to do my part as You do Yours. Please give me the faith of the Roman centurion and let me see Your miracles. I know that when I trust in You completely, You always show up and do Your will.*

August 22

> *The night before Herod was to bring him to trial, Peter*
> *was sleeping between two soldiers, bound with two*
> *chains, and sentries stood guard at the entrance.*
>
> ACTS 12:6 NIV

When we've done all we can, sometimes we have to just wait. Waiting is often part of the persevering. When we can't do any more, we're tempted to think everything's over, that we've failed, or God is disappointed in us. No.

In prison for preaching and teaching about Jesus, Peter could do nothing more to help himself—nothing but continue in his faith and rest a while. Jesus knew we'd need that kind of balance from all that happens to us: "Come to Me, all of you who work and have heavy loads. I will give you rest" (Matthew 11:28 NLV).

Rest isn't quitting—it's just a continuation of our work in peace and quiet confidence. Rest like Peter's requires faith and trust in who God says He is. It requires reminding ourselves that God is still at work, planning our release, even when our part is to wait a bit. We're not stopping, just resting.

> *Sometimes it's hard to rest, Jesus. Please help me to*
> *slow down when You say and trust You as I wait. I know*
> *that You'll take care of me. Remind me that abiding*
> *in You is an essential part of my Christian walk.*

MORNING

*Create in me a pure heart, O God, and renew
a steadfast spirit within me.*
PSALM 51:10 NIV

We fail others, we fail God, we fail Jesus. It's just part of life for human beings. While we strive to be more like Jesus every day, our failures hound us as if we're some spiritual Whack-a-mole.

But God is watching, helping us respond with His Word, fix the broken parts, and get back to work. It's hard to forgive ourselves when we fail, but failure changes nothing. Whatever we began is still there. Whatever is left undone will stay undone until we get back to it. And we do that with confession, renewal, and determination.

We ask forgiveness when we've messed up. We allow Jesus to move all the garbage out of our hearts and sweep them clean for a new round of grace and mercy. And we move to the next step with a little more understanding, a little more humility, a little more wisdom.

None of us likes to fail, fall backward, or lose momentum. But our saving grace is that it's all temporary. Success, completion, and redemption are next.

EVENING

Jesus, help me to remember that failure is not the end—it's just the beginning of a change. Thank You for never giving up on me. Help me to never give up on myself or on the dreams You have given me. Make me steadfast to accomplish what You've called me to do.

August 24

> *I know how to live on almost nothing or with everything.*
> *I have learned the secret of living in every situation, whether*
> *it is with a full stomach or empty, with plenty or little. For I*
> *can do everything through Christ, who gives me strength.*
>
> PHILIPPIANS 4:12–13 NLT

Every time we start again, pure and eager, Jesus is there. He's not looking back at our stumbles but forward to our victories—because they're *His* victories too.

Jesus taught us how to continue when we meet with opposition, how to live the truth we know despite what others say, how to have faith regardless of what we see. Our days might be a mess of delays and distractions, our nights restless with worry and fear—but our attitude of "yes, I can" is what counts. We know we don't fight any of these battles alone.

With that belief, attitude, and confidence as our foundation, we do not doubt or quit. We trust that Jesus has provided the solution to every problem well before it's needed. Then we fear nothing and trust that we will see a solution in the end.

EVENING

> *Lord, I'm thankful that You are with me in failures*
> *and victories. Keep me from ever quitting before*
> *I see Your victory. You are the source of all my*
> *hope and security. I'm grateful that I don't have*
> *to rely on myself, but only on Your power.*

August 25

MORMING

*Watch yourself how you act and what you
teach. Stay true to what is right.*

1 TIMOTHY 4:16 NLV

The apostle Paul wrote to Timothy with this instruction, and we can
learn a lot from his advice. Timothy was an eager student, an enthu-
siastic believer, and a representative of Jesus, just as we should be.
Whatever we do today is on display, and others will judge if we're
becoming more or less like Jesus each day.

Our private perseverance is public preaching. How we think and
what we believe is reflected in how we live.

A heart that keeps faith in Jesus looks like a person who is calm
and at peace, even in turmoil. A mind sure of Christ's grace and
direction no matter what looks like a person carrying on despite
mistakes and setbacks. Hands continuing to do work that shows
the love of God look like failures mended and forgotten. Fish are
caught even in broken nets.

We're all students learning from each other. Let's be sure that
what others learn from us is love that never stops. Grace is received
so it can be given away.

EVENING

*Lord Jesus, keep me in Your peace as I persevere
through trials. I'm thankful that even my troubles
can be successes for You. Remind me to watch how I
act and what I teach, that I am staying true to what
is right in Your sight. May I never be self-serving.*

August 26

*For [God the Father] chose us in [Jesus] before the creation
of the world to be holy and blameless in his sight.*

EPHESIANS 1:4 NIV

When we're working productively and good things are happening, progress feels easy. We're secure, confident, full of purpose. But when our balance sheet is something even Matthew would light on fire, we're ashamed, discouraged, and empty of hope.

But God doesn't see that disappointment. His vision is better. A field that's producing nothing, a lack of tools to work with, or a growth plan that resulted in impressive failure is not a retreat but a call to trust.

God saw the nation of Israel as worthy of His songs of joy. . .despite the people's obvious weakness: "The LORD your God is with you, the Mighty Warrior who saves. He will take great delight in you; in his love he will no longer rebuke you, but will rejoice over you with singing" (Zephaniah 3:17).

God celebrates us too. He never gives up on us but trusts His Son, Jesus, to supply the strength we don't feel. He sees what we can't. He expects us to keep going until we see it.

EVENING

*Jesus, it's wonderful that You delight in me even
when I feel discouraged and hopeless. I praise
You for never giving up on me. What a wonderful
thought that You delight in me and rejoice over me
with singing. Renew my passion to keep working
even when I don't yet see the fruit of my labor.*

MORNING

"For sure, I tell you, whoever puts his trust in Me can do the things I am doing. He will do even greater things than these because I am going to the Father."

JOHN 14:12 NLV

As part of God's plan, Jesus recruited those first trusted followers, and they recruited more and more workers. Now, here we are. Our work today, tomorrow, and always is to continue Jesus' work, and He says we'll be great at it.

Jesus entrusted the whole world to those who would follow Him, and He did not leave us alone or powerless. We have Him in our hearts in the person of the Holy Spirit, who empowers us to continue everything Jesus began.

And when we do, the effect is cumulative. Whatever you do for someone gets passed to the next person—and on and on it goes. When we begin with small things, we may think they're insignificant or won't amount to much. But every good thing we do accomplishes exactly what God intends.

Nothing is wasted, nothing is small, because Jesus' footsteps just look like yours and mine now. And that's pretty great.

EVENING

Lord Jesus, keep me faithful in Your work, though it may not seem like much today. I thank You for blessing all that I do. Show me how I can do even more to impact the world for Your kingdom.

August 28

> *"As long as it is day, we must do the works of him who sent me. Night is coming, when no one can work."*
>
> JOHN 9:4 NIV

God assigns each of us our work. Whatever we have to do is part of the whole, so that nothing will be left incomplete. It is hard sometimes, but we can make everything better, easier, and more effective. The way we talk to others, the attitude with which we give to others, and the heart of forgiveness we open to others is all tied up in the way we show God to them.

We don't do our work behind a curtain—we're exposed, watched, even judged. May our relentless habits of joy, prayer, and gratitude blind all who see with God's grace.

Find the joy in the tasks you've been given, joy in doing your small part each day. Let's stay in constant prayer for strength, wisdom, abilities, and grace to do the parts no one else can. Let's thank the Lord for today's work and the bigger, grander work-in-progress we're already entrusted with for tomorrow (1 Thessalonians 5:16–18).

Jesus plans big. Let's keep up with Him.

EVENING

Thank You for making me part of Your big plan, Jesus. May others clearly see You in all that I say and do. Let me do all of the work You've given me with joy in my heart and my eyes fixed on heaven.

MORNING

*Now finish the work, so that your eager willingness to do it may
be matched by your completion of it, according to your means.
For if the willingness is there, the gift is acceptable according
to what one has, not according to what one does not have.*

2 CORINTHIANS 8:11–12 NIV

Do you know what sometimes gets in the way of our work, that work we began so joyfully, just us and Jesus? Comparison. If we start comparing our work with that of others, we can feel inadequate, unnecessary, unworthy of God's time.

That stacking of your work next to another's should never be for comparison or judgment—it should be for advancement and building, for getting the best from yourself and other believers so that all our efforts together produce what God has planned.

Our work follows our willingness. When Jesus sees our hearts ready, He rejoices in our eagerness and expects us to follow Him through whatever happens. Then we finish that job and move on to the next because God's building all the time. We start with what we have and finish with something better so we can start all over again.

EVENING

*I'm grateful, Lord, that You don't judge me by what I
can't do. You always accept the gift of my willing heart.
Please use me to successfully complete Your work.*

August 30

> *"The LORD is my strength and my defense; he has become my salvation. He is my God, and I will praise him, my father's God, and I will exalt him."*
>
> EXODUS 15:2 NIV

The saying goes "once begun, halfway done" because beginning is often the hardest part. But finishing is the other half, and everything in and out of this world conspires to keep us from getting there.

Of course, we must keep away from everything that even looks like sin, the apostle Paul said, aware of all that threatened believers' faith and work (1 Thessalonians 5:21–22). But we must also beware of other temptations, like moments of ease and relief when we're tired. . .or those times we question our abilities, our inclination, our commitment. Not knowing the end can make the middle harder.

But when we focus on the promise and example of Jesus, we find our strength, stamina, enthusiasm, and belief. We won't allow our good progress to become a casualty of fatigue or insecurity. Let's make a new saying: Once begun, with Jesus, done!

> *Lord Jesus, help me to begin with strength and avoid the distractions that take me from Your work. I want to serve You well and reap Your good harvest. Let me not procrastinate or grow weary when the work I'm doing is for You and Your kingdom. Keep me on track!*

MORNING

> *I have fought the good fight, I have finished*
> *the race, I have kept the faith.*
> 2 TIMOTHY 4:7 NIV

The apostle Paul had come from so far behind but near the end of his life, he focused only on completion. Sensing his life on earth was almost done, he had peace.

When we've done all we can for as long as we can, overcome the obstacles, endured the waits, come back from the setbacks, and leaned on our faith in the Savior who never leaves us, we'll know peace today and forever (Matthew 28:20).

Jesus has not changed His mind about entrusting us with His work... or about our responsibility to it. Every fight is a good fight if we battle the bad along the way. We live in a troubling world that works against us, but God gives us fierce grace to walk the challenging road, to reach the blessing at the end.

The work Jesus left us is a privilege. Let us go at it with focus, fearlessness, and faith because we know we never go alone.

EVENING

> *Jesus, please help me fight the good fight and*
> *reach Your blessing in the end. I'm grateful that*
> *You walk with me all the way. I cannot wait to*
> *hear the words "good and faithful servant."*

September 1

> *Jesus spoke to all the people, saying, "I am the Light*
> *of the world. Anyone who follows Me will not walk*
> *in darkness. He will have the Light of Life."*
>
> JOHN 8:12 NLV

This month, as kids go back to school, we'll focus on guidance. No teacher, even the very best one, knows everything. But Jesus does. He has absolute knowledge of everything, everywhere, at all times and in all places.

He always knows what to do, and He told us how: "The Father has not left Me alone. I always do what He wants Me to do" (John 8:29).

He does what pleases His Father. *Our* Father.

How do we do what God wants us to do? How do we know if we're doing that today? It's a big question, and we can shade the answers in our own fear and uncertainty. But Jesus throws holy light on them—revealing direction, guidance, and companionship as we go.

Jesus says *know* Him and *follow* Him. When we learn what that means, we'll know how to do what God wants us to do too. We'll never take a single step blind, unaware or alone.

EVENING

> *I want to draw closer to You, Jesus, so I can always sense*
> *Your guidance in my life. I have the road map I need*
> *in Your Word. Thank You for Your perfect direction.*

MORNING

Jesus told them, "This is the only work God wants from you: Believe in the one he has sent."

JOHN 6:29 NLT

Those who lived and walked with the Son of Man saw the miracles and heard the voice of the Son of God. They could ask Jesus anything and He would answer. They could literally act on what they heard Him physically speak, if they chose to believe. They could enjoy instant direction and follow-through.

If we choose to believe, Jesus will gladly lead us too. Spiritually speaking, we're in the classroom, sitting at His feet, asking questions, learning who He is, and putting our faith in Him to take charge of everything we do. If we commit everything we are and everything we'll become to His care, we can enjoy an intimate, undoubted knowledge of our Savior.

This belief in Jesus is much more than simply agreeing that He lived. It's knowing He still lives and that He knows us personally. It's choosing to walk through this life with Him leading the way. His voice is still the same.

EVENING

Lord, all You ask is that I believe in You. Thank You for giving me faith; help me to walk in Your footsteps each day. I trust that You will lead and guide me through Your Word and my prayers. I never have to wonder if You will lead me astray.

September 3

> *When he was at the table with them, he took bread,*
> *gave thanks, broke it and began to give it to them.*
> *Then their eyes were opened and they recognized him.*
>
> LUKE 24:30–31 NIV

Jesus delights in spending time with us when we're hungry for Him. The two men He met after His resurrection knew their way home to Emmaus, but they needed far more direction for their lives. Jesus began to guide them—and He wanted more time.

As they approached the village to which they were going, Jesus continued on as if He was going farther. "But they urged him strongly, 'Stay with us, for it is nearly evening; the day is almost over.' So he went in to stay with them" (Luke 24:29).

Jesus waits for us to ask for more time at His table, getting to know Him and understanding more. And He always says yes.

Those men from Emmaus recognized Jesus when He broke the bread. He's still offering Himself to us in that way today. May we "urge Him strongly" to stay with us and fill us with His presence. May His brokenness for us make us wholly His.

EVENING

> *Oh, Jesus, after a day full of hurry and*
> *demands, I want to slow down and be with*
> *You. I urge You to stay with me and fill me with*
> *Your presence. I want to know more of You.*

September 4

Simon Peter answered him, "Lord, to whom shall we go?
You have the words of eternal life. We have come to
believe and to know that you are the Holy One of God."

JOHN 6:68–69 NIV

Sometimes the road we're walking with Jesus looks a little too hard and uncomfortable. We hope for a better way, a more palatable and pleasing path.

Some of Jesus' early followers chose that way, perhaps because they didn't know their Guide well enough. So Jesus questioned those closest to Him, the Twelve: "You do not want to leave too, do you?" (John 6:67).

He asks that question of us too when we wobble in our walk. When we behave as if we're lost, weak, and alone, He wants us to recognize that we've forgotten who He is. Simon Peter made the answer that should stay front-and-center in all our minds, all the time: "You are the Holy One of God." No one else even vaguely compares. To whom else would we ever go?

Lord, I need not go to anyone but You. Please
always be front and center in my mind. I think
of Peter walking on water as long as his eyes
were on You. Please hold my focus so that I don't
sink. I know You will always guide me.

September 5

> *I have wandered away like a lost sheep; come and find
> me, for I have not forgotten your commands.*
> PSALM 119:176 NLT

"Come get me, please!" We pray this plea more often than we'd like to admit. Even with the clear path of obedience stretched out in front of us, we wander off with no clue how to find our way back.

Our sense of direction is a constant work in progress, but we improve a bit with every lost-and-found journey. That's because our plea for help comes from the right place—from our trust and belief in the One who does know the way.

Lost or confused or just feeling way too far from Jesus, we admit our weakness. Thankfully, we know where our help is found—not in forging ahead on our own but in humbly asking God to bring us back to His pasture. When we finally trade our own selfish direction for His perfect guidance, we find ourselves on a path paved with His grace.

EVENING

> *I am a sheep, Jesus, but I am Your sheep, and You
> never desert me. Bring me back to Your pasture
> when I stray. When I wander off the right path,
> please find me and remind me whose I am. I know
> You offer me second chances without number.*

September 6

> *"Do not let your heart be troubled. You have put your trust in God, put your trust in Me also."*
> JOHN 14:1 NLV

Choice is a wonderful thing. We cherish it and claim it as a God-given gift. And it is, so let's make a choice that will make all the ones that follow far less scary.

Jesus prayed for those who trusted their way to Him: "O Father, Lord of heaven and earth, thank you for hiding these things from those who think themselves wise and clever, and for revealing them to the childlike" (Matthew 11:25 NLT).

The child who doesn't know where she's going asks someone she knows and trusts, believes the answer, and moves forward with confidence. It's a simple choice but one of total faith and surrender. That choice is ours today and in a thousand ways every day.

The choice comes with a comfort we can't reason or buy. That comfort is Jesus in the lead. He is the One we know and trust, and when we believe the answer He gives, we can move forward with confidence. We are His surrendered children.

EVENING

Lord, in choosing to follow You, I have made the very best choice. Thank You for taking on my troubles and giving me peace. Help me to be childlike as I trust You in even the smallest of decisions.

September 7

*"Bring them here to me," he said. . . . Taking the
five loaves and the two fish and looking up to heaven,
he gave thanks and broke the loaves. Then he gave them
to the disciples, and the disciples gave them to the people.*

MATTHEW 14:18–19 NIV

Sometimes the problem in front of us is big and overwhelming, certainly beyond our ability to solve. That's what Jesus' disciples saw in the thousands of hungry people on the hill. Their instinct was to send the problem away, but Jesus replied, "They do not need to go away. You give them something to eat" (Matthew 14:16).

Solve it, instead, He said. I can imagine the disciples' surprise—and Jesus' delight in knowing what was about to happen. We only have a little, they say, but He says it's enough. And that's what He tells us when we stand in front of big problems: "Run *toward* whatever you think is too much for you. Just bring whatever you have to Me."

Jesus knew what to do then and He'll know what to do with our offering now. It doesn't matter how small or unimpressive it might be. He can take any small gift we bring and multiply it to increase His glory.

*Lord, today I give You both my overwhelming problems
and the little things that trouble me. Please help me
work out a solution for each one. You know how to
turn them into situations that give You glory.*

September 8

MORNING

*Every good and perfect gift is from above, coming
down from the Father of the heavenly lights, who
does not change like shifting shadows.*

JAMES 1:17 NIV

We all know the brutally quiet times when God's voice seems silent. Scared, pressured, feeling the weight of a wicked world—or worse, the weight of our own guilt and regret—we can't seem to find even the tiniest comfort. The shards of our trust are buried in a crime scene of choices gone bad, but no sirens sound, no flashing lights signal help is on the way.

That's because the answer to any question we have has already arrived in the person of Jesus Christ. No matter how much it hurts or how abandoned we feel, His help is already here. No new answer doesn't mean no answer at all.

We'll never be so lost that Jesus can't find us, and maybe that's what God's saying in our times of silence: the promise of His grace and guidance remains. He doesn't change. No matter how crazy our world becomes, God's good and perfect gift of Jesus is always with us.

EVENING

*Lord Jesus, Your silence doesn't mean You don't care.
Please remind me to trust that Your aid is always on its
way. There were centuries of silence between the Old
and New Testaments—before You came on the scene and
changed everything. Remind me to wait for the things
You've promised, even in the times that You are silent.*

September 9

*"When the shepherd walks ahead of them, they
follow him because they know his voice."*
JOHN 10:4 NLV

An angel visited young Mary and told her an unlikely story: she would become mother of the Savior of the world, Jesus Christ. Surprised more than anyone has ever been, she responded out of a faith that knew and trusted God so well she could recognize His will in her life. Mary's one question was out of genuine practicality, a request to understand what would happen next: "How will this happen?" (Luke 1:34).

Mary's attitude was one of confident acceptance: *If God says so, it must be true, and I will act on it.* Joseph made the same choice, trusting God's voice that led him in the same unlikely direction.

Here is an example of the way we should respond when God's direction goes against our common sense. Sheep should never question the shepherd. . .especially when the Shepherd is the Lord of all creation. You know His voice. Just follow.

EVENING

*What need have I to doubt You, Lord? You know
everything beforehand. When doubts enter my mind,
please remind me of the scriptures and personal
experiences that prove I can always trust You.
I know that You have my best interests in mind.*

September 10

MORNING

> *"Keep on asking, and you will receive what you ask for.*
> *Keep on seeking, and you will find. Keep on knocking,*
> *and the door will be opened to you. For everyone who*
> *asks, receives. Everyone who seeks, finds. And to*
> *everyone who knocks, the door will be opened."*
>
> MATTHEW 7:7–8 NLT

Jesus doesn't play hide-and-seek with us, but He's not the town crier either. He's present, eager, and able, but rarely pushy, interruptive, or loud. He knows how we often panic when we're lost or confused. He knows we're desperate for answers, and He understands our pain when the answers seem slow or incomplete. But even in those times, He's teaching us trust.

When we ask for guidance and direction because we believe Jesus will supply it, we're demonstrating trust. When we beg for help from the only One we know can help, He honors that trust.

When we don't know what to do besides turn to Jesus, we always end up knowing the one next step. And one step at a time is all that's required of us. Keep on asking, seeking, and knocking. The door will ultimately open.

EVENING

> *Lord Jesus, I am turning to You, asking for Your help.*
> *Show me the next step and help me to trust in You for*
> *each step after that. You alone can open doors that I*
> *can't. I believe You will open the right ones for me.*

September 11

Do not keep good from those who should have it, when it is in your power to do it.

PROVERBS 3:27 NLV

Jesus was never about the audience, always about the affected. He based His actions on His unchanging mission. Unmoved by critics or complaints, He continued to help and heal. When He saw the need of a man in pain, He answered it. But the lovers of the law who watched Him so carefully missed Jesus demonstrating real love right in front of them.

So Jesus said to His critics, "I will ask you one thing. Does the Law say to do good on the Day of Rest or to do bad? To save life or to kill?" (Luke 6:9).

Just as Jesus was Lord of Israel's Sabbath day (and every other), He is Lord of our lives in every particular. As we encounter people we can help, may we follow His lead by keeping our focus on them, regardless of any criticism from others.

The best choice is always the one of mercy, help, love. . .and whatever else looks like Jesus.

EVENING

Lord, I want to serve You faithfully. Help me to do good without being distracted by the critics. Please keep my focus on the choices that look like You. I want to be concerned only with Your approval, not the nitpicking of others.

MORNING

*And this is my prayer: that your love may abound
more and more in knowledge and depth of insight,
so that you may be able to discern what is best and
may be pure and blameless for the day of Christ.*

PHILIPPIANS 1:9–10 NIV

Jesus gives us a lot of credit, trust, and opportunity to exercise the power of our relationship with Him. He believes that if we *know* what is right, we're more likely to *do* what is right. . .that's why He's so interested in making Himself known to us.

The more we know Jesus, the more we'll love Him. We'll see that everything He did for us was and is because He loves us—that's what guides Him. We hear it when He says we're not alone, we rejoice over it in answered prayer, and we see it in the care and help of a friend.

Jesus, Savior of the whole world, is the center of yours—just Him and you, together, navigating your way through this puzzling, temporary home. You grip the steering wheel, but His direction is what you need to know. You'll discover your way *with* Him.

EVENING

*Knowing You, Lord Jesus, I know where to go, because
Your love guides me. I thank You for leading me through
life and into eternity. I want to have Your knowledge and
insight to help me discern the best choices in my life.*

September 13

*"If you take your gift to the altar and remember your
brother has something against you, leave your gift on
the altar. Go and make right what is wrong between
you and him. Then come back and give your gift."*

MATTHEW 5:23–24 NLV

We start our day with requests for Jesus to guide us on the right
path, to give us answers and direction. We ask Him for the roadmap
to the mountaintop. Of course, He says, but the way may not be as
direct as you'd thought.

Before we know it, He's led us toward the tree line, straight into
the undergrowth. Clear the path, He says, and then we'll be moving
forward again.

We don't always like this part of the journey. But that thick,
twisted undergrowth of offenses, resentments, and simple misun-
derstandings between us and others needs to be addressed. Left
unattended, it will get in the way of everywhere we want to go with
God. Jesus tells us to go and clear up the mess so we can just go!

EVENING

*Lord, I want things to be right with my spiritual brothers
and sisters, so I can also be at peace with You. Help
me to clear away the underbrush in my life so that
I can walk with You. Help me to be humble and ask
forgiveness for the things I've done wrong and the
grudges I've held. I want to be free of any offense.*

MORNING

*Be wise in the way you live around those who are not Christians.
Make good use of your time. Speak with them in such a way
they will want to listen to you. Do not let your talk sound
foolish. Know how to give the right answer to anyone.*

COLOSSIANS 4:5–6 NLV

Every time we ask Jesus for direction and do what He says, people notice. We go forward in renewed strength and a well-exercised trust that never fails. Our walk becomes our witness, so let us be ever mindful of our words and actions so that Jesus is never misrepresented.

Sometimes those in pain are so lost that they can't imagine the Jesus we know. What an opportunity! If we step out on the faith and joy and dependence we know, if we keep stepping out because of our confidence in the One who knows us, perhaps others will come to know Him too.

Maybe when the lost and hurting see that Jesus guides our steps, the way we walk and talk won't be so hard to understand anymore. Others are always watching, so let's invite them along for the journey.

EVENING

*Oh, Jesus, I want to be wise in the way I live, making
good use of time and speaking carefully to all. I
never want to misrepresent Your character by living
in a such a way that dishonors You. Help me to live
so that others will clearly see You through my life.
Draw them to Yourself through my example.*

September 15

> *"Do for other people whatever you would*
> *like to have them do for you."*
> MATTHEW 7:12 NLV

We can complicate anything with our procedures and protocols, rules and regulations, history and histrionics. We listen to those who've studied more than we have or traveled more than we have and wonder how we'll become the disciples Jesus wants. We see the many times we've gone in the wrong direction and wonder how He'll ever find us useful. We can stop worrying.

Jesus made things simple. He told us to love, forgive, and share. He told us to be honest, fair, and hospitable. His every reaction was straightforward and uncomplicated.

If we want to follow Him, we can start today with the simplest of questions: Ask yourself what your next move will mean to those around you. How will your choices affect those you know and love? How will we model Jesus when we cross paths with others?

No need to worry—just ask and answer one simple, useful question each time. We don't need any information we don't already have.

> *Thank You, Jesus, for making things simple when*
> *others complicate them. Help me to ask the basic*
> *questions that ultimately reveal Your path. I*
> *want to follow Your "golden rule" of treating*
> *others exactly how I want to be treated!*

MORNING

Set my steps in Your Word. Do not let sin rule over me.
PSALM 119:133 NLV

Given long ago but so needed now, the apostle Paul's advice to believers is simple and profound: "Do not act like the sinful people of the world. Let God change your life. First of all, let Him give you a new mind. Then you will know what God wants you to do. And the things you do will be good and pleasing and perfect" (Romans 12:2).

That "new mind" is a daily challenge for us—and a daily comfort. Each day in our ordinary lives, in all the ordinary things we do, we can renew ourselves in God's extraordinary grace through Jesus Christ. So much is waiting! The new mind is learning new things from God's Word, understanding ever more what we should do.

The behavior we reflect is either that of the world or that of Jesus. Deciding which way we'll go is a conscious act of either defiance or obedience. Welcoming renewal begins with a small step in His direction.

EVENING

Lord Jesus, You have given me a new mind. May it overcome my old, sinful self in all I think and do. Please renew me day by day through the power and guidance of Your Word. Let me do what is good and pleasing in Your sight.

September 17

> *"These things dominate the thoughts of unbelievers, but
> your heavenly Father already knows all your needs. Seek
> the Kingdom of God above all else, and live righteously,
> and he will give you everything you need."*
>
> MATTHEW 6:32–33 NLT

We spend time and effort "gathering," worried about getting everything we need and want. When commonsense preparation devolves into a crazed preoccupation, we're in trouble. That overlooks our whole reason for being on earth.

Life isn't about how much we can hold but about where we are held. It's not about overcoming our needs but about needing only one thing.

When we know, believe, and trust Jesus to be who He says He is, we find peace. We live in a place where we are completely loved and cherished and directed. We can go about our days in total confidence, not trying to *get* so much as to *give*, not trying to build a kingdom but living in the one God's already designed for us.

It's a place of plenty, where we've learned to follow Jesus' lead.

EVENING

> *You provide all I need, Jesus. I'm grateful that I
> can trust in You instead of worrying about every
> unimportant thing. Help me to seek You above
> all else, and I will have all I need in You.*

MORNING

"I have given you an example to follow. Do as I have done to you."
JOHN 13:15 NLT

We can learn a lot by watching those around us live their lives of faith. We may not even realize all the examples of grace, patience, discernment, and forgiveness we've seen—until we need to find those qualities in ourselves. Then we'll remember, discovering help from others' experience.

Jesus always was and is the picture and pattern of love, no matter the situation. And at least one time, He thought it important enough to point that out. He washed His disciples' feet as a demonstration of love, showing humility and service. At other times, He modeled love and grace with His forgiveness, compassion, and wisdom. Whatever question or confusion we face, Jesus in some place and at some time demonstrated the best response.

If we watch and learn from Him (and those who love Him), we'll know what to do too.

EVENING

Lord Jesus, help me to model Your love to my family
and friends, and everyone else I meet. May I always
aspire to Your perfect example of grace and truth.
You gave me the perfect example to follow—help
me to do to others as You have done to me.

September 19

"But go and learn what this means: 'I desire mercy, not sacrifice.'
For I have not come to call the righteous, but sinners."

MATTHEW 9:13 NIV

Jesus was never afraid to go to untidy places, to talk to unschooled people, to bet on unproven hearts. He did what He always did because He could do nothing else. He did exactly as the Father told Him.

At a public dinner, facing criticism over His choice of friends, Jesus drew on the Old Testament prophet Hosea, who spoke of God's love and how we should love Him in return by loving others.

God is not interested in showy-but-empty declarations of our devotion—He wants to see mercy and loving-kindness toward others. At some time or another, we've all been the one who looks undesirable, unworthy, unlikely to share the Lord's company. . .but He came to us anyway. Following Him is about showing up for dinner but not showing off, letting compassion be our guide.

Jesus is looking for true hearts, the ones that wade in their own humility and seek ways to see others, not to be seen.

EVENING

I am not the judge of others, Lord, You are. Please
keep me from unmerciful attitudes, because You
have shown me so much mercy. Give me a heart of
compassion for others that draws them to You.

September 20

"Go and do likewise."
LUKE 10:37 NIV

Jesus' stories hit His followers where they lived. When that Good Samaritan helped a wounded traveler, Jesus was providing guidance for us all. When the unmerciful landowner, blessed and forgiven of his debts, offered no such treatment for the one who owed him, Jesus meant conviction for us all.

We've been the selfish, uncaring character in the story too many times. But Jesus never lets the vast distance between His perfection and our self-centered human nature interfere with His mercy. He doesn't plan our path based on the number of our mistakes in the rearview mirror. . .but He certainly uses our every experience to direct us.

The right choice is always mercy. The requirement is always faith, not fanfare. He's not looking for our grand ability, but our anchoring to forgiveness, love, and grace already received. We never know who will help us. . .or who will need us.

Let us be the conduit for Jesus' love. Fellow travelers are waiting.

EVENING

Oh, Jesus, forgive me for the times I've failed You. Guide me into the right and merciful choice as I live each day of this life. I want to follow You so closely that mercy and compassion become my natural instinct when I see someone in need—that I help without hesitation.

September 21

> *But whoever obeys His Word has the love of God made perfect in him. This is the way to know if you belong to Christ.*
>
> 1 JOHN 2:5 NLV

With great sadness we remember the times we ignored God's guidance. The guilt is heavy. But His mercy says, "Follow Me now. Let us make the best of all that remains."

Released from captivity, the Israelites went home to rebuild their ruined temple. They started working on their own houses, though, and the results weren't good. Through the prophet Haggai's guidance, with sincere remorse, they repented for the wrong way they'd gone. God forgave *them* and focused on going forward, on filling their lives to the full: "Is the seed still in the store-house? The vine, the fig tree, the pomegranate and the olive tree have not given any fruit. Yet from this day on I will bring good to you" (Haggai 2:19).

Peter's fragile faith led to his momentary betrayal of Jesus, but the Lord didn't let that change His plan for the great apostle. Jesus knows what great temples obedient believers can build. Anything in ruins is irrelevant. Looking back will not change anything that's been, but looking toward Jesus will change everything to come.

EVENING

> *Lord Jesus, thank You for forgiving me all the times I've failed. Show me how to move forward in righteousness as I keep my eyes on You. I want to focus on building Your kingdom, not my own. Shine Your love through me.*

September 22

MORNING

"It is bad for him who says to a piece of wood, 'Wake up!' or to a stone that cannot speak, 'Get up!' Can this teach you? See, it is covered with gold and silver. There is no breath in it."

HABAKKUK 2:19 NLV

Moses understood the principle of never looking back, of overcoming the past to get to a future. Because Moses had faith, he left Egypt. He was not afraid of the king's anger. Moses did not turn from the right way but "kept seeing God in front of him" (Hebrews 11:27).

Jesus leads us forward, through anything in the way. He won't get so far that we can't see Him, and He stays in front, awaiting our commitment to follow. We certainly can't lead ourselves out of any kind of captivity, but God can.

Maybe we're held back by guilt, addiction, illness, or debt—it doesn't matter. Looking anywhere except toward Jesus is what keeps us captive to these things. Going forward in our faith is what guides us away from them and toward the good work we'll do with Him.

EVENING

Lord Jesus, I want to keep my eyes on You as You lead me forward. Don't let anything hold me back from Your will. Nothing and no one in this world compares to You. I put my trust in You alone.

September 23

For God is not a God of disorder but of peace.
1 CORINTHIANS 14:33 NIV

Jesus always gave clear, forward-moving direction that said simply, "follow Me." In His encounters with the sick or hurt or lost, His words were straightforward and without confusion. He told the lame man to pick up his mat and walk. He told the guilty woman to go and sin no more.

Jesus always focused on the immediate task, and that led to eternal triumph. That's order and control, not worry and disarray. As we think about the obstacles in front of us, we see a tangled, scary mess...but Jesus sees a box of choices. He points out the most obvious one, the one that will lead us where He wants us to go. It's up to us to believe and follow.

Yes, there's another box, full of the choice to worry and fuss. We'll get to that box too. But first, today, do this one thing: simplify the confusing. Listen, understand, obey, move.

EVENING

*Lord Jesus, keep me focused on Your simple way
and the task You have for me for today. I don't
want to worry—I want to obey You. As I conclude
this day, let me rest in Your peace and wake up
ready to choose Your peace again tomorrow.*

MORNING

Make it your goal to live a quiet life, minding your own business and working with your hands, just as we instructed you before.

1 THESSALONIANS 4:11 NLT

Practical, gimme-a-plan types find great comfort in the apostle Paul's three-point directive above. The answers we need usually fall in there somewhere.

Yes, it's hard to find the "quiet life" in our cymbal-clanging, attention-demanding world, but Jesus modeled that life for us. His singular focus—following only God's direction—kept His life in peace.

When we see too much chaos, too much drama, and we don't know what to do, let's listen carefully for the quiet voice of God, which drowns out all the other voices saying they know better. What does *He* say?

Quiet means focused, confident, committed, and unafraid to trust Jesus' lead.

EVENING

Lord Jesus, all the chaos and drama of this world can be so distracting. Help me to listen for Your quiet voice today. I want to hear You clearly and live a life that honors You.

September 25

His mother said to the helpers, "Do whatever He says."
JOHN 2:5 NLV

No matter how smart we think we are, we can get lost trying to take someone else's road. Many of those around Jesus wanted Him to be the warrior king that would save them in worldly battles with stunning heads-on-sticks victories. He said no.

It was Jesus' business to save His people from this world and teach us how to help save others. *That's* the plan Jesus followed to the end. He never wavered or tried to do anything other than what He began. That's a practical focus that says "tend to your work where you are." That was John's approach—he baptized where there was "much water" (John 3:23). With no worries about what wasn't there, he used what was and carried on.

God's guidance always fits *you*, not another person. And when you put it on, then you can really go places with Jesus, minding the business He says is yours. Do whatever *He* says.

EVENING

I want to do what You say, Jesus, instead of following anyone else's plan. Strengthen me to tend to the work You have given me. You alone can guide me in what You tell me to do. Help me never to waver or grow distracted.

MORNING

*Do not merely listen to the word, and so
deceive yourselves. Do what it says.*

JAMES 1:22 NIV

We want that big purpose, that world-changing mission that only we can do. We want what we do to matter. And we don't have to wait. Jesus' mission *did* change the world, but it also changed one person at a time.

Sometimes the most important thing Jesus could do was a very small thing He did willingly. He paid attention and didn't overlook the chance to help, to be in the flesh what He was in the Spirit. We can too.

Yes, our big purpose will take all the days God's given us—just like Jesus—but the way is one day at a time. Let each of us ask, *What can I do right now in my family, my job, my church, my community?* Let us pay attention, as we consider the whole big world, to the one person we see in front of us.

EVENING

*Lord, if I listen to Your Word and don't do it, I
am spiritually empty. May I follow Your teaching
and example and change the world one person
at a time. Teach me to truly see each person with
whom I come in contact each day. Open my eyes
even to those the world has overlooked.*

September 27

> *"You have done well. You are a good and faithful servant.*
> *You have been faithful over a few things. I will put*
> *many things in your care. Come and share my joy."*
> MATTHEW 25:21 NLV

Jesus told the story of a man who gave three servants bags of gold. He was pleased with the two who were unafraid to go forward and used what they had been given to make more. That's our story every day: our trust must match our bag of gold.

Let us receive what Jesus gives us and hide nothing. Let us know that every divine touch is meant to be used in the most human ways. When He gives us boldness, wisdom, compassion, and talent—and He will, regularly—let us ask who needs the blessing of those gifts passed on. Let us listen and follow Him.

Others will see when God elevates the most ordinary and humble to "good and faithful." We become effective representatives for Jesus when we're grateful for all we've been given and let Him direct us to use it all well.

EVENING

> *I don't want to hide my gifts in the ground, Lord Jesus.*
> *May I faithfully use everything You give me to shine for*
> *Your glory. Show me how I can best invest the talents*
> *that You have given me to advance Your kingdom.*

MORNING

> *"We have no power to face this vast army that is attacking us. We do not know what to do, but our eyes are on you."*
>
> 2 CHRONICLES 20:12 NIV

"What now?" we ask when our enemies—even those who never carry arms—approach, and we see no good way to go.

When Judah's King Jehoshaphat was outnumbered and about to be attacked, his completely dependent response was to put it all on God. His was a confident, expectant faith.

What a comfort that leadership must have been to his men! In his transparency, Jehoshaphat showed everyone that prayer and surrender to God's control is the first move to make, not the last. The king couldn't see himself doing anything on his own, but he believed that God would show him the way.

Sometimes we're the warriors who need to see a faithful disciple live out that faith in a frightful time. And sometimes it's up to us to lead others into the fray, encouraged and unafraid. When the first step is always in Jesus' direction, perfect direction will follow.

EVENING

> *When I have no idea where to turn, Jesus, may I turn to You. Thank You for defending, protecting, and guiding me, in every circumstance. My eyes are on You, waiting for You to lead me in the way that will bring You glory and welcome others into Your family.*

September 29

In everything set them an example by doing what is good. In your teaching show integrity, seriousness and soundness of speech that cannot be condemned.

TITUS 2:7–8 NIV

We often learn the most when we teach someone else. We become quick studies of the tips and tricks that make our tasks easier. Knowing what Jesus wants us to do isn't a formula or a spreadsheet, but it is something we learn even better by teaching.

When your life offers you a choice between different roads, you must choose. Sometimes those roads are major highways with lifelong implications. They matter greatly. But far more often, the choice is a tiny little trail that reveals far more about who (and whose) you are.

The "least of these" (Matthew 25:40) moments are everywhere, and others see when we act with love, courage, humility, and compassion. Jesus walks among us, giving us the opportunity to walk with Him and bring others along too. What an awesome privilege! We travel this world in His footsteps, and we teach those around us how to follow Him too.

EVENING

Lord Jesus, keep me faithful to You so I can help lead others into Your loving arms. May I follow You closely and set an example for others by doing exactly what You have me to do. Help me to show integrity and sound speech that represent You well.

MORNING

For this God is our God for ever and ever;
he will be our guide even to the end.

PSALM 48:14 NIV

Jesus once exclaimed, "I have come into the world as a light, so that no one who believes in me should stay in darkness" (John 12:46).

That's a promise that will never fail—and brings us right back where we started this month. When we know and believe in the most faithful Guide ever, we leave the darkness, never to return. We can let go of fear and confusion and worry and doubt and never be lost again.

We know how to put trust in the Savior who came to put Himself in our hearts. And we hold tight to the opportunities to obey and follow Him, even through the dimly lit times, with great courage and confidence so others may see their journey lighted as well.

Your life will cause others to ask in awe, "How do you know what to do?"

Stand in the light of Jesus, the One you know and love, the One who knows and loves you. Say in pure devotion, "I go where He leads."

EVENING

Light of my life, I thank You for Your guidance
through even the darkest of days. Empower me
to follow You everywhere, every day. I pray that
You will give me clarity for the questions I have
and the situations I will face tomorrow. Lead and
guide me through every aspect of this life.

October 1

His divine power has given us everything we need
for a godly life through our knowledge of him who
called us by his own glory and goodness.

2 PETER 1:3 NIV

Autumn is falling, and change is in the air.

Change can be good, but it often brings stress. Oftentimes, people who live apart from God (and sometimes even Christians) try to dig down deep and muster the strength and energy to power through difficult times of change. Then they crash.

But the relentless call from Jesus is "Come to Me. . . ." He wants to supply you with everything you need, including the power and endurance to do what He has called you to.

In times of change—really, all the time—welcome Jesus into every detail. Talk with Him, listen for His voice in return, and request His supernatural strength to help you. Then watch in amazement at what He does.

He is the unchanging, everlasting God. As you head into a season of change, remember to fall into the steady arms of Jesus.

Change can be scary, Lord. But I know I need not
fear when You are in every detail. Please hold
me fast in Your strong, steady arms. You make
the change into an adventure so that I don't
have to be afraid of the coming season.

MORNING

"I, even I, am the Lord. There is no one who saves except Me. . . .
I am God and always will be. No one is able to take anything
out of My hand. I do something, and who can change it?"

ISAIAH 43:11, 13 NLV

We live in a world of falsity. Fake smiles. Fake news. Fake people. Children and adults both are addicted to screens, finding it hard to relate to the real world. Surrounded by so much unreality, it's hard to know what is true and good. But God the Father wants you to know and live in the truth that *He* is. He is the unchanging, everlasting God.

And, to keep the theme of this book, so is Jesus. The writer of Hebrews reminded us that "Jesus Christ is the same yesterday and today and forever" (13:8). We know Jesus was loving and compassionate to the people He met two thousand years ago. He's still that way today. We know He was wise and powerful when He formed the universe (1:3). He's just as wise and powerful today. And, Christian woman, He is on your side!

EVENING

There is nothing false in You, Jesus. Thank You for
always being the same—and for always saving anyone
who comes to You. I never have to wonder about Your
character because You will always be who You have
always been. Help me to have the same unwavering
character and integrity that You have, Lord.

October 3

*So all of us who have had that veil removed can see
and reflect the glory of the Lord. And the Lord—
who is the Spirit—makes us more and more like him
as we are changed into his glorious image.*

2 CORINTHIANS 3:18 NLT

God's Word reminds us, over and over, that we are to be light in a world darkened by sin. Where do we get that light? It comes from God Himself, from spending time in His presence. Think of those solar lights people put along their sidewalks: the longer they're in the light of a sunny day, the brighter and warmer they glow.

When you spend time with Jesus, He lights up everything about you. Psalm 34:5 says, "Those who look to him for help will be radiant with joy; no shadow of shame will darken their faces." You can emanate His light, His love, His peace, even during times of change, because you've been soaking in it. Ask Jesus to give you a deep desire for His Presence. He'll answer, and you'll begin to light up your world.

*Lord Jesus, I am thankful You reflect Your light
through me into this dark world. Give me an ever
deeper desire for Your presence so that I can shine
more brightly for You. I want to be like a lighthouse
that protects sailors from the treacherous rocks.*

MORNING

> *"Do not be afraid. For I have bought you and made you free. I have called you by name. You are Mine! . . . You are of great worth in My eyes. You are honored and I love you."*
>
> ISAIAH 43:1, 4 NLV

During times of change, it's important to remember who you are and to whom you belong. Take another look at today's scripture: Can you picture Jesus saying these words directly to *you*? Do you really believe that God loves you this much?

When God Himself tells you who you are, it changes everything! Let Him speak to your heart every day and remind you of your worth—how much you matter to Him. Before you get out of bed every morning, thank God for a new day and ask Him to remind you of His truth.

You are God's child because you accepted Jesus' work on the cross. You have nothing to fear. God is always with you and calls you by name. You are of great value to Him.

EVENING

> *Lord Jesus, You have purchased me out of sin! You call me by name. May I never worry about other people's thoughts of me—Your attention is all that matters. You saw me as a lost sheep, and You left the beauty of heaven for a time to come to earth and restore me to Yourself.*

October 5

*The LORD is my strength and shield. I trust him with all
my heart. He helps me, and my heart is filled with joy.
I burst out in songs of thanksgiving. . . . Lead them like
a shepherd, and carry them in your arms forever.*

PSALM 28:7, 9 NLT

In times of change, Jesus is right there with you, ready to help in
any way you need. God values you and He is committed to caring
for you in every way.

The Lord leads you like a shepherd leading his sheep. He even
carries you in His arms! Jesus knows exactly what you need, and
He knows how to get you from one place to the next. When you let
Him help you work through your challenges and feelings and fears,
miraculous things happen. Things you didn't even think were possible
begin to take place before your eyes.

Picture yourself, a little lamb carried in the arms of Jesus. Nothing
in the world can disrupt the peace and security He provides. Rest in
His hold today and trust that He will face the battles for you.

EVENING

*Lord, I need You to carry me through my troubles. I look
forward to the miraculous things You'll do on my behalf.
While changes can seem overwhelming, I know that
nothing is impossible for You. I rest in Your promises.*

October 6

> *"For the Holy Spirit will teach you at that*
> *time what you should say."*
>
> LUKE 12:12 NIV

Some people thrive in high-pressure environments. Others tend to run from them. Whether you thrive, run, or land somewhere in the middle, Jesus wants to help.

Next time you find yourself in an intimidating situation, just take a deep breath and relax. *That sounds great*, you may be thinking. *But how?*

Here's the thing: if Jesus Christ is alive in you, then He is at work. If He wants you to do or say something in a particular situation, you can trust Him to give you the guidance you need. And you don't even have to worry about it ahead of time.

This is a faith thing, and it might take some practice—so whenever you know you're headed into a stressful situation, be sure to take Jesus with you. Invite Him to speak to you. Tell Him how you're feeling. Then let it rest in His hands.

EVENING

Lord, in stressful times I often don't even know how
to pray. Give me words that will glorify You, and
help me to wait for Your rescue from every crisis—
even the ones that I've gotten myself into. May
everything I say, Jesus, come from and honor You.

October 7

Don't worry about anything; instead, pray about everything. Tell God what you need, and thank him for all he has done. Then you will experience God's peace, which exceeds anything we can understand. His peace will guard your hearts and minds as you live in Christ Jesus.

PHILIPPIANS 4:6–7 NLT

Science and common sense both show that holding anxiety and worry inside can harm our bodies. It's actually dangerous to carry such heavy burdens, but it often seems as though they're inevitable during stressful times of change.

God wants you always to take your fears and worries to Him. He wants you thankful rather than stressed—and He alone can help you with that. When you turn to Him in grateful prayer, He gives you His peace. It's a peace that won't make sense to anyone but you and God. . . a peace that floods your heart no matter what you're facing.

Just sit down with Jesus and say, "Lord, it's too much. I don't know what to do." Release everything into His hands and allow Him to carry your burdens.

EVENING

Lord Jesus, right now I cast my cares on You. I thank You for everything You have done and all You will do for me. You know what I need and what is best for me. Help me to guard my mind against fear and worry. Please fill me with Your peace.

MORNING

*A cheerful heart is good medicine, but a
broken spirit saps a person's strength.*

PROVERBS 17:22 NLT

Change and stress go hand in hand. And we know that stress is hard on us, both physically and mentally. That's one reason God doesn't want us to carry everything on our shoulders.

Life can be hard. Traumatic things do happen. Does God want you to just sweep them under the rug and paste on a fake happy face? No... Jesus invites you to go to Him with all your struggles. He knows how hard life can be (He lived a pretty challenging human life Himself), and He wants you to know that He is with you. He will stay with you through anything you face, everything that could possibly sap your spirit's strength.

As you linger in Jesus' presence, give Him permission to comfort you and give you a cheerful heart. In times of stress and change, He will fill you with true joy, cheering your heart and mind. That's the best medicine you could ever take.

EVENING

*Lord, I invite You into all my struggles, to comfort me
and fill me with joy. May I show the world a cheerful
heart reflecting Your presence in my life. Heal my broken
spirit when it threatens to sap my strength. Your joy
is the very best medicine I could ever hope to find.*

October 9

Let the peace of Christ rule in your hearts, since as members
of one body you were called to peace. And be thankful.
COLOSSIANS 3:15 NIV

"Let the peace of Christ rule in your heart" means you have an inner calm that can only come from trusting Jesus. As problems arise (and they will), you are pacified by the Lord's power over anything and everything. Letting the peace of Christ rule in your heart means you'll begin to see life as an adventure of overcoming. Along with Jesus, you'll anticipate challenges and changes instead of fearing them, knowing that God will bring good out of everything that you submit to Him.

Get in the daily habit of praying, taking all of your problems, worries, and concerns to Jesus—then enjoy the peace He offers. And thank Him for His peace, working in your heart, as you make your way through the changes of life. He's walking through them with you and leading You with joy.

EVENING

Jesus, I thank You for Your peace. I know I can face
every problem with Your calmness in my heart. Help
me to give thanks and walk in peace with Your people
so that we can advance Your kingdom here on earth.

October 10

When I am afraid, I put my trust in you.
PSALM 56:3 NIV

Have you ever wasted time and energy worrying about something that ended up working itself out? The uncertainties of life can put us in a place of almost overwhelming fear, and fear of the unknown brings sleeplessness and stress.

Ever since Adam and Eve's disobedience brought sin into the world, humans have struggled with fear of the future. But Jesus has said, "Who of you by worrying can add a single hour to your life? Since you cannot do this very little thing, why do you worry about the rest?" (Luke 12:25–26).

Jesus calls you to come to Him for rest. You can unload your biggest worries and fears and trust Him with all of them. Remember, He has promised always to be with you. So place your questions, your concerns, your unsettled fears in His capable hands. He will calm your anxious heart.

EVENING

Lord Jesus, why do I worry when I can trust You for everything? This is such a common problem, but as a believer, I know that You always have my best in mind. Remind me that You can handle whatever happens in my life. I thank You for replacing my fears with peace.

October 11

"I have told you these things, so that in me you may
have peace. In this world you will have trouble.
But take heart! I have overcome the world."
JOHN 16:33 NIV

C. S. Lewis has written, "Life with God is not immunity from difficulties but peace within difficulties." These words reflect Jesus' warning that we *will* have trouble in this world. After all, this world isn't heaven, so we can't expect our lives to be perfect. But Jesus offers something amazing in the midst of our troubles: His presence, which in turn brings perfect peace.

The world God created is a beautiful place. But because of sin, it's also a messed-up place—a constantly changing place that quickly causes fear and worry. We live in a fallen world, and things will never be wholly right until Jesus returns. In the meantime, He promises to be with us, helping us overcome this world and the heartburn it causes us.

Don't expect an *ideal* life on this earth. Just embrace the reality of God's peace and presence in your life.

Lord, my life has never been "ideal," but it has often
been good—especially since I met You. I know that I no
longer have to bear the burden of fear and troubled
thoughts. You have already overcome this world. Please
help me to overcome it too, by walking in Your peace.

October 12

"Anyone who listens to my teaching and follows it is wise, like a person who builds a house on solid rock. Though the rain comes in torrents and the floodwaters rise and the winds beat against that house, it won't collapse because it is built on bedrock."

MATTHEW 7:24–25 NLT

The Leaning Tower of Pisa is famous for its poor foundation. It leans precariously, and vast amounts of time and money have been expended trying to correct the problem. All this because the tower was built on soft land, with a foundation only about ten feet deep.

Without doubt, foundations are important—for construction projects as well as for life. That's especially true when the earth below us starts to shift and change.

Is your foundation built on the solid rock of Jesus Christ? Aligning your heart and mind with God's truth will keep you firm and steady, no matter what's happening around you. When the earth below is shifting, you can hang on to the truth of Jesus' great love for you. If your hope is built on Him, you will not fall (Psalm 121:3–5).

EVENING

Jesus, I want You to be my firm foundation. I know I can always stand firm in Your love. Please help me do that in my daily choices. May I send my roots deep into Your good ground—may I be firmly anchored in You.

October 13

Cast all your anxiety on him because he cares for you.

1 Peter 5:7 niv

In the Amplified Bible, today's scripture reads like this: "casting all your cares [all your anxieties, all your worries, and all your concerns, once and for all] on Him, for He cares about you [with deepest affection, and watches over you very carefully]."

Have you ever cast a specific care on Jesus, only to later reel it back in? This amplification of this famous verse implores us to cast all of our cares, anxieties, worries, and concerns onto Jesus—and then leave them with Him once and for all. But how do we do that in reality?

It's a test of your faith. Do you truly believe that Jesus cares about you with the deepest affection and concern? Do you really believe that He constantly and carefully watches over you—today and every day? If you can answer "yes" to those questions, you will trust the Lord's faithfulness to care for you. You'll allow Him to handle every one of your worries—today and every day.

EVENING

*Lord, when I cast my anxiety on You, I don't want
to reel it back again. Help me to trust that You
will take care of that problem—that You will
never fail me. I know that You care for me.*

MORNING

> *Give your burdens to the LORD, and he will take care of you. He will not permit the godly to slip and fall.*
>
> PSALM 55:22 NLT

"Lord, I don't know what to do right now!" That's a valid prayer. Though you feel helpless in the telling, Jesus wants you to come with that kind of humility. Not every challenge has a good solution, humanly speaking. You can't fix everything, even when you want to. Some things were never yours to fix in the first place. When you're in over your head, Jesus is there.

A modern paraphrase of today's scripture verse says, "Pile your troubles on GOD's shoulders—he'll carry your load, he'll help you out. He'll never let good people topple into ruin" (The Message).

When you're going through times of change, ask Jesus to help you discern His voice. Ask Him to make Himself clear. Then simply rest and trust, knowing that He is faithful and that He has good plans for you.

EVENING

> *Oh, Jesus, how many times have I not known what to do! Help me to discern Your voice when I am confused. I turn over my burdens to You so that You can take care of them—and take care of me. I want to trust You and enjoy Your peace.*

October 15

> *When anxiety was great within me, your*
> *consolation brought me joy.*
>
> PSALM 94:19 NIV

You probably already know that Psalm 119:11 urges us to hide God's Word in our hearts. And that Jesus said, "The Advocate, the Holy Spirit, whom the Father will send in my name, will teach you all things and will remind you of everything I have said to you" (John 14:26).

Hide the following scriptures in your heart and ask the Holy Spirit to remind you of them when you need them most:

- "Peace I leave with you; my peace I give you. I do not give to you as the world gives. Do not let your hearts be troubled and do not be afraid" (John 14:27).
- "I keep my eyes always on the LORD. With him at my right hand, I will not be shaken" (Psalm 16:8).
- "God has said, 'Never will I leave you; never will I forsake you.' So we say with confidence, 'The Lord is my helper; I will not be afraid. What can mere mortals do to me?'" (Hebrews 13:5–6).

EVENING

> *Lord Jesus, I want to hide Your Word in my heart so*
> *that I can know and follow You well. Remind me to*
> *turn to Your Word when I need comfort and joy. Your*
> *promises bring me peace when I feel anxiety rising.*

October 16

*"I have loved you just as My Father has loved Me.
Stay in My love. If you obey My teaching, you will live in
My love. In this way, I have obeyed My Father's teaching
and live in His love. I have told you these things so
My joy may be in you and your joy may be full."*

JOHN 15:9–11 NLV

Jesus very plainly told us how we can show God that we love Him:
by obeying His commands. What are those commands? To love Him
and to love others. Everything in God's law, Jesus said, depends on
those two things (Matthew 22:36–40).

The Bible warns us never to forget our first love, Jesus. Here's what
He Himself told the church in first-century Ephesus: "You do not love
Me as you did at first. Remember how you once loved Me. Be sorry
for your sin and love Me again as you did at first" (Revelation 2:4–5).

This world is ever changing, but our love for Jesus must remain
firm. He has given us clear direction for staying in His love and returning to it when need be. What an amazing Lord we serve!

*You loved me first, Jesus, so I could love others. Help
me to obey Your teaching—to love You first and then
love others as You have loved me. I know that love is
the basis of all Your commands, so may I love well.*

October 17

There is no one like You among the gods, O Lord. And there are no works like Yours. All the nations You have made will come and worship before You, O Lord. And they will bring honor to Your name. For You are great and do great things. You alone are God.

PSALM 86:8–10 NLV

Time spent with Jesus will accomplish more than anything else you could ever do. Worry and stress cause harm but taking everything to Jesus in prayer shifts the burden onto His capable shoulders.

Make Jeremiah 32:17 your sincere prayer today: "O Lord God! See, You have made the heavens and the earth by Your great power and by Your long arm! Nothing is too hard for You!"

Over the course of the day, repeat that verse again and again. Ask God to help you, believing that He can do anything. No problem is too hard, too big, or too small for His help. Remember, Jesus said His Father cares when sparrows fall to the ground. . .and that He cares for *you* in much greater measure (Matthew 10:29–31).

EVENING

Oh, Jesus, You said that Your Father knows every sparrow that falls. . .and every hair on my head. That level of knowledge—and the love You showed when You died on the cross—is beyond my comprehension. There is no one like You, Lord. I worship and honor You today for who You are and all You've done.

October 18

*Trust in the LORD with all your heart and lean not on
your own understanding. In all your ways submit
to him, and he will make your paths straight.*

PROVERBS 3:5–6 NIV

Good decision-making is a vital life skill—especially when we face
the stressful uncertainties of this world. But we often make things
harder than they need to be. Why? Because we forget that Jesus
wants to help us make our decisions. When we leave Him out of
the process, it causes us unnecessary trouble. But it doesn't have
to be that way.

Go to Jesus in prayer. Talk to Him about the decisions facing
you. Ask Him to forgive you for the times you've left Him out of the
equation. Ask Him to transform your thinking. Then listen for His
voice as you go through your day, trusting that He will be with you.
Jesus, your good Shepherd, will always lead you in the right way.

EVENING

*Forgive me, Lord, for all the times I've left You out of
my decision-making. Transform my mind so that I can
always follow Your will. May I trust in You with all
my heart and leave my own understanding behind.*

October 19

MORNING

Now may the Lord of peace himself give you peace at all times and in every way. The Lord be with all of you.

2 Thessalonians 3:16 niv

Imagine being taught by someone who really knows the answer to everything. That's the case with Jesus, and the amazing news is that He *wants* to teach you. Centuries before Jesus' birth, the prophet Isaiah wrote, "All your children will be taught by the Lord, and great will be their peace" (54:13). If you've committed your life to Jesus Christ, His Spirit is within you to teach you all things—and that results in peace.

Jesus has authority and power over *all things*. It's important to remember that truth in every moment, every challenge, every circumstance, because it means you can go to Him with every question. He is bigger than all of your problems, failures, and fears—bigger than the changes, uncertainties, and struggles of your life.

You have access to this divine power at every moment!

EVENING

You have power over my whole life, Jesus—let me never forget that. I offer all I have and am to You. May I sit at Your feet and learn from You like Mary did. Teach me to live in Your power and peace.

October 20

He reached down from heaven and rescued me; he drew me out of deep waters. He rescued me from my powerful enemies, from those who hated me and were too strong for me. They attacked me at a moment when I was in distress, but the LORD supported me. He led me to a place of safety; he rescued me because he delights in me.

PSALM 18:16–19 NLT

Ever been in big trouble—or, as today's scripture puts it, "deep waters"? At some time or another, we all face situations that just seem too big to handle, times we feel we have nothing firm to stand on. And we're not sure we can tread water long enough for anything to change.

But you know what? The Lord supports you. Jesus cares about everything that has happened, is currently happening, or ever will happen to you. . .and He wants to reach down from heaven to help. He will lead you to a place of safety, and He can use any means He chooses to meet any need you have.

Just talk to Jesus about your struggles. He loves to change things for the better.

EVENING

Lord Jesus, I trust that You will rescue me from every trouble. Thank You for caring about my trials and bringing me to safety. Thank You for coming down from heaven to prove how much You care.

October 21

> *The LORD gives his people strength.*
> *The LORD blesses them with peace.*
>
> PSALM 29:11 NLT

On our own, we'll never find lasting peace. But when we obey God, He gives us true peace. That's good news! Though there is a bit of a catch. . . it's definitely not a once-for-all thing.

Here's what the psalm writer David told us to do: "Turn away from evil and do good. Search for peace, and work to maintain it. The eyes of the LORD watch over those who do right; his ears are open to their cries for help" (Psalm 34:14–15). This means we have the privilege of giving our worries to Jesus and replacing them with obedience. . .every single day.

Turn away from evil and toward God to find peace. You can't assume that trouble won't find you. . .the enemy is constantly looking for ways to destroy our peace by getting us to turn away from God (1 Peter 5:8). Ask Jesus to keep you facing in the right direction.

EVENING

Jesus, please turn me from evil and toward
You. May I continually seek Your peace by my
obedience. Let me not be fooled by the enemy's
attempts to draw me away from You.

MORNING

You will lead me by telling me what I should do.
And after this, You will bring me into shining-greatness.

PSALM 73:24 NLV

Moment-by-moment, Jesus is with you, ready to guide you through any and every situation. He wants to speak to you. He wants to share in your joy during times of blessing and comfort you in pain and sadness. And He wants to give you wisdom for times of change and choices.

The prophet Isaiah wrote, "Your ears will hear a word behind you, saying, 'This is the way, walk in it,' whenever you turn to the right or to the left" (Isaiah 30:21). For Christians, that means you don't have to figure things out by yourself.

The Holy Spirit is inside you, always speaking wisdom. He will guide you as you listen for Him. He will make the Lord's expectations clear. If Jesus wants you to know something, you will hear it again and again—through the Word, through a song, through the voice of a faithful friend. The ways God speaks are limitless. Be listening!

EVENING

I want to walk in Your way, Lord Jesus. Help me to listen
to Your Spirit so I can live in Your glory. Your still, small
voice will direct me on the path, telling me which way
I ought to go. Give me the humility to listen and obey.

October 23

> *When they saw the courage of Peter and John and realized that they were unschooled, ordinary men, they were astonished and they took note that these men had been with Jesus.*
>
> ACTS 4:13 NIV

Peter and John obeyed Jesus' command to go tell the world about Him. These apostles weren't educated people; they were simple fishermen. But they spoke and acted courageously because they knew Jesus personally. Peter and John had been with Jesus and that made all the difference. He had given them authority, and it showed.

You have received authority from Jesus too. Are you walking in it? Are you living and speaking with the courage you receive from knowing Him? Can people around you tell that you've been with Jesus?

Through Him, supernatural power is available to you. Jesus is ready to help you in whatever challenges you face. Spend more time with Him. Like Peter and John, you'll become the courageous believer He wants you to be.

EVENING

> *Oh, Jesus, I need Your supernatural power to live with confidence. Remind me that education and experiences are good, but they cannot compare to time in Your presence. Help me to desire and pursue more time with You, in Your Word and prayer.*

MORNING

> *Rejoice always, pray continually, give thanks in all circumstances; for this is God's will for you in Christ Jesus.*
> 1 THESSALONIANS 5:16–18 NIV

If, as a follower of Jesus, you've ever wondered what God's will is, you can start right here. Sometimes things are spelled out so clearly that you simply can't miss the truth: "Rejoice always, pray continually, give thanks in all circumstances."

This is a clear directive. But we might read the apostle Paul's words and think, *How could I possibly rejoice all the time? How can I pray continually? How can I be thankful in every situation? How can I do those things during times of challenge and change?*

Well, the Bible answers those questions too. You *can't* do these things on your own. You can only succeed through the power of the Holy Spirit, who is alive and working in you (Romans 8:26–27). Jesus sent His Spirit to fill His followers. As always, He has you covered.

EVENING

> *Lord Jesus, I cannot succeed in my own power. I ask You to live through me, through the Spirit You have put inside me. Guide me to pray in all situations and give thanks even when things get hard. Help me to always rejoice.*

October 25

For You have set my soul free from death. You have kept my feet from falling, so I may walk with God in the light of life.

PSALM 56:13 NLV

Jesus wants you to take a long walk with Him. . .a walk that truly never ends.

Walking with Him means having a relationship with your Creator and Savior. It is knowing Him, loving Him, trusting Him, worshipping Him in each moment. What does that look like in everyday life? It's more than just reading a Bible passage and checking God off your to-do list for the day. It's knowing that Jesus is with you in every moment and inviting Him to be part of your daily experience. It's allowing Him to be involved in every conversation you have, every thought you think, and everything you do. It's starting each day with gratitude, seeing your life from an eternal perspective.

As you pray, invite Jesus to take your hand on this walk. See Him as a friend, a confidant, a lover of your soul. He needs to be the focus of your whole day. When He is the center of your life, you will go places you've never imagined you could. Where will He lead you today?

EVENING

Jesus, please take my hand and walk with me today. May You be part of everything I think and say and do. Be the center of my world.

October 26

I know how to get along with little and how to live when I have much. I have learned the secret of being happy at all times. If I am full of food and have all I need, I am happy. If I am hungry and need more, I am happy. I can do all things because Christ gives me the strength.

PHILIPPIANS 4:12–13 NLV

Happiness may not seem like a choice, especially when circumstances have you down. But the book of Philippians suggests otherwise. The apostle Paul said he figured out "the secret."

Spoiler alert: the secret is contentment, a conscious decision to allow Jesus Christ to be your source of strength and happiness no matter what.

Are you content? Take an honest inventory. If you often find yourself wishing for some "better" thing, ask Jesus to fill you with contentment instead. Intentionally thank Him for the place you live, the job you have, the family you're part of, the friends He's given you.

It takes a supernatural power to choose happiness each day, but notice the end of today's scripture: "I can do all things because Christ gives me the strength."

You get to make this choice, every single day. Jesus will help.

Give me Your power to be content today, Lord Jesus. I want to find peace, joy, and the ability to accomplish the work You've set before me. You have blessed me in amazing ways—help me to recognize and acknowledge each one.

October 27

Christ was before all things. All things are held together by Him.

CoLOSSIANS 1:17 NLV

Jesus holds the whole world together—and He holds you too. He is more powerful than anything you can imagine, yet He loves you and cares for you, deeply and personally. He knows everything about you, including those hard things you're enduring right now. And He will show up and be very real in your life. . .if you let Him.

Jesus wants you to go to Him every day, talking with Him about everything. Whether your problem feels too small (or too big?) for God, tell Jesus what you're thinking and how you really feel. Ask Him to help you believe how much He cares.

The closer you get to Jesus, the more you walk with Him every day, the more your thoughts will begin to match His thoughts. Your problems will seem much smaller as you experience the greatness of Christ, who holds the whole world together.

EVENING

*You, Lord Jesus, hold everything together—including
my little world. Let me sense Your power and presence
in my life and know that You walk with me every
moment. May I never be so stressed by this world
that I forget that You hold it in Your hands.*

MORNING

Jesus said, "Come!" Peter got out of the boat and walked on the water to Jesus. But when he saw the strong wind, he was afraid. He began to go down in the water. He cried out, "Lord, save me!"

MATTHEW 14:29–30 NLV

It seems Jesus loves a good adventure. Today's scripture describes a moment when He welcomed His friend Peter to step out of his boat and walk on top of the water. You already know how the story goes: Peter jumped out of the boat and walked on the wind-whipped waters, like Jesus. But then he noticed the swirling seas and took his eyes off the Lord. In that split second, realizing he was doing something impossible, Peter grew frightened and sank like a stone.

It's easy to become frightened when we take our eyes off Jesus. But none of us need to live in fear. Here's what Jesus says to you: "Take hope. It is I. Do not be afraid!" (Matthew 14:27). Keep your eyes on Jesus and no storm can touch you.

EVENING

Lord, as we go through life's adventure together, I want always to keep my eyes on You. Please banish my fear and remind me that You are constantly keeping me safe. When the waves threaten, I know that You are controlling the storm.

October 29

> *You, God, are awesome in your sanctuary; the God of Israel*
> *gives power and strength to his people. Praise be to God!*
>
> PSALM 68:35 NIV

Times of hardship and change are inevitable. But something powerful happens when you take your gaze off your situation and turn it to Jesus. Today, let worship be your focus and see how it changes things.

Music, scripture memory, telling a friend what God's doing in your life—they're all forms of worship. Thank God, through Jesus Christ, for all the blessings He's given you. Thank Him for pulling you up out of darkness and placing you into His light. Thank Him for His daily provision, for you, for the people you love, for the entire world.

Ask Jesus to strengthen you through your worship of Him. He is the awesome God of all creation, and He calls Himself your friend. He is worthy of all of your praise.

EVENING

> *Jesus, You have blessed me with all my daily needs,*
> *the people I love, the beautiful world, and salvation.*
> *Keep me worshipping You by Your own strength.*
> *Remind me to live each day in thankfulness to You.*

October 30

> *"See, God has come to save me. I will trust in him*
> *and not be afraid. The Lord God is my strength*
> *and my song; he has given me victory."*
>
> Isaiah 12:2 nlt

It's a leap of faith to sing and praise God during times of trouble, change, and stress. But there is great power in our praise. We tone our faith muscles when we praise and thank God in difficult times.

When you feel like running away from your problems, hide out in Jesus instead. He's the one who longed for sinful Jerusalem, saying, "How often I have wanted to gather your children together as a hen protects her chicks beneath her wings" (Matthew 23:37). He feels the same way about you. . .so thank Him, honor Him, and praise Him.

Praise will keep you healthy in so many ways. Worry only holds you back. Which will you choose today?

EVENING

> *Today, Lord Jesus, I choose praise instead of worry.*
> *I know I can turn to You in every situation, sing of*
> *Your greatness, and receive victory through You,*
> *my strength. Let me trust You completely, holding*
> *nothing back from the victory You long to give me.*

October 31

> *"For the LORD your God is going with you! He will fight for you against your enemies, and he will give you victory!"*
>
> DEUTERONOMY 20:4 NLT

Spiritual warfare is real. There is a major battle ongoing in the unseen world (Ephesians 6:12). The Word tells us to be alert because our enemy, the devil, prowls around looking to devour us (1 Peter 5:8). One of his main weapons against us is fear.

In unsettled times, fear is natural. That's why we need supernatural help. Through Jesus, we have been given everything we need to overcome. We don't fight these spiritual battles in our own human strength! Jesus has told us not to worry, since He has overcome for us (John 16:33). And Jesus' lead disciple, Peter, elaborated on that theme: "By his divine power, God has given us everything we need for living a godly life. We have received all of this by coming to know him, the one who called us to himself by means of his marvelous glory and excellence" (2 Peter 1:3).

Stand firm in God's truth, always remembering that "the Spirit who lives in you is greater than the spirit who lives in the world" (1 John 4:4)!

> *Lord, it's good to know that I need not fear, no matter what lies in front of me. I thank You for Your supernatural help. You are greater than anything the enemy could try to throw at me. You are greater than any anxiety I may have.*

November 1

Now all glory to God, who is able, through his mighty power at work within us, to accomplish infinitely more than we might ask or think. Glory to him in the church and in Christ Jesus through all generations forever and ever! Amen.

EPHESIANS 3:20–21 NLT

We all have a choice to make every morning—we can be thankful for the new day, knowing that Jesus is with us and for us in whatever challenges come our way. . .or we can take that day's matters into our own hands. The latter choice usually brings stress and worry; the former brings peace. And why wouldn't it? We serve a God who, through Jesus Christ, does "infinitely more than we might ask or think."

Kingdom life is not natural—it's supernatural. It is a daily choice to invite the Spirit of Jesus to come and fill us with goodness and peace and joy (Romans 14:17). It's thanking our Savior for all that He is and does, minute by minute, hour by hour, day by day. He's infinitely more worthy than we can even think!

You do more in my life than I could ever think to ask, Jesus. Every day I experience Your deep blessing. You are indeed worthy of all the praise I can offer You—and then some. Let my life be a sacrifice of praise to You.

November 2

> *Let my soul be at rest again, for the Lord has been good to me. He has saved me from death, my eyes from tears, my feet from stumbling. And so I walk in the Lord's presence as I live here on earth!*
>
> Psalm 116:7–9 NLT

Have you ever taken time to count your blessings? Really. . .as in stopping to think about each one, even writing them down on paper? Literally counting your blessings can transform your outlook. When life feels overwhelming and out of control, your grateful reflection on God's past goodness will encourage your soul with His goodness now and in the future.

Take a few minutes today to jot down all the ways Jesus has been good to you. Then, when you're tempted to stress over the difficulties of life (and those days are sure to come), look at your list and remember His goodness.

Jesus Christ is the same yesterday, today, and forever (Hebrews 13:8). What He's done for you in the past, He'll do for you today, and He'll continue to do for all eternity. Now that's reason for gratitude.

> *Oh, Lord, forgive me for the times I've overlooked Your blessings—or worse, complained. I want to acknowledge You as the giver of all good things and thank You. Remind me of Your goodness first thing each morning so that my day is set on the good track of gratitude.*

MORNING

Jesus said to them, "I am the Bread of Life. He who comes to Me will never be hungry. He who puts his trust in Me will never be thirsty."

JOHN 6:35 NLV

There's nothing like the smell of homemade bread. Somehow, that combination of flour, yeast, and other ingredients fills a kitchen with a mouth-watering aroma. It's really one of life's simple pleasures . . .and then there's the joy of actually *eating* the bread!

Our Lord Jesus likened Himself to this essential and enjoyable foodstuff: "I am the Bread of Life." Each and every day, let's enjoy the aroma of His presence, then take Him in for the spiritual nourishment we need. Only He can satisfy the hunger in our souls.

And that's a perfect reason to stop and say, "thank You." Jesus provides everything we need for life, on this earth and throughout eternity.

EVENING

Lord, please be the Bread of my life, filling up my every hunger. I thank You for Your lavish provision. Even though You're totally satisfying, I still find myself wanting more. Draw me ever deeper into Your wonderful love.

November 4

*Let all that I am praise the LORD; with my whole heart,
I will praise his holy name. Let all that I am praise the LORD;
may I never forget the good things he does for me.*

PSALM 103:1–2 NLT

Pastor and author John Piper has said, "Genuine thankfulness is an act of the heart's affections, not an act of the lips' muscles." Put another way, true gratitude begins in the heart before it comes out of our mouths.

Look at all that God has done for you through Jesus Christ and say, "Thank You! Thank You! Thank You!" Then go out and actively live your life in a spirit of genuine gratitude. Notice the psalm writer's commitment to praise the Lord with "all that I am" and "my whole heart."

A heart of gratitude can transform you—how you think, how you talk, and how you live your daily life. If you need help in this area, Jesus stands ready. Ask Him to change your heart so you too can live a life marked by deep gratitude.

EVENING

*May every atom of my being thank You, Lord Jesus,
not only my lips. I want to live out that thankfulness
through everything I say and do. I recognize that
You've done things for me that I could never do
on my own. And I humbly say, "Thank You."*

November 5

MORNING

*The faithful love of the LORD never ends! His mercies never cease.
Great is his faithfulness; his mercies begin afresh each morning.*

LAMENTATIONS 3:22–23 NLT

In the classic novel *Anne of Green Gables*, heroine Anne Shirley says, "Tomorrow is always fresh with no mistakes in it." That line is reminiscent of today's scripture, which celebrates the faithful love of God. It never ends. His mercies begin afresh each morning.

When you feel the need for God's mercy—and we all will, regularly!—bring your failures to Jesus. Because of what He did on the cross, God won't punish you. Our sins deserve punishment, but because of Jesus, the Father now showers us with mercy.

When you've failed God, lift your head and thank Him for mercy and forgiveness. God the Father sees you through the lens of Jesus. . . you can move forward confidently knowing that Christ has made your way.

"Tomorrow is always fresh with no mistakes in it." Let tomorrow begin right now.

EVENING

*Oh, Jesus, I'm thankful for Your mercies that are
new every morning. Your love and faithfulness
never end. May I respond in grateful obedience to
You each day. When I walk in faithfulness I know
that I will experience Your unceasing mercy.*

November 6

> *The blessing of the LORD makes a person*
> *rich, and he adds no sorrow with it.*
> PROVERBS 10:22 NLT

God's blessings—both large and small—do indeed make life rich. So instead of just asking "What's next, God?" take time to thank Him for what He's already done for you. When God blesses people around you, don't ask, "Why not me, God?" Gratefully celebrate His goodness in their lives.

God has placed joy and beauty and blessing all through His created world. Take pleasure in nature and the beauty of each season. Smile at the children you see and learn from their simple faith and trust in Jesus. Invest in the people He's placed on your path, experiencing the joy of loving and being loved. These simple blessings are truly gifts of our generous Lord. Don't take any of them for granted.

EVENING

> *Lord, I want to take pleasure in the good things*
> *of life, whether they come to me or someone else.*
> *May I never become jealous or covetous. I want to*
> *cheerlead for others, always being gracious in my*
> *response to the blessings they've received. I thank*
> *You now for every blessing You've given me.*

November 7

> *"Those the Father has given me will come to me, and I will never reject them."*
>
> JOHN 6:37 NLT

When you turn to Jesus, you can be sure that His arms are open. He will never turn you away—even if you've messed up badly. The apostle Paul told us something amazing about our Lord: "Don't you see how wonderfully kind, tolerant, and patient God is with you? Does this mean nothing to you? Can't you see that his kindness is intended to turn you from your sin?" (Romans 2:4).

It's God's kindness that leads us away from our sin and to Jesus! Is that your perception of God? If not, ask Him to lead you to a full understanding of this wonderful truth.

When we sin, the best thing we can do is go straight to Jesus. Don't run away. Don't try to hide. Jesus has promised that He will never reject you. He'll simply assure you of His love and forgiveness, then grant you power to change.

EVENING

Thank You, Jesus, that You will never turn me away, even after I've sinned. When I fail You, help me to go straight back to You. I have no reason to hide. You have already given me the forgiveness and mercy I need.

November 8

> *"The robber comes only to steal and to kill and to destroy.*
> *I came so they might have life, a great full life."*
>
> JOHN 10:10 NLV

Solomon wrote Ecclesiastes to remind people that life on earth is meaningless—unless we follow God and obey His commandments (Ecclesiastes 12:13–14). Ecclesiastes is a bit of a dreary book, apparently written as the king looked back on his own life. He had wealth and power and everything he wanted but confessed it meant nothing when he chose to ignore God for many years.

Solomon wrote: "I know that there is nothing better for men than to be happy and to do good as long as they live. And I know that every man who eats and drinks sees good in all his work. It is the gift of God" (Ecclesiastes 3:12–13). This is a reminder that God wants us to enjoy life—but *with* Him, not apart from Him.

Jesus is the One who brings us to God. He brings true joy and meaning to our lives. How can we not express our gratitude every day?

EVENING

> *Without You, Jesus, this life would be terribly dreary.*
> *May I enjoy every minute with You on this earth*
> *as I anticipate Your perfect eternity to come.*

MORNING

The commandments of the LORD are right,
bringing joy to the heart. The commands of the
LORD are clear, giving insight for living.

PSALM 19:8 NLT

God's Word can generate a sense of freedom and gratitude. . .if we allow it to. Where Jesus tells His followers to "obey my commandments" (John 14:15), some people see that as constrictive and joy killing. Nothing could be further from the truth. In fact, today's scripture says God's commands give joy to our hearts.

God didn't create rules to make us unhappy or spoil our fun. Jesus didn't reemphasize God's laws to make us feel unfulfilled, as if we're missing out on something. No. . .like wise parents who set rules and boundaries for their children, God has given us precepts to keep us from trouble and help us to enjoy life. This truth should bring gratitude to our hearts.

EVENING

I thank You for Your commandments, Lord. May they
bring joy to my heart as I seek to bring joy to You by
my obedience. I never want to look back on my life,
as Solomon did, and see that the things I lived for
were meaningless. I want to live wholly for You.

November 10

*How abundant are the good things that you have
stored up for those who fear you, that you bestow in
the sight of all, on those who take refuge in you.*

PSALM 31:19 NIV

When we trust God, He becomes our "ever-present help in trouble" (Psalm 46:1). Think about that: God is *ever* present. . .meaning He is with you this very moment, even as you read these words. His power and comfort are constantly available. He is good and He wants to show His goodness to you on a daily, hourly, minute-by-minute basis.

When we focus on problems and worry about things that haven't even happened, we're taking our eyes off God. But when we focus on the Father and His gracious provision of Jesus Christ, He will show Himself to us in each moment. He will make ways for us when we didn't believe there could be one.

Jesus, our refuge, is a perfect reason to thank God every day.

EVENING

*Thank You, Jesus, for providing for me publicly
and for being my private refuge. How abundant
are the good things You have stored up for
me! You truly bless me in every way.*

MORNING

I will give thanks to you, Lord, with all my heart; I will tell of all your wonderful deeds. I will be glad and rejoice in you; I will sing the praises of your name, O Most High.

PSALM 9:1–2 NIV

If you praise Jesus daily with a heart full of love, others can't help but notice. "Praise and worship" isn't just about songs at church on Sunday—it's about living your life with daily thankfulness to God and allowing that gratitude to motivate everything you do.

A life of praise and worship means there's an ongoing song of contentment in your heart. As you trust Jesus to guide you and meet your needs, your faith grows. Are you experiencing that kind of contentment and faith right now? If not, talk to Jesus, asking Him to do any necessary "heart surgery." Ask Him to place a song of gratitude inside and fill you to overflowing with His joy.

EVENING

Jesus, please put a song of joy in my heart. Your deeds are so wonderful that I must stop and say, "Thank You." I want my whole life to worship You so that others can't help but notice and praise You too.

November 12

The Word became flesh and made his dwelling among us.
We have seen his glory, the glory of the one and only Son,
who came from the Father, full of grace and truth.

JOHN 1:14 NIV

When God made a way for us to be saved, He showed us the true meaning of love. Jesus—who is the Way—told His followers, "Greater love has no one than this: to lay down one's life for one's friends" (John 15:13). Giving up your life for someone else is true, unselfish love, and that's what exactly Jesus did for us.

God the Father chose to send His Son into the world to live a life like ours, then to eventually lay down that life and die an excruciating death on the cross. Jesus knew the physical pain He would suffer, and He knew there would be emotional pain too, when He was betrayed by Judas and deserted by His other disciples. But He faced it all so we could be made right with God.

Be thankful for the "Word made flesh". . .there is no greater love.

EVENING

I thank You, Jesus, for giving up Your earthly life for
me. And that was after giving up the glories of heaven
to take on human flesh! Your love was big enough to
overcome the suffering and pain You faced. I am so
grateful for Your willingness to experience that for me.

MORNING

"I call heaven and earth to speak against you today. I have
put in front of you life and death, the good and the curse.
So choose life so you and your children after you may live.
Love the Lord your God and obey His voice. Hold on to Him.
For He is your life, and by Him your days will be long."

DEUTERONOMY 30:19–20 NLV

Life with Jesus is the most wonderful thing a human being can experience. The Bible says eternal life is knowing God through His Son (John 17:3) and Jesus came to give us abundant life (John 10:10)—not only in eternity but here, now, on this earth.

We all have a choice to make every day of our present, earthly lives: to follow Jesus and stay close to Him. . .or not. Following Jesus isn't always easy. But it is always worth it.

If we experience persecution or even martyrdom for Jesus' name, we are blessed (Luke 6:22). And the apostle Paul says any trouble on earth can't even compare with the glory to be revealed in us (Romans 8:18). No matter what, we have a reason for gratitude.

EVENING

Lord Jesus, remind me that my daily troubles are small
and short compared to the incredible future You have
planned for me. There is no trouble or pain that could
ever separate me from Your love. I praise You for being
so much bigger than any difficulty I could ever face.

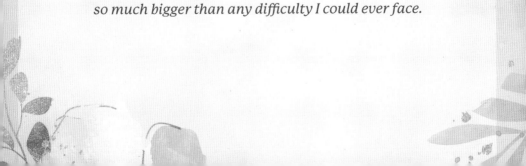

November 14

> *"Have I not told you? Be strong and have strength of heart! Do not be afraid or lose faith. For the Lord your God is with you anywhere you go."*
>
> JOSHUA 1:9 NLV

The Bible teaches that God's Spirit is working inside followers of Jesus at all times. What an astounding miracle! Along with the apostle Paul, we can shout in gratitude: "Let us honor and thank the God and Father of our Lord Jesus Christ. He has already given us a taste of what heaven is like. Even before the world was made, God chose us for Himself because of His love. He planned that we should be holy and without blame as He sees us" (Ephesians 1:3–4).

Even when we feel like we're alone, God is with us. We have the Father's love, the Spirit's presence, and Jesus' prayers. The blessed Trinity will never leave or forsake us. Let's always thank our God for working everything out for our good and His glory.

EVENING

> *I have no reason for fear, Jesus, because You have promised to always be with me. You will never leave me or forsake me. Thank You for blessing me with a preview of heaven and making me worthy of being there!*

MORNING

Since, then, you have been raised with Christ, set your hearts on things above, where Christ is, seated at the right hand of God. Set your minds on things above, not on earthly things.

COLOSSIANS 3:1–2 NIV

Life bombards us with trouble: health issues, financial difficulties, relationship problems, and many other daily trials that can potentially break our spirits. But Jesus beckons us to focus on Him instead of our worries. Don't be like Peter, who miraculously walked on water until he took his eyes off Jesus. May we never miss out on life's blessings because we let our gaze wander from Jesus to our troubles.

God wants to bless you, right now, in the midst of the mess of life. But that will take action on your part: you need to set your heart on "things above." Look up, "where Christ is, seated at the right hand of God." Consciously leave the "earthly things" behind. When you do, you'll be filled with gratitude for the overcoming power God provides.

EVENING

Even on my best days, Jesus, life is a challenge.
I want always to have the help and protection
You offer. I commit to keeping my eyes on
You and my heart filled with gratitude.

November 16

*Trust in the LORD and do good; dwell in the land
and enjoy safe pasture. Take delight in the LORD,
and he will give you the desires of your heart.*

PSALM 37:3–4 NIV

It's easy to look at today's verse and think, *Hey, if I "delight" myself
in God, He will give me everything I want!* But what this verse means
is that our true submission to Jesus will change our hearts so completely that we'll want what *He* wants. When we commit everything we do to the Lord, we'll begin to see the desires of our hearts
matching God's own desires.

Practically speaking, how do you take delight in the Lord? Start
your day with gratitude. Go to Jesus first, before everything else gets
in the way, and thank Him for His love. Ask Him to bless your day
and give you opportunities to bless others. Talk to Him about every
opportunity and problem you face. Commit your entire self to Him
...and thank Him in advance for the blessings that will come your way.

EVENING

*Lord Jesus, I commit all my ways to You. May I truly
delight in You and gain what I most desire. Help
me to see that the thing I need and should want
most is You. Nothing could be more important
to my life than Your love and presence.*

November 17

MORNING

Yes, even if I walk through the valley of the shadow of death, I will not be afraid of anything, because You are with me. You have a walking stick with which to guide and one with which to help. These comfort me.

PSALM 23:4 NLV

Jesus has promised to be with us through everything. He has the tools we need for every job and the map we need for every journey. If He asks us to go somewhere or do something, He promises to be with us, providing exactly what we need, when we need it. And we can count on Him to keep His promises.

Look at what Psalm 139:7–10 says: "Where can I go from Your Spirit? Or where can I run away from where You are? If I go up to heaven, You are there! If I make my bed in the place of the dead, You are there! If I take the wings of the morning or live in the farthest part of the sea, even there Your hand will lead me and Your right hand will hold me."

No matter where you go, our Lord is always right there with you. Thank You, Jesus!

EVENING

Oh, Jesus, You guide and protect me no matter where I am in life. You always provide for me. I thank You for Your amazing love that has never once left me alone.

November 18

He giveth power to the faint; and to them that have no might he increaseth strength. Even the youths shall faint and be weary, and the young men shall utterly fall. But they that wait upon the Lord shall renew their strength; they shall mount up with wings as eagles; they shall run, and not be weary; and they shall walk, and not faint.

ISAIAH 40:29–31 KJV

Could you use a large helping of Jesus' power in your life? Who couldn't? The Bible says that those who wait for the Lord—the people who pray and depend on Him in everything—will gain new strength.

God gives strength and power to people who know they don't have any. . .if they simply "wait upon the Lord." That means we pray in the full expectation that He will show up and keep His promises, no matter how long it might take. It means looking for Him, longing for Him, putting your full hope in Him.

In a world that makes us faint and weary, how appreciative we are of a Savior who gives strength, who causes us to soar like eagles. Don't miss this blessing by rushing out of His presence.

EVENING

Lord Jesus, wait can be such a difficult word. Remind me that it means You're developing good things in my life. Help me trust in Your purposes. May I never rush through my time with You as though it were just a box on my to-do list. I want to linger in Your presence for as long as I possibly can.

November 19

MORNING

It is for freedom that Christ has set us free. Stand firm, then, and do not let yourselves be burdened again by a yoke of slavery.

GALATIANS 5:1 NIV

"Freedom in Christ" means we know that our eternal life is secure. But how grateful we should be to know that freedom in Christ also means we can be free *here and now*—free from our tendency to sin, free to live a life of purpose, free from the worry of what other people think or say about us.

Freedom in Christ gives us confidence to be all that God has made us to be. We are no longer held captive by fear, because the perfect love Jesus offers us casts out all fear (1 John 4:18), giving us true peace. We can enjoy a peace that transcends all understanding, here on earth, while we live our daily lives.

When we live in the freedom Jesus provides, our insecurities fade, our fears diminish, and love takes over. Praise and thank Him for such a gift.

EVENING

I want to live as You intended, Jesus, freed from sin and becoming the person You designed me to be. May your perfect love cast out any fear that still troubles me. I know that You have given me freedom through Your sacrifice on the cross. There is nothing greater than that!

November 20

> *"The God who made the world and everything in it is the Lord of heaven and earth and does not live in temples built by human hands. And he is not served by human hands, as if he needed anything. Rather, he himself gives everyone life and breath and everything else."*
>
> ACTS 17:24–25 NIV

Isn't it amazing that the God who established the earth is the same Lord who knows you intimately and wants a deeply personal relationship with you? His Word says He knows when you sit down and stand up, and even your words before you speak them (Psalm 139)! Long before you were born, God had already determined where and when you should live. Ponder these things and let them inspire thankfulness for everything the Lord has done for you.

What a comfort it is to know Jesus is in control of your life. He knows everything that has happened and everything that will happen to you. Everything that comes your way has passed through His hands first. You are safe and secure in the strong arms of Jesus.

EVENING

Oh, Jesus, sometimes I don't feel secure—but I know You are still in control of my life and preparing good things for me. You have placed me where I am for this exact time on earth. Please help me trust, and rest, in You and Your perfect plan.

MORNING

*There is no fear in love. Perfect love puts fear out of
our hearts. People have fear when they are afraid of
being punished. The man who is afraid does not have
perfect love. We love Him because He loved us first.*

1 JOHN 4:18–19 NLV

Sadly, many followers of Jesus waste time believing that God is angry with them. He's not. God sees you through the love and sacrifice of His Son, Jesus. That means you can always approach Him without fear.

Saved people who worry about punishment don't understand who they are in Jesus. We don't have to work harder or be "better Christians" to somehow earn God's love. Nothing we do would make Him love us any more or less than He does right now.

When you really understand who you are in Christ, it changes everything. You leave fear behind. You embrace perfect love. You live a life of thanksgiving.

EVENING

*Lord Jesus, I thank You for the salvation You provide,
which casts fear out of my life. I thank You for loving
me so I can live for You. I know that I could never
earn what You did for me, but I ask that You help
me live in such a way that it honors Your sacrifice.
May my life be a reward for Your suffering.*

November 22

*I remain confident of this: I will see the goodness of
the Lord in the land of the living. Wait for the Lord;
be strong and take heart and wait for the Lord.*

PSALM 27:13–14 NIV

We can all take great comfort today knowing that when we wait on the Lord, when we trust in His purpose and timing, we will see His goodness *in this life*. He promises that if we cast our burdens and cares on Him, He will sustain us. He won't let us fall (Psalm 55:22).

Jesus sees your situation. He knows your circumstances. He loves you and cares deeply about what you experience, and that will never change. He will make everything that happens in your life work together for your good (Romans 8:28).

Trust that the Lord is working in your life, often behind the scenes, orchestrating a grand finale that you can't yet recognize. Ask for His guidance and wait on Him. And be grateful for every miracle and blessing—big or small—that He sends your way.

EVENING

*Thank You, Lord, for giving me good things in this life.
When I can't imagine the big picture, help me to trust
that You are working through every experience to bless
me more. I can be confident in You because I've seen
You move and work in my life over and over again.*

MORNING

Keep your minds thinking about whatever is true, whatever is respected, whatever is right, whatever is pure, whatever can be loved, and whatever is well thought of. If there is anything good and worth giving thanks for, think about these things.

PHILIPPIANS 4:8 NLV

If we don't take control of them, our thoughts can get us in trouble. It's easy to get off track, thinking about things we shouldn't. . .even when we're praying. We start off with good thoughts, then get distracted. Nothing good comes from that.

Next time you find your mind going to a place that isn't good or helpful, ask Jesus to step into your thoughts and change them. Speak His name and call out for rescue. He can guide the direction of your thoughts, making them like His own—pure and true and lovely.

The name of Jesus has all power in heaven and earth (Philippians 2:10). Call on Him to turn your thoughts to love, praise, and thanksgiving.

EVENING

Lord Jesus, please control my thoughts and rescue me from the sin that seeks to entangle me. May I focus on the pure, true, and lovely, giving You all the thanks and praise. I want to only meditate on the things that bring You glory.

November 24

I will praise you, Lord, with all my heart; before the "gods" I will sing your praise. I will bow down toward your holy temple and will praise your name for your unfailing love and your faithfulness.

PSALM 138:1–2 NIV

Make it a practice to thank God for each new day, knowing that His mercies and compassion are new every morning. Keep a song of praise in your heart, expressing gratitude for His many blessings. Praise Him for the simple pleasures of life: family, friends, food, and a million other things.

Throughout your day, say "thank You!" out loud to Jesus. Tell Him how much you appreciate His love and His gift of life, now and for eternity.

And as you lay your head on your pillow at night, thank Him for the day, for all the blessings He sent your way, and for His presence with you through it all. You know He'll be with you through the night, the next day, and all eternity.

EVENING

Lord Jesus, I just want to say "thank You." Thanks for what You do for me, but especially thanks for who You are. You are my God and my loving friend! Please keep a spirit of thanksgiving in my heart and renew it when I begin to slip into discontentment.

MORNING

All praise to God, the Father of our Lord Jesus Christ. God is our merciful Father and the source of all comfort. He comforts us in all our troubles so that we can comfort others. When they are troubled, we will be able to give them the same comfort God has given us. For the more we suffer for Christ, the more God will shower us with his comfort through Christ.

2 CORINTHIANS 1:3–5 NLT

This is a season of thanksgiving. Why not take a moment to count and record your blessings? Write them in a journal, make notes in your Bible, capture them in your phone—whatever works best for you. Keep the list handy for those moments of stress or discouragement.

Remember that hard times will come your way. That's a guarantee in this life. But you'll find encouragement in the midst of your trials when you pull out your chronicle of God's blessings in your life—headlined by the salvation that comes through Jesus Christ. Not only will that take your mind off your troubles, it will generate thanks to God, who is absolutely worthy of your praise.

EVENING

Lord Jesus, may I never forget the blessings You have given me. I am grateful for the good things You send, but also for the hardships that push me closer to You. Let gratitude pull me ever closer to You as I focus on Your goodness and faithfulness.

November 26

> *Let the message of Christ dwell among you richly as you teach and admonish one another with all wisdom through psalms, hymns, and songs from the Spirit, singing to God with gratitude in your hearts.*
>
> COLOSSIANS 3:16 NIV

What does "the message of Christ" do for us? It saves us from sin and the punishment our sin deserves. It helps us to really understand who God is. It gives us purpose in a world that seems meaningless otherwise. And, as today's scripture indicates, it develops gratitude in our hearts.

Even nonbelievers recognize the value of gratitude. Good parents teach their kids to say "thank you," since that will help them throughout life. Thankfulness smooths off the rough edges of human interactions, making the world just a little bit kinder each time it's expressed.

We as Christians should be the most thankful people of all. The message of Jesus Christ has changed everything for the better. Let's "teach and admonish one another" to be more thankful. . .first to God, and then to each other.

EVENING

> *Lord Jesus, empower me to live in thankfulness each day of this life. I don't ever want to take Your good things for granted. May I encourage others to be thankful as well!*

November 27

Give thanks to the Lord for He is good!
His loving-kindness lasts forever!
PSALM 107:1 NLV

No one will be faithful to you all the time—no one, that is, except Jesus.

Here are some wonderful truths to bank your life on: Jesus will never leave you. He'll never give up on you. He'll never speak anything but truth to you. He'll never stop loving you. Nothing you do will ever change His mind about how much He loves you. Jesus is the embodiment of God's love—and that will never change because God never changes.

The Father looks at you with lovingkindness because He sees Jesus in you. You don't have to be afraid to approach Him or tell Him honestly what's going on in your life. He already knows, anyway ...He just wants to hear from you.

Be thankful for God's goodness and love, purchased for you by the blood of Jesus.

EVENING

I thank You, Jesus, for Your faithful love. You embodied Your Father's loving-kindness that lasts forever. You are the ever-faithful lover of my spirit. May I always live in the light of Your love.

November 28

> *I have seen you in your sanctuary and gazed upon your power and glory. Your unfailing love is better than life itself; how I praise you! I will praise you as long as I live, lifting up my hands to you in prayer. You satisfy me more than the richest feast. I will praise you with songs of joy.*
>
> PSALM 63:2–5 NLT

During this season of thanksgiving, focus your mind on gratefulness to Jesus. Ruminate on these scriptures:

- "Since we are receiving a Kingdom that is unshakable, let us be thankful and please God by worshiping him with holy fear and awe" (Hebrews 12:28).
- "All who are victorious will inherit all these blessings, and I will be their God, and they will be my children" (Revelation 21:7).
- "From his abundance we have all received one gracious blessing after another. For the law was given through Moses, but God's unfailing love and faithfulness came through Jesus Christ" (John 1:16–17).

Every blessing comes to us through Jesus. He is worthy of our thanksgiving. Not just one day of the year, but every single day.

EVENING

> *Oh, Jesus, I cannot give You too much praise! You have blessed every moment of my life. Lead me away from discontentment and into a life of true thanksgiving. Keep me on the path of gratitude for all that You've done for me.*

MORNING

> *"These people honor me with their lips, but their*
> *hearts are far from me. They worship me in vain;*
> *their teachings are merely human rules."*
>
> MATTHEW 15:8–9 NIV

The Pharisees were high-ranking religious leaders of Jesus' day. They knew a lot about the Old Testament laws and prided themselves on looking good on the outside. They thought they were pleasing God, but in rejecting Jesus, they were very far from Him.

As Christians, we welcome Jesus, and He reconciles us with God the Father. We have a real friendship with our Lord, who kindly teaches us every day. Unlike the Pharisees, Jesus doesn't pile up rules and duties that weigh us down. He takes us by the hand and helps us along. His yoke is easy and His burden is light (Matthew 11:28–30).

As our relationship with Jesus grows, we sense more and more His love for us. How can we be anything but thankful?

EVENING

Thank You, Lord Jesus, for Your light burden. Your
rules are meant to benefit me and keep me from harm,
and You give me the strength to obey them. May my
relationship with You be so close and warm that I delight
in obeying Your rules, to show Your love and respect.

November 30

> *I will sing of the LORD's great love forever; with my mouth I will make your faithfulness known through all generations. I will declare that your love stands firm forever, that you have established your faithfulness in heaven itself.*
>
> PSALM 89:1–2 NIV

God shows love for us in so many ways. One of the simplest ways to see that love in action is to go outside and enjoy creation—which came through Jesus (Colossians 1:15–16).

You can see His handiwork in the green plants of spring and summer, the colorful leaves of fall, and the white snow He sends in winter. The skies tell of His wonders in every season. Animals and creatures great and small know their Creator. The birds God created sing His praises as they go about their daily tasks. . .and you can too.

God gave you a voice to talk to Him, to tell others of the great love of Christ in saving us from sin, and to sing His praises every day of your life.

So spend some time with Jesus in creation every day. Allow His handiwork to spur thankfulness in your heart.

EVENING

> *Lord Jesus, please use Your creation to remind me of Your power and presence—and of my need to praise You. You are my Creator and You deserve all the glory. May I shout praise to You so that the rocks don't have to!*

December 1

MORNING

> The LORD is near to all who call on him,
> to all who call on him in truth.
>
> PSALM 145:18 NIV

December has arrived! Christmas is coming! In just twenty-four more days, we'll celebrate the birth of Jesus, that point in time and space when God came near in a truly unique way.

Who would have guessed that the almighty Creator of the universe would arrive on the scene as a baby? Nobody would expect salvation to begin in the womb of a godly young girl who'd never yet been with a man. What kind of Messiah is this?

Well, it's Immanuel, "God with us" (Matthew 1:23). It's Jesus Christ, the Son of God, second member of the Trinity, the focus of all history, before whom "every knee should bow, in heaven and on earth and under the earth" (Philippians 2:10). On that first Christmas, He came near physically to draw us near spiritually. Let's be sure to "call on him," the first time for salvation, then unceasingly for daily mercy, grace, and love.

EVENING

> Lord Jesus, I am amazed and grateful that You were willing to come to earth to save me. I want to draw closer than ever to You this Christmas season. This month, please reveal Yourself to me in ever deeper ways.

December 2

> *One who has unreliable friends soon comes to ruin,*
> *but there is a friend who sticks closer than a brother.*
>
> PROVERBS 18:24 NIV

Relationships are vital. There are times we want to share good news with someone, other times we long for a friend to walk with us through adversity. All of us need someone who journeys with us through life. We were not made to travel alone.

And every Christian has that person, "a friend who sticks closer than a brother." Jesus Christ is always with us, supporting, protecting, helping, guiding. He's always interested in our joys and trials. He's always ready and able to carry us through the rough places of life. He's like the perfect brother, only better—wiser, stronger, more loving, closer.

You'll never find a better friend. You'll never be nearer another person. Jesus made you, keeps you, loves you. . .and will continue to love you for all eternity.

EVENING

> *You are the best friend I could have, Jesus. I thank You*
> *for Your love, protection, and guidance. . .and the fact*
> *that I need never walk alone. Remind me to come to*
> *You first with my needs, desires, and even complaints.*
> *I know that You want and enjoy my company!*

December 3

MORNING

Come near to God and he will come near to you.

JAMES 4:8 NIV

After Adam and Eve chose to sin in the garden of Eden, they tried to hide themselves from God. Imagine, separating yourself from the One you'd walked with daily, the One who knows you intimately, and the One who had created you! That's how crazy sin is.

Of course, God knew exactly where Adam and Eve were, and He pursued them. . .as He pursues every sinful person born into their line. From the very beginning, God the Father had prepared a plan to restore human beings to a right relationship with Himself: He would send His Son, Jesus Christ, to die as a sacrifice for sin.

Jesus' obedience to His Father closed the gap that human disobedience had created. Jesus came near to us. In Him, we come near to God. The divine-humanity fellowship is restored.

EVENING

Oh, Jesus, please help me to bring my sins to You rather than running away. The fact that You died to save me just proves how loving You are. I know that You will always forgive and restore me because of Your great love.

December 4

Look for the Lord and His strength. Look for His face all the time.
PSALM 105:4 NLV

Some days are not so great. Others are absolutely wonderful. The latter are those kinds of days when everything goes right. You wake up well rested. Getting ready for the day goes smoothly, and you get out the door early. The weather is perfect, and the coffee shop nails your favorite flavor. The day speeds by with no hiccups, no one around you seems angry, dinner is fabulous, and you fall right to sleep when you get into bed.

On days like that, do you sense the nearness of Jesus? Often, we are quicker to call on Him in times of trouble than on the day when everything goes swimmingly.

But the fact is that we need Jesus at all times. Good days give way to less-good days which roll into atrocious days. But Jesus is always near. Let's look for His face at all times.

EVENING

Lord Jesus, I need You every day, not only the bad ones. Remind me to seek Your face daily and keep me from becoming distracted by the world. I know that the good days don't come because of my goodness, and the bad days aren't necessarily a punishment—they're all just aspects of living in this world. Please let me find You in every experience.

December 5

Then you will experience God's peace, which exceeds anything we can understand. His peace will guard your hearts and minds as you live in Christ Jesus.

PHILIPPIANS 4:7 NLT

A *guard*, as a noun, can be found in prisons, on basketball courts, or along the sides of roads (attached to the word *rail*). Guards protect other things, defending against harm. As a verb, *guard* indicates the action of protecting and defending.

When we are near Jesus—according to today's scripture, actually living "in" Him—our hearts and minds are protected and defended from the crazy world around us. We get a peace that goes far beyond our human comprehension. We'll weather the storms of life in ways that baffle our unbelieving friends and neighbors. But it's not because of our own strength. . .it's all thanks to the incredible nearness of Jesus.

May we always stay as close to Him as He is to us.

Jesus, You guard my life in so many ways. May your peace guard my heart and mind today, keeping me from the temptations that threaten to undo me. And, as You give me Your peace, let me also share it with others.

December 6

> *The LORD is close to the brokenhearted;*
> *he rescues those whose spirits are crushed.*
>
> PSALM 34:18 NLT

Brokenhearted and *crushed* are discouraging words. But they often accurately reflect our feelings. This world can crush our dreams and break our hearts in an instant. At times the pain seems more than humanly possible to bear.

There is good news, though. In these moments, Jesus comes near. He experienced the same emotions and adversity when He walked the earth, so He's sympathetic. But more than that, He also is capable of healing our wounds.

As God made flesh, Jesus is completely capable of carrying us through trials. What we learn on the way can deepen our faith and become lessons that we can then share with others. Has anyone ever stepped up to help you in such times? Sometimes, that's exactly how Jesus comes near.

EVENING

Thank You, Jesus, for being compassionate and capable.
I know I can bring You my fears and wounds, and You
will both understand and heal me. Show me how I
can be Your hands and feet to others who need help.

MORNING

He answered and said, Lo, I see four men loose, walking in the midst of the fire, and they have no hurt; and the form of the fourth is like the Son of God. Then Nebuchadnezzar came near to the mouth of the burning fiery furnace, and spake, and said, Shadrach, Meshach, and Abednego, ye servants of the most high God, come forth.

DANIEL 3:25–26 KJV

Nebuchadnezzar's law was that everyone would bow and honor him as a god. But there were three young Hebrews who would not bow to any but the one true God.

So the Babylonian king had the three thrown into a blazing furnace, only to be astonished at what he saw inside: the young men were completely unharmed and joined by a fourth person! According to the venerable King James Version of the Bible, the fourth was like "the Son of God."

Modern translations render Nebuchadnezzar's quote as "a son of the gods," but the fact is that "the Son of God," Jesus, goes with us through all the fires of adversity. We are never alone. Jesus promises always to be with us.

EVENING

Lord, whatever fires I face, You are right there with me. I thank You for never leaving me to face trouble on my own. When I trust You, even unbelievers can see that You are walking with me, always by my side.

December 8

MORNING

"For God so loved the world that He gave His only Son. Whoever puts his trust in God's Son will not be lost but will have life that lasts forever."

JOHN 3:16 NLV

The perfect creation was tainted. People were selfish, disrespectful, rebellious. And still God loved them.

Our human tendency is to associate with people who treat us well. Who would devote themselves to the worst of the worst, those who intentionally misuse others? But our all-loving God initiated a plan to forgive humanity and restore the relationship they had ruined. That plan was to send Jesus to earth as a man.

While He was here, Jesus invested tirelessly in people, only to have them intentionally mistreat Him. . .to the point of His death on a cross. But that was part of God's plan too. Jesus came near only to be pushed away. But He keeps coming near, keeps pursuing people, keeps reconciling to God. That's what love does.

EVENING

Jesus, I am glad You invest in me, though I have often failed You. I appreciate Your seeking me out to reconcile us forever. Thank You for pursuing me time and again, even after I've failed You and dishonored Your perfect plan. Continue to renew me and make me right with You.

MORNING

> *"Who can hide in secret places so that I cannot see them?" declares the LORD. "Do not I fill heaven and earth?" declares the LORD.*
>
> JEREMIAH 23:24 NIV

Has anyone *not* played hide and seek? In big groups or small, in daylight or nighttime, indoors or outside, the game is the same: the seekers pursue the hiders, who stay as quiet and still as possible. The hiders' goal is not to be found.

That's the way sinful people respond to God—they try to stay out of His sight. Of course, that's not possible, since God knows and sees all. But even Jesus plays the game: "the Son of Man came to seek and to save the lost" (Luke 19:10).

Be thankful He got close enough to "find" you. When Jesus tagged you, *you* won. . .eternal life, with pleasures at His right hand (Psalm 16:11).

EVENING

> *Oh, Jesus, how delightful that You tagged me and made me a winner, with eternal life as the prize. I thank You for the ongoing pleasure of Your presence. Remind me that I don't need to hide from You, even when I've done wrong. Help me to confess my failures so I can be free from my sin and shame.*

December 10

*And ye shall seek me, and find me, when ye
shall search for me with all your heart.*
JEREMIAH 29:13 KJV

Moving toward Jesus is not some kind of guessing game. The Bible
provides us with clear guidelines for coming to Him, both for our
salvation and for daily renewal. And He has promised that He will
be found when we search for Him with our whole heart.

"Search the scriptures. . .they are they which testify of me" (John
5:39). "Whosoever shall call on the name of the Lord shall be saved"
(Acts 2:21; Romans 10:13). "Come unto me, all ye that labour and
are heavy laden, and I will give you rest" (Matthew 11:28). "Abide in
me, and I in you. As the branch cannot bear fruit of itself, except it
abide in the vine; no more can ye, except ye abide in me" (John 15:4).

Seek Jesus, and He'll be found. Draw near to Him, and He'll draw
near to you.

EVENING

*Because You sought me out, Jesus, I need only to respond
in obedience—and You are there for me! I don't deserve
Your love, but I am grateful. You are so easily found when
I seek for You. Thank You for drawing me into Your love.*

December 11

See what great love the Father has lavished on us, that we should be called children of God! And that is what we are!

1 John 3:1 niv

What joy when an orphaned child is chosen as a member of a new family! With much anticipation and preparation, a family readies for an adoption. But the process is not finalized until the child is physically united with and welcomed into his or her new family.

When we came to Jesus, we were adopted into the family of God. We had heard about God's love for us and the forgiveness He offered though His Son. We had heard that He would accept anyone who came to Him. . .and we'd heard right!

Our spiritual adoption is finalized by our confession, "I want to belong to You." We can be no closer to God than when we're members of His family through faith in Jesus. May we never lose our thrill of the moment that became reality.

EVENING

Lord Jesus, You've made me a child of God and Your own sister! I am thrilled to know Your love and mercy. Thank You for welcoming me into Your marvelous family of believers.

December 12

MORNING

Pray in the Spirit on all occasions with all kinds of prayers and requests. With this in mind, be alert and always keep on praying for all the Lord's people.

EPHESIANS 6:18 NIV

Jesus performed countless miracles during His time on earth. He made the blind to see, the lame to walk, the deaf to hear, and the mute to talk. He raised people from the dead. He multiplied food and calmed stormy weather. Most of His miracles took place when a person was in the presence of Jesus, but He wasn't limited by their physical proximity (Matthew 8:5–13). Even from a distance, He could speak a word and heal the afflicted.

Jesus is not physically present with us, but He actually lives within us by His Spirit. His power is just as strong today as it was two thousand years ago. Whether we pray for healing or for provision, whether we ask for safety or for guidance, He is just as willing to work in our lives as He was with the blind, lame, deaf, and mute.

Jesus is near! May we boldly ask Him for His touch.

EVENING

Lord Jesus, Your miracle power is ongoing, and You do amazing work in my life. Please give me the boldness to ask You for all I need and to always keep other believers in my prayers so that You will touch them too.

MORNING

Taste and see that the LORD is good.
PSALM 34:8 NLT

So what does it mean to "taste" the Lord's goodness?

Think of it this way: tasting is a necessary step in enjoying food. A chef could explain exactly what he's put into a dish, even describing its flavors in detail. . .but until we actually taste the food, we can't really appreciate its goodness.

It is the same with Jesus. We can read all about Him in the pages of scripture. But until we actually "taste" Him, we cannot fully comprehend all that He is.

If you're a believer, you've tasted and seen that Jesus is good. (If you're not a believer, why not choose Jesus now?) But even after that first delicious taste of salvation, there are always deeper and more satisfying tastes to come. Draw near to Him in Bible study, prayer, and service. . . Jesus will become more flavorful with every passing day.

EVENING

*Oh, Jesus, I have tasted Your goodness—and I crave
more of it. Help me to be consistent in my Bible study,
prayer, and service, so I can draw ever closer to You.
Teach me to hunger after Your righteousness each day
so that I can experience Your goodness all the more.*

December 14

> *For we are to God the pleasing aroma of Christ among*
> *those who are being saved and those who are perishing.*
>
> 2 CORINTHIANS 2:15 NIV

A rose. Warm chocolate chip cookies. Ocean breezes. The interior of a new car. There are many aromas that please.

How about adding "Jesus follower" to that list?

The apostle Paul said God likes our smell when we walk in Jesus' triumphal procession. And our Jesus aroma, so pleasing to the Father, brings life to other people.

We typically hold flowers up to our noses. We lean over the oven to smell the cookies. We need to be on the beach to enjoy the salt breeze. And we need to get into the new car to enjoy its smell. In other words, we get close for the best experience of the aroma.

How close are you to Jesus today?

EVENING

> *Lord Jesus, I want to be a pleasing aroma that*
> *draws other people to You. May I spend much time*
> *in Your presence, soaking up Your goodness so*
> *that others will notice. Use that good sensation*
> *to draw others to Yourself through me.*

MORNING

Then a great and powerful wind tore the mountains apart. . .
but the LORD was not in the wind. After the wind there was
an earthquake, but the LORD was not in the earthquake.
After the earthquake came a fire, but the LORD was not
in the fire. And after the fire came a gentle whisper.

1 KINGS 19:11–12 NIV

At times in biblical history, God thundered. Sometimes He blasted trumpets. Yet other times, there was an audible voice clearly heard by many.

But when the prophet Elijah was told that God was going to "pass by," a mighty wind blew outside the cave. The Lord was not in the wind. An earthquake rumbled and a fire roared by, but God wasn't in them either. He came to Elijah in a "gentle whisper."

Our world is full of noise, and it always threatens to draw our attention away from Jesus. But even though He is the actual voice of truth, He doesn't scream to get our attention. Let's be listening closely for Him, waiting for that gentle whisper that says He is near.

EVENING

Jesus, tune my ear to Your gentlest whisper. I don't
want this world to drown out our quiet conversations.
Our time together is for You to speak to me. Teach
me to make listening closely my highest priority.

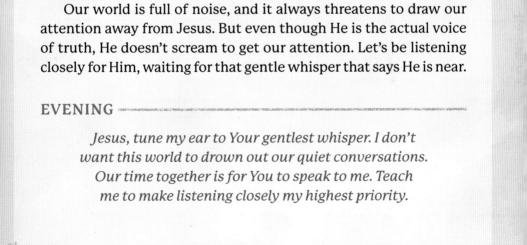

December 16

*For now we see only a reflection as in a mirror; then
we shall see face to face. Now I know in part; then
I shall know fully, even as I am fully known.*

1 CORINTHIANS 13:12 NIV

Physical distance plays a large role in our relationships. Most would probably agree that friendships are best in-person. But today's technology allows us to maintain relationships even when miles—maybe even oceans—separate us. Still, being in the same room with a dear friend, in that person's physical presence, brings the deepest levels of joy.

Our relationship with Jesus will look different from that. We can't see Him, so sometimes it may feel more like a long-distance relationship. But scripture assures us that He is present with each of His children at all times, wherever they are: "surely I am with you always, to the very end of the age" (Matthew 28:20).

Our "sight" for now is faith, but when we reach our heavenly home, we will see Jesus face to face.

EVENING

*Lord Jesus, give me the confidence that You are near
me today and every day—and the sure hope that
one day I will meet You face to face. I know You are
close by me when I pray and read Your Word. I look
forward to the day that I will know You fully.*

MORNING

> *A woman who had suffered for twelve years with constant bleeding came up behind him. She touched the fringe of his robe, for she thought, "If I can just touch his robe, I will be healed." Jesus turned around, and when he saw her he said, "Daughter, be encouraged! Your faith has made you well." And the woman was healed at that moment.*
>
> MATTHEW 9:20–22 NLT

You can't get much closer to Jesus than this poor woman did. . .but you can enjoy the same blessing.

Weighed down by twelve years (years!) of sickness, she believed that Jesus could provide healing. And so she crept up behind Him, hoping simply to touch the edge of His robe. She did, He knew it . . .and the story ended happily. Jesus commended the woman's faith and her decade-plus of wearying illness was history.

Those of us who follow Jesus, who know Him personally, who house His own Holy Spirit, never have to sneak up on Him. We can draw near in confident assurance that He will gladly welcome us and hear our requests. As with that hopeful woman, faith is the key.

EVENING

> *My loving Lord, I want to boldly ask for Your help—and then hear Your words, "Daughter, be encouraged." Please grow my trust in You. I want to be so convinced of Your power that I reach out in faith to grasp it in my own life.*

December 18

But as [Jesus] came closer to Jerusalem and
saw the city ahead, he began to weep.
LUKE 19:41 NLT

As Christians in the Christmas season, we celebrate Jesus' nearness. He came to earth. He comes to us. He knocks on the door of our heart (Revelation 3:20). But not everyone responds.

As He neared His death on the cross, Jesus drew near to Jerusalem. The city of His ancestor David, the favored place of God on earth, Jerusalem largely dismissed Jesus. And it made Him weep. "How I wish today that you of all people would understand the way to peace," He lamented. "Before long your enemies. . .will crush you into the ground, and your children with you. Your enemies will not leave a single stone in place, because you did not recognize it when God visited you" (Luke 19:42–44).

Having recognized the visitation of God ourselves, may we always stay close to our Lord Jesus Christ. And may we constantly encourage others to draw near as well.

Thank You, Jesus, for letting me recognize Your visitation
to this world. Help me to appreciate the sorrow and
suffering You experienced on my behalf—and to
respond in obedience and outreach. The calling You've
put on my life is to bring others into Your family.

MORNING

"But you, Bethlehem Ephrathah, though you are small among the clans of Judah, out of you will come for me one who will be ruler over Israel, whose origins are from of old, from ancient times."

MICAH 5:2 NIV

"A king is coming! A king is coming!" The Jewish people were ready for the pageantry of a king's arrival. What would He look like? When would He ride into town? Surely, there would be robes and jewels, evidence of the royalty they were expecting. But a baby? From tiny Bethlehem and then Nazareth (Matthew 2:23)? Nothing good comes from Nazareth, they concluded (John 1:46). This couldn't be the One. Their expectations did not match the reality.

We all have expectations. We picture the who, what, where, and when. And often the outcome does not match our anticipation. But God has a plan, even in those moments. What flummoxed our expectations can be something even more beautiful than we ever imagined.

The Messiah came near, looking much different than the people expected. But what perfection arrived in that little baby, the focal point of God's plan to save people!

EVENING

Lord Jesus, You were the perfect gift of the Father, the truly glorious blessing of grace and truth. May I always stand in awe of the salvation You bring. Thank You for Your willingness to humble Yourself on my behalf.

December 20

> *The angel said to him, "My name is Gabriel. I stand near God.*
> *He sent me to talk to you and bring to you this good news."*
>
> Luke 1:19 NLV

Angels are messengers of God. In Bible times, He sent them to many different people. The angel Gabriel, mentioned in today's scripture, appears by name three times in scripture: to the prophet Daniel, to the virgin Mary, and to the priest Zacharias, who would become father of John the Baptist. To Zacharias, Gabriel introduced himself by saying, "I stand near God." Imagine not just serving in the presence of God, but actually standing near Him.

Jesus takes that a step further. He didn't simply stand near God; He *is* God in the mysterious reality of the Trinity. God the Father sent Jesus from heaven to earth, to be born as a baby in Bethlehem. Unlike the angels, Jesus didn't come just with a message—He was the once-for-all sacrifice for sin. He came as both the messenger and the message. His nearness was an intentional, eternal gift offered to every person.

> *Thank You, Jesus, for being so much more than a*
> *teacher, a healer, or an example. You are all of those*
> *things, but You are the one-for-all sacrifice for sin.*
> *Thank You for being the message of salvation and*
> *redemption. I accept Your gift and praise You for it.*

December 21

> *The angel said to her, "Mary, do not be afraid.*
> *You have found favor with God."*
>
> LUKE 1:30 NLV

Who could be nearer to Jesus than Mary, His own mother?

An angel had carried the incredible news to the young virgin: she would give birth to God's Son, the Messiah, Jesus. Some quality of her heart had brought her to God's attention: she had "found favor" with the Lord. Mary's humble response was simply, "I am willing to be used of the Lord" (Luke 1:38).

We may feel as if our own calling is insignificant compared with Mary's. Yet all of us, as followers of Jesus, can fulfill God's purpose for our lives. And we can be just as near to Jesus as Mary was. "Who is My mother? And who are My brothers?" Jesus would ask, many years later. "Whoever does what My father in heaven wants him to do is My brother and My sister and My mother" (Matthew 12:48, 50).

EVENING

> *Lord Jesus, You have made me Your sister through*
> *salvation. Thank You for Your amazing favor. Help me*
> *to obey the Father's will and be used in building up Your*
> *kingdom. Like Mary, I am willing to be used of the Lord.*

December 22

> *The angel said, "Joseph, son of David, do not be afraid to take Mary as your wife. She is to become a mother by the Holy Spirit."*
> MATTHEW 1:20 NLV

Joseph was planning to wed Mary. But after he learned she was pregnant, he made the agonizing decision to break off their engagement. The news that she was expecting a child that wasn't his was just too much to take.

But then, in one of the most distressing moments of his life, Joseph was visited by "an angel of the Lord." He explained that Mary's child had been conceived by the Holy Spirit. "A Son will be born to her," the angel said. "You will give Him the name Jesus because He will save His people from the punishment of their sins" (Matthew 1:21).

God came near to Joseph. He stayed close to Mary. She bore Jesus Christ, who brings all who believe into God's presence. No wonder Christmas is a time of celebration!

> *Jesus, You bring me—and all who follow You—into Your Father's presence. I celebrate Your birth, Your death, Your resurrection, Your imminent return, and Your love for me.*

MORNING

> *When Joseph woke up, he did what the angel of the Lord*
> *had commanded him and took Mary home as his wife.*
> MATTHEW 1:24 NIV

We love the story of the first Christmas, with its picturesque characters like Mary, Joseph, and the shepherds. We love its drama, including a very pregnant young woman's awkward journey to Bethlehem. But though they may be less obvious, there are also some important lessons here too.

Notice in today's scripture that Joseph immediately obeyed the angel's instruction to make Mary his wife. And after the birth of Jesus, when the angel told Joseph to escape the wrath of King Herod by taking his little family to Egypt, the humble carpenter awoke from his visionary dream and left in the night (Matthew 2:14). Joseph was unquestioningly obedient to the voice of the Lord.

This kind of obedience draws us nearer to God. As Jesus Himself told us, "Whoever has my commands and keeps them is the one who loves me. The one who loves me will be loved by my Father, and I too will love them and show myself to them" (John 14:21).

EVENING

> *Lord Jesus, I want to obey You, even when Your call*
> *seems strange or difficult. Help me to hear Your*
> *commands and quickly keep them. I know that, to*
> *honor You, my obedience should be immediate.*

December 24

MORNING

Joseph. . .had to go to Bethlehem in Judea, David's ancient home. He traveled there from the village of Nazareth in Galilee. . . . And while they were there, the time came for her baby to be born. She gave birth to her firstborn son.

LUKE 2:4, 6–7 NLT

After learning that they had been chosen to parent Jesus, Mary and Joseph set out on a journey. Their travels, so they could be counted in a Roman census, would take them to Bethlehem. This little town was called the City of David, an ancestor of Jesus.

It had to be a challenging journey for Mary, so near to her due date. But the situation got even worse when she and Joseph learned there was no lodging available at their destination. Most likely, Jesus' birth was not at all what Mary had envisioned. . .but it was God's plan.

Think of the hardships Jesus experienced in coming near to us that first Christmas. Simply leaving the splendor of heaven is inconceivable, but then to be born in a stable? And yet, out of love, He was willing. This is the God we serve!

EVENING

Oh, Jesus, You suffered hardship Your entire time on earth. Help me to stay faithful when things become difficult, knowing that You have been there before me. I see how humble You were in Your life—may I always follow Your example.

December 25

Behold, a virgin shall be with child, and shall bring forth a son, and they shall call his name Emmanuel, which being interpreted is, God with us.

MATTHEW 1:23 KJV

For thousands of years, the Israelites had read about their promised Messiah. Many people knew those scriptures well and could recite them from memory. Yet when Jesus arrived, nearly everyone missed out. They were expecting some lavish kingdom, complete with all the fanfare associated with royalty. Instead, the Messiah arrived as a baby, wrapped in swaddling clothes and placed in a feeding trough.

How often does God perform an amazing work in our lives today, yet we somehow overlook it? We want fireworks when our prayers are answered. But the God who sent His Son in humility two thousand years ago is the same God today. He still works for our good.

God's provision may come quietly and in unexpected ways. But because of Jesus, we experience all the blessings reserved for children of God. God is with us! What a gift!

EVENING

On the day we celebrate Your birth, Jesus, I want to praise You for being "God with us." Here is my heart— please make me entirely Yours. Even when Your plan doesn't look like I expected, show me how to experience the blessings that come in even the smallest of gifts!

December 26

When the angels had returned to heaven, the shepherds
said to each other, "Let's go to Bethlehem! Let's see
this thing that has happened, which the Lord has told us
about." They hurried to the village and found Mary and
Joseph. And there was the baby, lying in the manger.

LUKE 2:15–16 NLT

Only God knows exactly how many shepherds were out in the nearby fields the night Jesus was born. Whether it was two or twenty-two, they found themselves participating in the most dramatic event in history.

You might think Jesus' birth would be announced to kings and senators, the educated and influential. But no. . .God chose some of the humblest people of all to be first to learn that He had come near, that in Immanuel—a prophetic name for Jesus—God was indeed "with us" (Matthew 1:23).

While the rich and famous are certainly welcome to come to Jesus, the good news of salvation is for *everyone*. As the apostle Paul said, "few of you were wise in the world's eyes or powerful or wealthy when God called you" (1 Corinthians 1:26). Praise Him for His kindness!

Oh, Jesus, I'm grateful that I didn't have to be anything
special to come to You. I praise You for Your kind
generosity that invited me into Your kingdom. When I
feel unqualified for the work You've given me, remind
me that I am just like those shepherds. I'm just a humble
person who had the privilege of hearing Your good news!

MORNING

> *"For my eyes have seen your salvation, which you*
> *have prepared in the sight of all nations"*
> LUKE 2:30–31 NIV

The "righteous and devout" Simeon spent his life waiting for the Messiah—and the Holy Spirit revealed that he would not die until he saw the promised One. Anna, an elderly prophetess in the temple, had devoted her life to worship.

Eight days after Jesus was born, Mary and Joseph took Him into the temple to "present him to the Lord" (Luke 2:22). . .and the faithful old-timers were blessed by His presence. Simeon recognized the Messiah, took the baby in his arms, praised God and spoke a blessing over Mary and Joseph. Anna also gave thanks to God, witnessing to all nearby that the Messiah had come.

Our experience of Jesus is purely through faith. But, by His Spirit, He is just as near to us as He was, as an eight-day-old baby, to Simeon and Anna. One day soon enough, we'll be in His presence forever.

EVENING

> *Lord Jesus, You came to earth two thousand years*
> *ago, but You are as real and present now as You*
> *were to Simeon and Anna. I look forward to Your*
> *second coming, when I will actually see Your face.*
> *Give me opportunities each day to enhance Your*
> *kingdom by bringing new souls into Your family.*

December 28

> *"But very truly I tell you, it is for your good that I am going away. Unless I go away, the Advocate will not come to you; but if I go, I will send him to you."*
>
> JOHN 16:7 NIV

At times we all need help. A couch is too much for one person to carry. Modern cars are way too complicated for the average person to repair. And God bless those people who wade through all the tax laws on our behalf.

Jesus lived some thirty years on earth, two thousand years ago. He lived a perfect life and accomplished amazing things, which were recorded for us in the pages of scripture. He was crucified, resurrected, and returned to heaven. But that, of course, wasn't the end of the story.

Just as promised, Jesus sent His Holy Spirit—the Advocate, the Comforter, the Helper—to be with His children. Jesus' presence through His Spirit is a tremendous blessing in itself, but He's more than just near us. . .He lives inside us. There is no greater nearness than that.

> *Thank You, Jesus, for living within me through Your Spirit. What more could I ask? May I always be pure and true in my thoughts and actions. Guide me into all truth. Go before me and lead me where I ought to go.*

December 29

*Then Jesus told him, "Because you have seen me,
you have believed; blessed are those who
have not seen and yet have believed."*

JOHN 20:29 NIV

Following His death and resurrection, Jesus appeared to many people. They saw Him and spread the news that He was alive. But one disciple, Thomas, was absent at the time and missed Jesus' first appearance. Thomas had heard the talk, but he wanted proof. "Doubting Thomas," as he is now known, said he wouldn't believe unless he saw the Lord in person.

In His compassion, Jesus went straight to Thomas. Entering the house through a locked door, Jesus invited His oh-so-practical disciple to touch His hands and side. And then came the directive: "Stop doubting and believe" (John 20:27).

Jesus drew near to Thomas and dispensed with his doubt. Then the Lord pronounced a blessing on *us*, we who have believed in Him without seeing. That is the essence of our faith (Hebrews 11:1).

EVENING

*Lord, I believe in You though You haven't yet
physically shown Yourself to me. I thank You for the
blessing of faith that believes without sight. I look
forward to the day when my faith becomes sight.*

December 30

Search for the LORD and for his strength; continually seek him.

1 CHRONICLES 16:11 NLT

As this calendar year draws to a close, we recognize the nearness of the new year. For some, this is a welcome and joyous thought. For others, the realization brings hesitation, sorrow, or fear. We have no guarantee of what the new year will hold. . .will it be good or bad? Happy or sad? Of course, God knows. Nothing that happens over the course of the next year will surprise Him.

So let's walk through the coming months in faith. There will be moments of delight. There will be seasons of adversity. But Jesus, our Savior, cares deeply about His own. . .and He will be with us through every experience.

As we approach the new year, know that your Lord is already aware of what you'll need, as well as what He, in His love, will provide for you. He's here right now. He'll be there tomorrow, and the day after that, and the day after that. . .throughout all eternity.

EVENING

Lord Jesus, I don't know what the new year holds,
but I know that You hold the year in Your hands. May
I trust in Your provision for all I'll need, every day.

December 31

MORNING

> *He Who tells these things says, "Yes, I am*
> *coming soon!" Let it be so. Come, Lord Jesus.*
> REVELATION 22:20 NLV

It is said that "all good things must come to an end." A good movie. A delicious meal. A perfect vacation. Often times, an end—of a relationship, of a job, of our good health—can be painful.

But when our days on earth come to an end, God has provided something so much better. We see the Bible's description of heaven with our limited human understanding, but know this for sure: it will be far better than we could ever imagine.

The promise of an eternal home with Jesus will be reality sooner than we know. We will see Him face to face!

"Yes, I am coming soon!" Jesus said. And when He does, we will enjoy eternal nearness with our Creator, Redeemer, and Friend.

EVENING

> *Oh, Jesus, this life can be hard. But I know Your*
> *promise is true—You will return to make everything*
> *right. You will make all things new. Thank You*
> *for that sure hope. Come quickly, Lord Jesus!*

Author credits

Writers for the *Jesus Each Day* devotional include

Glenn Hascall
Jennifer Hahn
Josh Mosey
Karon Phillips
Lee Warren
MariLee Parrish
Pamela L. McQuade

Scripture Index

More Devotions for Women

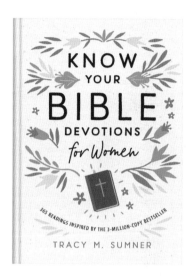

Inspired by the 3-million-copy bestseller, *Know Your Bible Devotions for Women* provides 365 readings focusing on important verses of scripture, offering background, insight, and encouraging takeaways. You'll get a fascinating overview of all 66 books—an excellent primer if you're new to God's Word, and a helpful refresher if you're already familiar with scripture.

Hardback / 978-1-63609-427-4